WHY ARE WE STILL FIGHTING?

**How to End Your Schema Wars and Start
Connecting with the People You Love**

Maureen Kirby Lassen

MAUREEN KIRBY LASSEN, PH.D.

New Harbinger Publications, Inc.

Publisher's Note

Author's Note

Distributed in the U.S.A. by Publishers Group West; in Canada by Raincoast Books; in Great Britain by Airlift Book Company, Ltd.; in South Africa by Real Books, Ltd.; in Australia by Boobook; and in New Zealand by Tandem Press.

Copyright © 2000 by Maureen K. Lassen
New Harbinger Publications, Inc.
5674 Shattuck Avenue
Oakland, CA 94609

Cover design by Blue Design
Edited by Kayla Sussell
Text design by Michele Waters

Library of Congress Catalog Card Number: 99-75282
ISBN 1-57224-186-1 Paperback

New Harbinger Publications' Web site address: www.newharbinger.com

02   01   00

10   9   8   7   6   5   4   3   2   1

First printing

To my mother,
Fern Lee Kirby,
whose courage and resilience in the face of adversity
throughout her life has been an inspiration.
With love and admiration.

Contents

Foreword

Some people seem to be happy with their lot in life. Others don't ever seem to have enough. But when outsiders look at their situations, it is often hard to see any objective differences. Some people have good lives despite their need to cope with many challenges, while others don't seem to be happy no matter how fortunate they appear to be. How do we explain these differences? Or more to the point, how can we help people learn how to achieve as much as they can, and be happy with the result? Psychologists, philosophers, religious thinkers, and many others have devoted decades of study to understanding and helping people achieve that elusive joy in their lives. The result of their efforts is a new industry that turns out scores of new "how-to-be-happy" books every week.

Many years ago, before I wrote my first mass-market psychology book, I thought it would be a good idea to begin by studying the best-sellers to see whether I could discover the formula for their success. I did find it—but to my dismay I couldn't use it. The formula for six-figure sales has three key elements:

1. The author must begin by convincing readers that their personal flaws and unsatisfying experiences are all the result of other people's mistakes.

2. Then, in addition to absolving readers of any responsibility for their unhappiness, the author must assure them that they alone deserve credit for all of their positive qualities and for any positive experiences they might enjoy.

3. Once the stage has been set by creating the right mix of self-pity and self-righteousness, the author should then share a disarmingly simple "secret" that is known only to the

author, and to several hundred thousand fortunate readers. The secret, which the author must have developed through a personal odyssey that led to great success, must be something both easy to remember and easier still to carry out. Tasks like eating only rice, not eating fruits or vegetables, thinking only positive thoughts, meditating for three minutes every morning, venting anger so it doesn't build up, or expressing every thought are some examples of the nostrums competing on bookstore shelves.

Interestingly, these overly simple recommendations actually do work for at least a handful of readers. But they don't work for the vast majority. Life, and the process of enhancing it, are both far more complex than most authors acknowledge. Although most readers know deep down that there are *no* too-easy-to-be-believed solutions, hope triumphs over experience as they travel from one book, tape, or self-help group to another.

Dr. Lassen understands the complexity of human behavior. She makes the mysterious understandable, and the seemingly insurmountable obstacle achievable. Wisely, she has heeded the wisdom of scholars like Bradford Keeney (1983) who cautioned that human life is so richly complex that studying just one part of it can only build misunderstanding; and changes to only one part of life cannot be sustained for long. Taking a one-step approach to life is like making the mistake of putting gas in a car's tank, but neglecting to put oil in its engine, water in its battery, or fluid in its transmission. Because people are at least as complicated as cars, only multifaceted changes can be sustained. Knowing this, Dr. Lassen offers a set of very powerful recommendations that address the readers' need to make changes in the way they think, feel, and act in virtually every area of their lives.

Dr. Lassen has woven her tapestry by wisely choosing threads from decades of research on human behavior. For example, she drew on the work of George A. Kelly (1955) who was one of the first to point out that we can't see things if we don't have words to describe them, and we can't make plans unless we can visualize their effects. Dr Lassen's use of "schemas" is similar to Kelly's ideas about "constructs." For her, schemas are more than beliefs; they automatically create functioning mental models of the self and everything else in the realms of the interpersonal and physical worlds. She shrewdly recognizes that schemas have negative and positive poles, and that the schemas that help the most are those balanced between the extremes. She also acknowledges that schemas are more than words and include a rich texture of emotions that truly give them meaning.

The power of this book lies in Dr. Lassen's skill in helping readers to identify the elements of their most important schemas, and then in how to decide which ones to keep and how to replace the ones that don't work. Her research has led her to the conclusion that our ideas about the potential rewards and risks of bonding with others are among our most important schemas. She builds on the beliefs of attachment theorists that babies' relationships with their principal caregivers early in life profoundly influence the emotional quality of all of their subsequent relationships. These early dramas are replayed throughout life in the extent to which individuals manifest one of three dominant bonding styles, Easy, Anxious, and/or Distant. These schemas influence our choice of partners, and the ways we act so as to co-create relationships that bring us either joy or grief.

Dr. Lassen brilliantly presents readers the opportunity to identify their usual bonding styles, before offering guidelines on how to nurture or to change them. She is not a fatalist who believes that we are all doomed to repeat every mistake we have made. Rather than suggesting that schemas are fixed and immutable, she presents them as undergoing a never-ending process of evolution and change. She offers readers a choice: They can acquiesce and allow history to go on repeating itself or they can take an active role in creating the kinds of experiences they would like to have. Like Harville Hendrix (1988), she admonishes her readers to create "conscious" relationships in which they make wise decisions rather than being passive and complaining about the sad results.

Dr. Lassen guides her readers through a careful protocol for identifying their core beliefs, tracing the roots of these core beliefs, and identifying their impacts. She calls on them to take an inventory of beliefs about themselves, their significant others, and about every other important feature of their lives. Then she suggests specific ways to change thoughts and feelings to support new actions that will lead to more satisfying results. And she does this without making any false promises because she is aware that we can't always have everything that we want. She also helps her readers to understand when and how to forgive others for failing to meet their expectations, how to know when it is appropriate to accept what they receive, and how to know when to exit.

In summary, Dr. Lassen has written a very hopeful book without making false promises. Inherent in her message is the idea that every life can be made better and some can become great. She empowers her readers to seek improvement not by redefining their suffering as someone else's fault but by accepting responsibility for self-change. Everyone who reads this book and completes its exercises is certain to achieve greater self-understanding, the knowledge of how to plan a course of self-change, and the motivation to take the steps that can make their most cherished goals attainable.

—Richard B. Stuart, D.S.W., A.B.P.P.
Clinical Psychology Faculty,
The Fielding Institute
Clinical Professor Emeritus,
Department of Psychiatry,
University of Washington

Acknowledgments

The seeds of this book were planted with New Harbinger editor Kristin Beck's invitation and encouragement to write a book for the general reader that explains the critical role schemas play in our social lives. Schemas are the mental models or images we have of ourselves and others that contribute to the happy and unhappy patterns that we unknowingly repeat in our relationships. In spite of Trojan efforts to change, without understanding schemas, relationship strain and emotional crises continue to resurface. This book presents a model of human social behavior that is an integration of decades of work by social scientists in the areas of social cognition, attachment theory, and cognitive behavioral therapies with the schema polarity model developed by Chuck Elliott and myself. This integration produces a model of human interaction that recognizes the consistencies and contradictions common to all of us and describes how and why we often drive ourselves and others to distraction. I am greatly indebted to Chuck and the hundreds of other social scientists who have invested their lives in trying to explicate the sources of interpersonal peace and turbulence.

Writing this book has been a long and illuminating journey. I am grateful to Kristin Beck for letting me make it. Ron Giannetti, Dean of the Psychology Program at the Fielding Institute, was instrumental in helping me find the time to undertake this project and follow it to completion. I am especially indebted to Kayla Sussell, whose meticulous and incisive editing skills are evident throughout this text. Kayla's professional expertise and personal support have been invaluable. I want to thank Matt McKay for his helpful suggestions for illustrating the schema concept. Thanks are also due to New Harbinger's Kirk Johnson and Gretchen Gold for their creativity and enthusiasm for this book. Linda Meyer Hansen, Joan Hill, Monica Langefeld, Kristine Lassen, and Sheryl Mumford were infinitely kind to agree to serve as a test audience to make this book reader-friendly for nonprofessionals. Their helpful feedback was instrumental in making this text easily understood by all those who want to improve their relationships.

This book would not have been possible without the love, support, and encouragement that my husband, Gary L. Lassen, provided me throughout this process. For almost thirty years he has been a constant source of strength, stimulation, and good humor. Thank God for the asthma that sent me to Arizona and led me into his life. I also must acknowledge the role our border collies, Wiley and her son, Walker, played in the development of this manuscript. Without their constant harassment to play ball every hour, this text would have been completed months earlier. Should I ever write another book, they know they are in danger of being exchanged for cats.

Writing this book has increased my awareness of how I have been blessed with many loving relatives and friends throughout my life. I want to acknowledge the people who have been most critical in my realization of the joy and fulfillment that loving relationships can provide: Gary; my mother, Fern Lee Kirby; my late grandparents, John and Marian Draper Lee; my brothers, Patrick and Michael Kirby; and Linda Meyer Hansen, my best friend since we met shyly standing on the sidelines at first-grade recess. These seven loving, dynamic, and funny people have enriched my life beyond words. After twenty-five years of clinical practice, I think you are blessed if you find one person during a lifetime who truly loves you. In spite of my many shortcomings, I have experienced an abundance of such good fortune and will be forever grateful for that.

Introduction

Are you frustrated and unhappy with your relationships? Are you worn out from fighting the same old battles in spite of repeated promises and efforts to change? If so, this book can help you stop the harmful interactions and destructive patterns that sap the joy from your relationships. These emotionally draining cycles of conflict are the result of a common psychological mechanism called *schemas*. Without understanding schemas and knowing how to change them, you often are powerless to make lasting changes in yourself or in your relationships. This book can help you put an end to arguing and anger and replace them with deeper intimacy and acceptance of yourself and others.

Reading this book will help you to:

- Understand why you have repeated problems with the same person or many problems with different people.

- Understand how to change the underlying psychological mechanisms that generate emotional distress and relationship crises.

- Analyze your own relationships using the most current knowledge that behavioral scientists have accumulated on how people behave and the ways they interact with each other.

- Identify whether you are an Easy, Anxious, or Distant bonder and learn how your bonding style is critical to your relationships.

- Identify the bonding styles of the other people in your life and learn how their styles affect you.

- Change lifelong patterns that strain and destroy relationships.

- Guide your children to develop bonding styles that will enrich their lives and allow them to avoid the pitfalls you have experienced.

- Make relationship choices to achieve the peace and happiness that you have long been seeking.

This book will only achieve these purposes through our collaboration. We are both experts. You have expertise on yourself and the people in your life. No one else has the same knowledge that you have on these topics. I have expertise in psychological principles and human relationships and on how to analyze problematic relationships and make constructive changes. Only together can we achieve the goals of this book. However, I have an advantage. I have already done my work. Yours is just beginning.

This book is designed to be an interactive experience. With my guidance, you can apply your knowledge of yourself to analyze your relationships and make the changes that you think will enhance your life and improve the quality of those relationships. You also will discover what choices you have and how to be judicious in the actions you choose to take. But be forewarned. This book is not a cakewalk to relationship nirvana. Individuals are complicated. Together their complexity increases exponentially. This book reflects and examines that complexity in ordinary language. The general reader is much more capable of understanding complexity than many authors acknowledge. This book does not underestimate you. You need to understand the intricacies of your own social world. Within these pages you will discover why it is amazing that people get along at all!

Because this is a thought-provoking, interactive text, you will find it helpful to keep a notebook handy as you read it. You will want to record your thoughts and observations to the various questions and exercises as you go through the chapters. After you finish the book, you will be able to continue to use your notes in ways suggested throughout the text. Meaningful change never stops with the end of a book. You will need to continue to work on sustaining the changes you choose to make. This book is just a beginning. Together, we can open doors for you to find a new way of being with yourself and with others.

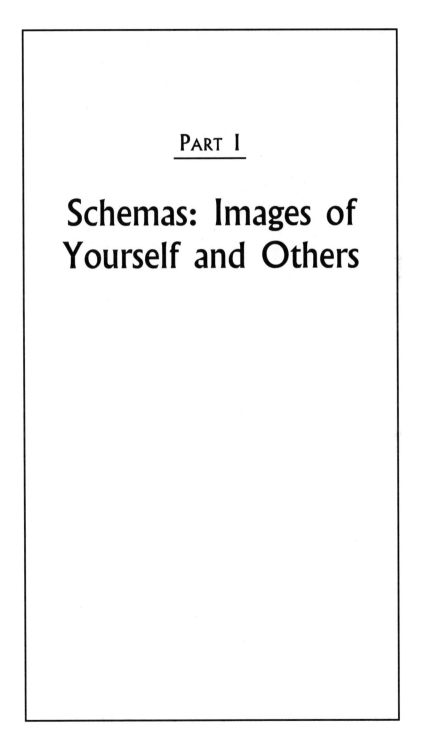

PART I

Schemas: Images of Yourself and Others

1

The Problem with People

"How can someone who says such mean and hateful things really love me?"

"If my own mother didn't love me, who will?"

"We have been having the same argument for ten years. Will it ever stop?"

"My dad has never said he loved me in the entire thirty-three years of my life."

"I would rather have her throw something at me than sulk. She is the Queen of Sulk."

"After she hurt me, I never let myself get close to anyone again."

"She was such a sick baby I was afraid to love her, for fear I couldn't take it if she died."

"He doesn't believe me, but the affair really wasn't about sex."

"Why should I get close to my stepdad? He'll just leave me too."

Therapists hear statements like these every day. They see the anguish people experience over the troubled relationships in their lives and they witness the heartbreak of betrayal and deception. They see the humiliation their clients have experienced at the hands of others, and they also witness the shame their clients feel at the way they have mistreated other people. They hear the regrets over past relationships, at actions not taken, or words spewed out in anger. Indeed, the majority of therapy time is spent in discussing the interpersonal aspects of individuals' lives. No wonder. It is impossible to fully understand anyone without understanding the social contexts of their lives. Our relationships with others are fundamental to our sense of self. Relationships are not only essential for life, they are the essence of life.

Nevertheless, satisfying, close relationships remain elusive for many. Not just marital relationships, but also those between parents and children, siblings, friends, and co-workers. For most of us, troubled relationships with particular individuals in our lives, even our relatives, are not uncommon. Why is that? Are people just difficult? A few of them may be, but certainly not most. The answer is much more complex than that. Hopefully, this book will simplify that answer and provide you with greater insight into your own relationships.

Getting Along with Others Is Better Than an Apple a Day

Human beings are social animals. We need each other. The inability to form meaningful emotional connections with other human beings has been shown to impair health and shorten life span. People with limited social connections are at greater risk for both disease and death. Over a ten-year period, people with the fewest social contacts had a death rate three times higher than those with the most social contacts (Berkman and Syme 1979).

Just one close confidant will increase a person's life span and decrease the risk of disease (Berkman and Syme 1979; House, Robbins, and Metzmer 1982). Social support also can reduce the likelihood of illness and speed recovery (Fontana, Kems, Rosenberg, et al. 1989; Kulik and Mahler 1989).

However, relationships are not always beneficial. People who experience repeated interpersonal conflicts exhibit both emotional and physical distress. Tense relationships at work impair productivity and contribute to demoralization. Troubled marriages that lead to separation and divorce increase the risk for emotional distress, automobile accidents, physical illness, suicide, and homicide (Gottman 1998). Physical harm, even death, are not infrequent outcomes of abusive relationships. Partner violence occurs in millions of marriages every year (Straus and Gelles 1986). Estimates of violence among heterosexual couples range from 35 to 50 percent of all couples (Malik and Lindahl, 1998). Similar rates of violence also are found among gay and lesbian couples, with higher rates reported for lesbians than for gay relationships (Bologna, Waterman, and Dawson 1987; Lie and Gentlewarrior 1991). Partner abuse occurs across all socioeconomic classes, religions, and racial and ethnic groups. In America, people are at greatest risk for assault and murder by their loved ones.

Hostile, antagonistic relationships are present in many of our lives. Every year millions of dollars are spent paying professionals to mediate family disagreements and employment disputes. Over one-half to two-thirds of all marriages end in divorce. Not only do thousands of couples seek relationship counseling annually, relationship distress is a primary precipitant for individual psychotherapy. Individuals experience betrayal, neglect, intimidation, and abusive behavior. They describe depression, anxiety, despair, and rage from mistreatment by others. Such feelings can be of recent onset or have simmered for decades from acts committed by others who are long since dead. There are few absolute truths in the behavioral sciences, but this is one of them: *Psychological and physical well being are enhanced by supportive, nurturing relationships with our families, our friends, and our co-workers.* We need to get along with each other. Our very existence depends upon it.

If we are social animals—and the prehistoric record indicates we are—then why are relationships so often difficult? Why is it so hard for some people to get along with others? There is no easy answer to these questions, but there are answers. You will discover those answers in the following pages. You will see why psychologists emphasize the role of early social experiences in the ability to develop satisfying relationships throughout life. You will understand the potential devastation that divorce, death, and extramarital affairs can have on interpersonal and intrapersonal functioning and how to prevent or limit such damage. How differences are resolved is fundamental to your relationship satisfaction.

The material in this book offers new ways to approach relationships and describes how to create peace with others without sacrificing self-respect. Acceptance and forgiveness are critical qualities for emotional well-being and loving relationships. You will discover the obstacles to developing those processes and learn how to overcome them.

People have certain styles for approaching other people. Your styles influence how you relate to other people, just as their styles affect how they relate to you. You don't relate to everyone in the same way. As you interact with different individuals, you may make subtle shifts in your style, or you may switch styles altogether. Such styles are called *bonding styles* and form the basis of how people treat each other. Some styles make interactions easy, while others can be problematic and painful. Bonding styles are instrumental to relationship happiness. Before you can determine what your styles or anyone else's are, however, you first need to understand what makes up a bonding style.

Bonding styles are made up of *schemas* (pronounced *skee-muhs*). Schemas are the images or mental representations that your brain creates to pull together your views of yourself, others, and your experiences. Your schemas play a critical role in your interpersonal life, and so do the schemas that others have. By understanding schemas, you will learn to recognize the different bonding styles that lead to positive and negative outcomes. You also will learn how to change the schemas that contribute to frustrating styles of interaction. This book's goal is to enable you to enhance the way you interact with others and to decrease the distress you experience with certain people. To achieve this goal, you first need to understand schemas, the fundamental units of relationship interactions.

Schemas: Your Mental Models

Your brain needs a way to organize your various experiences and knowledge about others and yourself. Otherwise, your life would be absolutely chaotic. You would have to make sense of every encounter and experience anew. You could never make any generalizations. You might know how to drive your 1997 Honda Civic, but you would not be able to figure out how to drive a 1999 Ford Taurus. Fortunately, your mind automatically clusters together information about similar subjects. These clusters of information are called schemas. For example, a schema of car-driving gives you a pretty good idea of how to drive a Ford if you know how to drive a Honda. You know there will be an ignition key that you turn to start the engine, that you put the gears in Reverse or Drive depending on the direction you want to go, and that you step on the gas pedal for power and the brake pedal to stop.

Your *car-driving* schema includes examples of specific cars and generalizations about cars. The more experience you have with cars, the more extensive your car-driving schema will be. For example, a generalization might be, "The ignition is usually on the dashboard, but with some models it is on the steering column." Then you might have several specific images of cars with their ignitions on the dashboard and other images of cars with their ignitions on the steering column.

In a sense, a schema is like a wheel. The hub of the wheel is a core set of generalizations about a particular subject, and the spokes are examples of the generalizations. Schemas about yourself and others are similar to the car-driving schema. Each schema includes generalizations and specific examples. Essentially, *schemas are the mental models that your mind creates to represent your knowledge about yourself, others, and the world.* Schemas help you make sense of your experiences. They identify patterns in yourself and in others.

For example, you may have a schema of your mother that tells you that the best time to borrow money from her is right after she has received her paycheck, and the worst time is right after the first of the month when she has paid the bills. Schemas allow you to organize your experiences, to process information rapidly, and to make predictions about yourself and others. *Schemas function as your personal theories of reality.* They guide you in interpreting your experiences and in selecting your responses.

Schema Types

There are three types of schemas that are particularly important in interpersonal functioning: *self schemas, person schemas,* and *role schemas.* Each type of schema includes both generalizations and specific examples of a particular subject.

Self Schemas

Your most elaborate mental models, or schemas, are those you have of yourself. Self schemas are your views of yourself in many different areas or domains, such as worthiness or competency. Your self schemas are more elaborate than your other schemas, because you know more about yourself than you do about anyone else. For example, if you have a self schema of *entitlement*, you view yourself as deserving privileges, having a right to the best of everything, feeling you should not have to wait for your needs to be met, and considering your needs to be more important than others'.

Although a self schema of entitlement emphasizes the self, you can see that it also has interpersonal connotations. If your needs are more important than everyone else's, then the needs of others are less important. If you should not have to wait, then others should be willing to stop whatever they are doing to accommodate you. Clearly, self schemas often have interpersonal implications, too.

Another example of a self schema is *dependent.* A self schema of dependency views the self as not capable of handling everyday responsibilities, needing to rely on others for most things, and not being capable of being independent. Again, this self schema includes an interpersonal view: "Others need to take care of me. Others need to be strong and reliable for me to survive. Otherwise, I could be overwhelmed." You can easily see how a self schema of dependency would influence relationships by maximizing clinging, dependent behavior on others and by seeking friends or lovers who are willing to assume responsibility for someone else.

If you are obsessed with the need to be in a relationship and require constant reassurance of being loved, you could be described as having an *intimacy driven* self schema, which includes an unremitting fear of being alone in the world. The interpersonal effects of an intimacy driven self schema are obvious. Such a self schema will create intense levels of distress when someone loses a relationship and even produce distress during a relationship because of continual worrying about the relationship ending.

You can see from these three examples of self schemas that although their primary focus is on the self, each also has important interpersonal meanings. Furthermore, not only do you have self schemas, so does everyone else. Their self schemas influence their thoughts, actions, and feelings and, thus, will influence their behavior with you, just as your self schemas influence your interactions with them.

Person Schemas

Just as you have schemas about yourself, you also have schemas about other people. These mental models are called person schemas. *Person schemas* are the mental representations you have of specific people. A person schema will include the thoughts, feelings, and behavior that you attribute to that particular person in various circumstances. Your person schema of someone will include general and specific information and images of that person in various situations. The more you know about someone, the more elaborate your person schema of that individual will be.

For example, your person schema of your mother will be more elaborate than that of your bank clerk. Your person schema of the bank clerk may include visual images of her appearance and impressions of her friendliness based on the extent of your interactions or your observations of her interactions with others. In comparison, your person schema of your mother will be considerably more complex and extensive. You may view her as nurturing, but also as domineering, critical, and demanding of perfection. Your schema of your mother may depict her interacting differently with her children than with her parents or at her job as a department store manager. You may see her as soft-spoken in public but mercurial at home. Your person schema of your mother will include many generalizations about her and a vast number of specific memories.

The person schemas you have of others influence the way you interact with them, how you approach them on various matters, and how you expect them to respond in different situations. However, person schemas are not infallible.

For example, sixteen-year-old Brian refused to tell his widowed father that he was gay because Brian's person schema of his dad viewed his father as religious and moralistic. Brian was sure his father would disown him if he knew of his son's sexual orientation. After his father found some of Brian's personal correspondence, he went to Brian and asked him if he were gay. Trembling, Brian acknowledged that he was. His dad sat down on the bed and said softly, "Brian, I love you and I know you are a good person. I don't understand homosexuality, but maybe we could see a counselor and figure it out together. I know I don't want this to drive us apart." Brian was speechless. He reached out and hugged his father, whom he had never loved more than at that moment.

Brian's dad did not react at all the way Brian's person schema of his dad had predicted. This illustrates how schemas, of any kind, are not always accurate. Your schemas are based on your experiences and your interpretations of events. Sometimes your impressions are simply inaccurate. At other times you don't have enough information to predict how you or others will react in certain circumstances. Brian's person schema of his dad was based on Brian's observations of his father during Brian's life. Brian had never seen his father confronted with this particular situation, so he could only guess, and in this situation, his schema misled him. As you learn more about schemas, you will discover that schema inaccuracies and distortions can be particularly problematic in relationships. Schemas are essential to your functioning, but sometimes they can mislead you.

Your Person Schemas

How do you figure out what your person schemas are? Actually, it is simple. In a notebook, make a list of the people who are important to you, from your present and your past. Be sure to include on your list anyone with whom you have a troubled relationship. Then, write the name of each person on a separate piece of paper. For each person, write down your general impressions of the individual, such as, "Jack is generous." For each generalization, give a brief example. Here, you might put, "Jack always gives a donation to any charity drive."

Be as comprehensive as you can. Try to include both positive and negative aspects about everyone on your list. To help you make your generalizations, here is a checklist of what to consider for each of the people on your list. You may not know all of this information for some on your list, but for a few people you will know most of it.

Your answers to these questions will be the generalizations you have about the person.

The specific instances you provide for each generalization are the examples of that generalization. Together the generalizations and the specific examples will give you a fairly complete picture of your person schema for each individual. When you are finished with this exercise, be sure to save the pages in your notebook about each person, because in later chapters you will be asked to add more information to those people's pages.

Your Generalizations About the Important People in Your Life
How do they view themselves? • What is their self-image? • What are their values and goals? • What motivates them? • What do they seem to want in life? • How do they react to stress and adversity? • What makes them happy? • What makes them sad? • What makes them angry? • What do they fear? • How do they express their emotions? • How do they act when they are happy, sad, angry, or worried? • How would you describe their typical emotional state? • Are they kind, thoughtful, and considerate? • Are they trustworthy, reliable, and responsible? • Do they have a sense of humor? • Are they outgoing? • Are they open about their thoughts and feelings? • How do they act in situations when they don't know anyone? • How do they feel about socializing? • How do they treat strangers? • How do they treat acquaintances? • How do they treat the people who are close to them? • How do they treat you? • How do you think they view you?

On each sheet of paper, when you have finished you will have written something like this:

Jack

- *Is generous: always gives some kind of donation to any charity drive; paid for his mom to take a cruise on her seventy-fifth birthday; let me borrow his car when mine broke down and I had a job interview.*

- *Is trustworthy: never told anyone what I told him about the way my dad treated me; has never been unfaithful to his wife.*

- *Has a good sense of humor: is witty; enjoys jokes; can take a joke on himself.*

- *Can be opinionated: when he thinks he is right, he will not give up in an argument.*

- *Is judgmental: he has strong religious opinions and views people in black-or-white terms; when his seventeen-year-old niece got pregnant, he was angry with her and wouldn't speak to her for months.*

And so forth. Don't worry if some of the things you say seem to contradict each other. People act differently in different situations, so their actions can be contradictory. In fact, you could even have "contradictory" as a generalization about some people and then list examples of how they are contradictory.

Role Schemas

Your images or mental representations of different social and professional roles are called *role schemas*. Role schemas include information about the kind of activities and responsibilities involved in a particular role, how people act in that role, the thoughts and feelings of those in that role, the kind of people who can fill the role, and specific examples of those who are in that role. Role schemas always imply how someone in that role will interact with other people.

In this book we are more concerned with social roles, such as husband, wife, mother, father, sibling, and friend than we are with professional roles, such as teacher, physician, computer technician, or paralegal. A role schema can be based on people whom you personally know who have filled that role or on imaginary figures, such as Bill Cosby's portrayal of the father on television in *The Bill Cosby Show* or Helen Hunt's portrayal of the wife in *Mad About You*. Most role schemas are a combination of real examples and imaginary possibilities. The role schemas you have can influence you as a standard—or model—of what you are seeking or trying to avoid, such as in a partner or a friend or even in yourself. In the following example, Lindsay's role schema of mothers is someone who is critical, put-upon, exhausted, angry, and chronically unhappy.

Lindsay. When Lindsay was six her parents divorced and her dad moved to another state. Her mother worked full-time while raising Lindsay and her two older sisters. Lindsay remembers how unhappy her mother always was. Nothing the girls did made her happy. She seldom smiled and rarely laughed. She was exhausted when she came home from work in the afternoon and impatient and critical of her daughters the moment she walked through the door. She would make them get up early on Saturday to begin their chores. If they did not do everything just right, she would yell at them and make them stay inside all day. She reminded the girls constantly of what a burden they were and how she had to work herself to death to buy their clothes and provide for them.

In view of that, Lindsay has no desire to become a mother and turn into that kind of person. When she accidentally became pregnant early in her marriage, her role schema of mothers created a dilemma for her. Later, we will discuss what happened to Lindsay, but for now you can see why she dreaded motherhood in view of how her role schema for mothers depicts the role.

If a role schema is extreme in either a negative or a positive direction, it can create problems. In Lindsay's case, her role schema for mothers is terribly negative, but extremely positive role schemas also can be troublesome. An unrealistically positive role schema can make it impossible for any real person to meet the associated criteria. For example, a woman might have an idealized role schema for a husband that he must be physically affectionate, emotionally supportive, protective, assertive, financially successful, athletic, witty, and love children. There are husbands like that, but even they have some negative attributes, such as occasionally cranky, frequently sloppy, and badly dressed. A real person can have a very difficult time trying to match someone else's idealistic role schemas. The discrepancies between our role schemas and the real people in our lives often create problems in our relationships.

Role schemas are not limited to individual or singular roles, such as a husband or a sibling. A role schema also can refer to two or more parties that constitute a unit, such as a role schema of families or role schema of marriage. These role schemas include generalizations and specific examples of all the parties included in that role schema. This book addresses only two role schemas that include multiple parties: family role schemas and marriage role schemas.

Family Role Schemas. A *family schema* would include views of how parents, children, and possibly grandparents, uncles, aunts, and cousins treat each other, what they think of each other, and how they feel about one another. Your family schema is based on real and imaginary information. The information in your family schema depends on the families that you have observed, heard about, or experienced directly plus imaginary families, such as those you have seen on television or simply imagined.

Other role schemas provide some of the information for a family schema. For your family schema, your role schemas of father, mother, son, daughter, and extended relatives all influence the way you think different parties are expected to behave in a family and how they treat different members of the family in different circumstances. In a sense, your family schema is a *mega-role* schema, because your family schema includes all your role schemas of the people involved in a family. A mega-role schema includes other role schemas in it, as illustrated by the family role schema.

Marriage Role Schemas. These schemas also illustrate how one schema can include other schemas in it. Your *marriage schemas* include your role schemas for husbands and wives. Marriage schemas often contribute to marital distress because they include expectations of how spouses should treat each other, express feelings, resolve differences, show love, and share household and child care responsibilities. When spouses have different role schemas for marriage, they may misinterpret each other's behavior.

For example, Megan and Michael had been married for less than a year when they sought counseling. Megan thought that their marriage was fine, but Michael thought they weren't getting along well. During Megan's childhood, her parents were very vocal, expressing anger loudly and intensely but quickly getting over such outbursts, and seldom holding a grudge. Snapping at each other was typical and holding in bad feelings was rare. Laughter and loving expressions were common, and they readily expressed physical affection with each other.

During Michael's childhood, his parents never raised their voices. When they were upset with each other, they withdrew and were subdued for a period of time. Physical affection was uncommon, and verbal expressions of love were even less frequent. Yet Michael felt his parents truly loved each other. They never showed each other any disrespect and each seemed devoted to the other, doing various things to be pleasing.

Naturally, Megan and Michael had marriage schemas consistent with their own previous experiences. Consequently, during the several months after their wedding, they behaved toward each other in ways consistent with their different marriage schemas. Megan snapped at Michael about minor household issues and raised her voice, even yelling at him occasionally, over bigger issues. Michael reacted by becoming subdued and then trying harder to please his wife. Over time, their interactions made Michael fearful that their marriage might not last. When he finally raised his concerns, Megan was stunned. She thought that he was as happy as she was. In turn, Michael was surprised by her reaction. He had assumed her behavior reflected how disappointed she was in him. In counseling, they discovered how their different marriage schemas were contributing to their marital distress. Clearly, your marriage and family schemas have a powerful impact on your expectations for yourself and others in those relationships.

Your Role Schemas

What are your role schemas? You can figure that out by doing the same thing you did to identify your person schemas. First, list the generalizations you have about the role and then give examples for each generalization. Your generalizations can include the beliefs, attitudes, feelings, and actions typical of someone in that role.

Roles that are important in relationships are listed below. Next to each role, describe the generalizations you have for that role. Then list the names of people in that role who illustrate your generalization. You may want to do this in a separate notebook.

Single adult female _____

Single adult male: _____

Wife: _____

Husband: _____

Daughter: _____

Son: _____

Father: _____

Mother: _____

Sister: _____

Brother: _____

Aunt: _____

Uncle: _____

Grandfather: _____

Grandmother: _____

Friend: _____

Boss: _____

Co-worker: _____

Employee: _____

Marriages: _____

Families: _____

Schema Interactions

Self schemas, person schemas, and role schemas all influence the way we function with others. These three types of schemas also interact with each other in your mind to influence your interpersonal actions and reactions. In the following example, you will see how Sarah's self schemas of *intimacy driven* and *entitlement* interact with her person schema of her stepson, Aaron, in a destructive way.

Sarah. Several years after her first husband left her for another woman, Sarah married Jason. She and her first husband had had a stormy relationship. Sarah, having no training or education, had been financially dependent on him and had been afraid to leave, hoping things would improve. His departure temporarily panicked her when her standard of living dropped drastically. She was barely able to survive on her clerical salary. By the time she met Jason, though, she had achieved financial stability. Jason had been divorced for two years and had a son, Aaron, from his first marriage. His first wife, too, had become involved in another relationship and left Jason, taking Aaron with her.

Jason and Sarah married after several months of dating. When their daughter, Emily, was born, Sarah quit her job although she had ambivalent feelings about doing so. She was anxious about relinquishing the financial security she had established, but felt confident that Jason was as devoted to her as she was to him. Jason told her he would be happy with whatever choice she made. Sarah wanted to stay home to raise their children, and Jason willingly worked harder to compensate for the loss of her income. Subsequently, Jason received a promotion that included a cross-country move. The move was especially difficult for Jason, because it was so far away from his son, Aaron. However, Jason felt that refusing to move would jeopardize his future with the company.

Sarah admits that Jason's relationship with Aaron threatens her. Jason seems much more playful and relaxed whenever his son visits. He stops obsessing about work, takes time off, and spends money freely on Aaron. Aaron married while in undergraduate school. Although Aaron's wife works, Jason continues to pay Aaron's tuition.

Sarah feels that Aaron has an expectation that he deserves to get whatever he wants. Sarah realizes that her *entitled* and *intimacy driven* *self schemas* are triggered by Jason's interactions with Aaron. When Aaron and his wife come to visit, she feels tense and resentful at how much easier their lives are than her life was as a young adult. Sarah feels angry that she has to negotiate with Jason for household expenses when he gives money so freely to Aaron. She feels "entitled" to have what she wants because she went without for so long.

Sarah's *intimacy driven* self schema originated in her childhood. Her parents always had a volatile relationship. Although her parents provided for their children, they fought about money and Sarah lived with chronic anxiety because she feared her father would follow through on his angry threats to leave. Sarah married right after she graduated from high school. In hindsight, which is always more illuminating than the present, she realizes that the primary appeal her first husband had was his job. He offered her the financial security that had eluded her parents. When he left her, Sarah's chronic fears of being abandoned and financially vulnerable were realized, which confirmed her *intimacy driven* self schema.

Sarah knows that Jason's relationship with Aaron triggers her *intimacy driven* self schema. When Jason acts so happy around Aaron, Sarah wonders if Jason loves his son more than he loves her or their daughter and she feels anxious that if forced to make a choice, Jason would pick Aaron over them. Her *entitled* self schema also is activated by Jason's generosity with Aaron, as she feels that Jason's money should be spent only on her and Emily. Her person schema of Aaron, which views Aaron as spoiled, selfish, and thoughtless, intensifies her feelings. Sarah sought counseling because she knew that her feelings toward Aaron are damaging her relationship with Jason.

This example illustrates how Sarah's self schemas and person schemas interact with each other. Sarah's *intimacy driven* self schema make her afraid of being abandoned. Jason's affection toward Aaron triggers that self schema and the associated fear that Jason will choose Aaron over her if she cannot find a way to accept Aaron. Her *entitled* self schema causes her to feel jealous and resentful of Jason's generosity with Aaron, although she acknowledges that Jason maintains a high quality lifestyle for her. Having gone without for so long, she feels "entitled" to everything, but she can see that this is an unfair expectation. Sarah's person schema of Aaron is that he is spoiled, self-indulgent, and lazy, because he lets his father help support him.

Schema Accuracy

Self, person, and role schemas are schemas that everyone has. However, the content in the schemas of one individual will not be exactly the same as the content in the schemas of someone else. *Your* schemas are *your* perceptions of reality, based on *your* experiences. For example, Sarah's person schema of Aaron is quite different from Jason's person schema of Aaron. Sarah's *Aaron* schema is predominantly negative and assigns few positive attributes to Aaron. In contrast, Jason's *Aaron* schema is predominantly positive, depicting Aaron as loving, devoted, playful, energetic, motivated, and bright. The different person schemas that Sarah and Jason have of Aaron are the result of different experiences with Aaron and the fact that Sarah and Jason each have different self schemas that influence their perceptions of Aaron.

Which person schema is more accurate? Is Sarah's person schema of Aaron more accurate than Jason's, or vice versa? Sarah's person schema might be based on several examples consistent with her schema, but the same is true of Jason's. Jason can describe numerous examples illustrating Aaron's fine qualities. So does accuracy depend on who has the most examples? Not exactly. In the next chapter you will see how schema accuracy is not quite as definitive as you might think. You also will see how schema conflict between people is a primary source of misunderstandings in relationships.

Conclusion

Supportive, nurturing relationships are essential to emotional and physical well-being. Yet relationship distress occurs in everyone's life. Getting along with other people can be difficult. Strained, hostile relationships can be tortuous, even debilitating. Everyone needs to and can become a relationship expert. Understanding schemas and the roles they play in your interpersonal life can help you attain that expertise.

A schema is a constellation of information on a topic that includes both generalizations and specific examples. Self schemas are the mental models you have about different aspects of yourself, such as your worthiness or your desirability. Although self schemas are the schemas you have about yourself, self schemas also contain interpersonal perspectives that have a major impact on the way you interact with other people.

Schemas organize your experiences on a particular topic. They expedite how you process information. They increase your ability to make accurate predictions about yourself and the people around you. Schemas are invaluable in your functioning. You can enhance the quality of your interpersonal life by understanding schemas. Even though *schema* is a very old term in psychology, most people have never heard of schemas. And though they may be an unfamiliar concept to you now, as you go from chapter to chapter, you will complete a paint-by-the-numbers picture of schemas. By the end of the book, you will have a clear vision of what schemas are and why they are so important in your relationships. You will be able to identify your own schemas and the schemas of other people as well.

2

How Accurate Are
Your Images?

The truth is balance, but the opposite of truth, which is
unbalance, may not be a lie.

—Susan Sontag, "Simon Weil,"
Against Interpretation

The schemas people have about others and themselves are the source
of many arguments. In the last chapter you saw how the different
person schemas that Sarah and Jason have of Jason's son, Aaron, create friction and hurt feelings between them. Schema differences are
seldom resolved by a simple determination of accuracy. Of course,
differences that are measurable can be evaluated for accuracy. For
example, if Sarah thinks Aaron is 5'9" and Jason thinks he is 6', accuracy easily can be determined by a yardstick, or if they disagree on
Aaron's eye color, accuracy can be resolved simply by closer examination. But measurable factual data comprises only a small part of
the content of a schema. *Schemas also contain memories, beliefs, assump-*
tions, generalizations, and expectations, most of which can not be objectively
measured and all of which can generate much disagreement and hostility
between people.

Schema Contents: What Is in There?

Schemas contain much more than simple factual information. They
accumulate a variety of information on a particular subject. Schemas
include both memories of specific events and memories that integrate
several similar past events, such as the way a family celebrated
Thanksgiving holidays. They also contain visual images of material
related to a particular topic. These images can be drawn from past

experiences, dreams, or fantasies. Other sensory memories can be included, such as the smell of your mother's perfume or the sound of her voice. Over time, schemas will include assumptions and generalizations based on the information within the schema. Beliefs, assumptions, and generalizations all generate expectations.

For example, children develop role schemas of fathers that consist of specific examples of the fathers they know and have observed in real life and those they have seen in movies or on television. From these various examples, one girl's schema might develop the conclusions and generalizations that fathers are young, more likely to be involved with their sons than their daughters, like sports more than movies, and yell when they are angry. Another girl may have a father who attends all of her school and extracurricular activities, spends his free time equally with her and her brother, and seldom raises his voice. She would develop very different generalizations about fathers.

The observations, specific examples, and memories that accumulate within a schema will influence the assumptions and generalizations that develop within that schema. In turn, these assumptions and generalizations then produce expectations. Your schema expectations then influence the goals you choose. To achieve those goals, you develop different plans and strategies. In the previous example, the first daughter may want to marry a man who is not so consumed by sports and who will be as attentive to his daughters as to his sons. This goal can influence the strategies she uses to evaluate future partners for herself. She might pay considerable attention to the way a man spends his leisure time and the way he interacts with his nephews and nieces. The second daughter may assume that fathers enjoy their sons and daughters equally, and her strategies for evaluating future partners might not even consider this issue.

Schemas can be viewed as constellations of information on different subjects, such as a role schema of daughters, a person schema of a particular individual, or a self schema about your desirability. All the information on that particular topic will be linked together in your brain. This constellation of information is a schema. The contents of a schema and the connections between a schema and goals, plans, and strategies are depicted below, with the box representing a schema.

Although different people may have schemas on the same subjects, the content within their schemas can be very different. These differences within schemas have the potential to create havoc in relationships. For example, both a husband and a wife will have marriage schemas but the actual content of their marriage schemas may vary greatly due to their different experiences. Those different experiences will produce different memories, observations, beliefs, conclusions,

Schema Contents and Connections

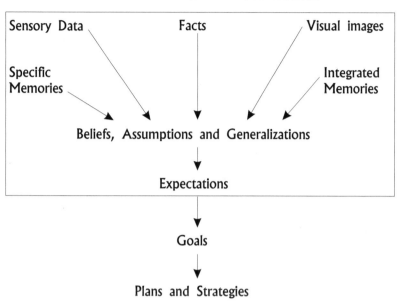

generalizations, and expectations about marriage. As a result of the differences in the schema content, considerable tension and frustration can develop between partners. To illustrate, let's look at the *marriage* schemas of George and Frieda.

George and Frieda

George and Frieda are in their late twenties and have been married for three years. In many ways their marriage schemas are quite similar. They both believe that the husband should be responsible for financial management and planning and that spouses do not have to share all the same leisure activities. They value fidelity and attending church together. They expect that children will be a part of their marriage and that parents should save for their children's college education.

However, significant differences between their marriage schemas also exist. According to George's schema, the husband should be the breadwinner and the wife should be responsible for household tasks and child care. George's schema also views frequent sexual relations as an important marital activity. His schema includes the beliefs that each partner will be receptive to the other's sexual overtures, and that the wife will initiate sexual activity as often as the husband will.

Frieda's schema views sex as an exclusive marital activity but the frequency of sexual activity will vary with the demands on their time and their feelings of emotional closeness. Frieda's marriage schema views the initiation of sexual activity as the husband's responsibility, and assumes the husband should understand when the wife is not inclined to sex at all. Frieda's schema views the husband as the breadwinner but also includes the belief that the husband should voluntarily help with household and child care responsibilities when the wife needs assistance.

George and Frieda have never discussed their schema differences but they have many heated arguments about their sexual relationship. They agree that for the last several months they have had sex once a week, but except for that simple fact, agreement between them disappears. George views weekly sex as too little. Frieda sees it as too much. George interprets this frequency data to mean that Frieda is no longer sexually attracted to him. He concludes that nothing he can do will increase her sexual desire for him. He wonders if she ever loved him or if she only wanted a husband.

On the other hand, Frieda interprets the frequency data as being the result of having a six-month-old baby and of her lack of rest, because George does little child care or housework. Frieda interprets George's unhappiness as evidence that George is concerned only with his own sexual needs and concludes that he is a selfish, thoughtless person. Frieda's conclusions cause her to feel resentful toward George and interfere with her sexual feelings toward him.

This example illustrates how the nonfactual content of schemas can contribute to personal unhappiness and relationship distress even when people agree on the factual content. In this situation George and Frieda have *marriage* schemas with different assumptions about how husbands and wives ought to behave. Their different assumptions create different expectations, which subsequently produce disappointment and resentment.

Expectations

Schema expectations are particularly important in our relationships. Different expectations between schemas on the same subject can create hostility between people. When expectations are unspoken, frustration can increase. George and Frieda have never spoken to each other about their sexual expectations. Many people feel uncomfortable discussing their sexual expectations, but people often do not discuss their expectations because they think their expectations are shared or are obvious. In the marriage schemas above, what if George and Frieda valued college education for their children differently, too. Let's consider that possibility.

Imagine that Frieda values a college education, assumes George shares that value, and expects George to develop a college savings fund as part of the husband's responsibility. Also imagine that George does not share that value. Several years might pass before it becomes obvious to Frieda that George has no intention of saving money for their children's education. At that point considerable distress would ensue, with Frieda feeling betrayed and George feeling unfairly blamed for not pursuing a goal that he never espoused. Expectations play a critical role in our relationships. Being able to identify the expectations of your schemas and those of the people around you often can help you to recognize the source of friction between you and others.

Although both spoken and unspoken schema expectations can be a major source of frustration and emotional distress, one particular expectation deserves mention here. I would be a wealthy woman if I had a dollar for each time I've heard a client say about a loved one, "He (or she) should know what I want. I shouldn't have to say it." Many people seem to have the expectation that love increases the psychic abilities of their loved ones. It does not. This expectation generates great misunderstanding and hurt feelings. Love means that someone will *care* about what you want, not *know* what you want.

Attention and Memories: Sources of Conflict

George and Frieda agree on the frequency data of their sexual activity, but therapists who work with couples and families will tell you that even supposedly factual information can generate many angry exchanges. I have heard two people describe the same events to me, and I would have sworn that one of them must have been somewhere else. Factual agreement is much more elusive than you might think. The mere frequency with which an event occurs can be intensely debated. Agreement might occur but only if both parties pay attention to the same aspects of an event and if they have infallible recall. Both of these premises are often absent.

Attention and memory are cognitive, or mental, processes that have a reciprocal relationship with schemas. In other words, attention and memory influence schemas, and, likewise, schemas influence what commands your attention and what you remember. As stated earlier, George concluded that Frieda is no longer sexually attracted to him. Over the past several months George's person schema of Frieda had begun to change. Originally, he believed that Frieda found him physically appealing. Her more recent lack of sexual interest in him has caused him to doubt that. Now he worries that she has no desire for him at all. George's person schema of Frieda has begun to shift toward seeing her as lacking any sexual desire for him.

In an earlier discussion, Frieda had explained that she was not feeling romantic since the baby's birth. George thought that was just an excuse to avoid telling him that she had lost interest in him. To test his hypothesis, George came home from work one evening with a bouquet of flowers. He thought, "This should stir some romantic feelings in Frieda if what she said is true." He walked into the kitchen and gave the flowers to her with a flourish. She said, "Thanks," and without offering a kiss or hug, lay the flowers on the counter, and rushed down to the laundry room where the dryer was buzzing. Not until after dinner did she put the flowers into a vase. At bedtime when he snuggled up to her, she rolled over on her stomach and mumbled, "Let's just go to sleep." She did not mention the flowers then or later.

George ruminated about that evening for days. The flowers had not made any difference. Frieda was not interested in him. After several weeks of harboring hurt feelings over this incident, George's person schema of Frieda changed. Now he viewed her as no longer being in love with him. One evening he blurted out that he knew Frieda did not love him anymore. When pressed to explain, George reminded her of how his gift of flowers had been virtually ignored. For a moment, Frieda did not even remember the flowers. George, having dwelled on his memories daily for six weeks, remembered the chain of events almost minute to minute and described them. Frieda then recalled the flowers, but she also remembered that the baby had had diarrhea all day and that she had been exhausted by bedtime and angry that George had not been more helpful. George's description of events had not included the baby being ill, Frieda's exhaustion from caring for the sick baby, or George's lack of assistance.

George had been keenly attentive to the events that night that were relevant to *his* schema concerns. He was testing his hypothesis about Frieda's feelings toward him and he focused his attention on her reactions to the flowers. Frieda's exhaustion and worry about the sick baby were less relevant to his concerns and thus received less of his attention. Frieda was exhausted and distracted by the baby and the laundry. The flowers barely got her attention. As a result, the information that got stored into George's memory was very different from what made it into Frieda's.

The more intensely we focus our attention on something, the more likely we are to remember it. However, two people never remember exactly all the same details of any event. Their attention will not be identically focused. Thus, they cannot remember what they did not notice.

Likewise, the more you review particular memories, the more likely you are to remember them. Because this event seemed to confirm George's fears of Frieda's lack of feeling for him, George thought about it for weeks. With each mental replay of the evening, his memory of how he perceived those events was strengthened. However, his memory was restricted to what seemed relevant to his schema. He had not associated Frieda's behavior with the baby's illness or with her exhaustion, so that information had received very little of his attention and subsequently was not entered into his memory.

People's memories of the same event can vary because they pay attention to different aspects of that event. This difference in attention is one reason that witnesses who see the same occurrence can describe it so differently. What each person remembers may be accurate, but those memories will not include everything that took place. Hence, there will be differences between people's memories of the same event.

Unfortunately, heated disagreements about what happened can cast doubt on each other's integrity. Although integrity can be the problem, people often overlook the simple fallibility of memory (Schacter 1999). Events that are not attended to are unlikely to create memories, but your memories are not infallible even when you are paying attention. Memories that are not recalled for long periods of time can be lost due to lack of use or interference from other memories. Information about similar experiences can become intermingled, making it hard to differentiate similar events.

You can even have memories of events that never happened to you, which are called "false" memories. False memories can be events that actually happened to someone else a long time ago and are now remembered as having been experienced by you. They also can be dreams that are no longer remembered as dreams but as actual events. False memories also can be created by the questions or comments of others when you are trying to recall an experience. Even the processes of recall and review can alter memories, by omitting old information and adding new information from other memories. There is one other significant detriment to accurate memories: your biased brain.

Your Brain Is Biased

Sometimes your memories are inaccurate because the original input was inaccurate. You might misinterpret what you see or hear, especially if that information is not quite clear. You can misinterpret a gesture or not quite catch a word. George and Frieda's example illustrates the cognitive process that psychologists refer to as confirmatory bias. *Confirmatory bias* is the tendency your brain has to interpret information in a way that is consistent with your current knowledge. This means that both your attention and your memory are biased.

Confirmatory Bias

You tend to pay attention to what is relevant to your schemas, and to interpret what you perceive in a way that is consistent with your schemas. Over time, you are more likely to remember information that is compatible with your schemas. All of this is the result of the confirmatory bias process. George's attention, interpretations, and memories all were consistent with his schema's hypothesis about Frieda's feelings for him. Once a schema has jelled, that schema influences your attention, interpretations, and memories. Confirmatory bias actually is a good thing. It expedites information processing and helps you make sense of bits of information.

For example, a woman walking to her car at night in a poorly lit parking lot of a shopping mall noticed a man running toward her with something held in his hand. This information triggered her rapist schema. She rushed to her car, jumped in, locked the doors, and started the engine as quickly as she could to pull away from him. This rapid response, which could have saved her life, is made possible by her brain's ability to pick up disparate pieces of information and in a nanosecond trigger a closely fitting schema which then assembles the information and allows her to immediately develop a strategy. When information is ambiguous, sketchy, or subject to different interpretations, one's schemas will strongly determine the way the information is processed.

While confirmatory bias is very helpful in processing most information, it does not always lead to correct conclusions or reactions. In the example above, the man hurrying toward the woman actually was carrying the wallet that had fallen from her purse when she pulled out her car keys. However, the impression that the woman received when she glanced over her shoulder and saw him running triggered her rapist schema because it was more easily activated. When the woman left the department store she realized that she had parked her car in a now darkened area of the parking lot. She felt very vulnerable as she walked out into the darkness alone, worrying about her safety and looking furtively about her. Her rapist schema was easily activated by the glimpse of a strange man running toward her with an object in his hand. This example also illustrates how schemas that have been recently active will be more easily triggered by relevant stimuli. The rapist schema was easily triggered, because the woman had been worrying about being assaulted when she first left the store.

Confirmatory bias is an extraordinarily helpful cognitive process, but it is not infallible, as the previous example demonstrates. Remember, the confirmatory bias process takes the information that is available and tries to fit that information into existing schemas. It makes sense that the results of this process occasionally will be flawed. Because confirmatory bias is a fallible process, the wrong schemas can sometimes be activated and the wrong conclusions drawn. When that happens, the result can be hurt feelings and intense disagreements between people, as occurred with George and Frieda. Confirmatory bias is one reason you have trouble changing your impressions of yourself and others. Once you have developed a schema, that schema tends to bias how you perceive things.

George finally heard Frieda's complaints about his lack of help around the house. He decided to try to change his behavior to see if that would make Frieda less irritable and more loving toward him. For several nights he unloaded the dishwasher and picked up after himself. He continued his efforts into the weekend, but he did not detect any change in Frieda's attitude toward him. So he pointed out to Frieda that he had been more helpful all week and it had made no difference. She had not even noticed. Frieda replied that she had noticed but that he was only doing this so she would have sex with him, so his different behavior didn't count.

Their discussion went downhill from there, but this illustrates the confirmatory bias process. Frieda did notice that George was being helpful in ways he had not been before, which did not fit her schema of him. Her schema was able to make sense of George's behavior only by attributing it to ulterior motives, in this case, to change Frieda's sexual response to him. So, Frieda's schema of George did not see his helping around the house as some permanent change on George's part but interpreted it as consistent with his obsession with sex. Thus, Frieda's schema of George remained unchanged.

When someone acts differently from their usual behavior, you either assume you have misunderstood their behavior or you develop an alternative explanation to make the perception consistent with your schema, as Frieda did. In many cases, your confirmatory bias is correct, but you can see how it can be a major obstacle to legitimate efforts to change. How to change schemas will be discussed in later chapters. There you will learn how to prevent confirmatory bias from sabotaging attempts by you or others to make genuine changes.

Schemas: A Matter of Balance

You now know that schemas contain much more than simple factual data. Schemas contain memories, which may or may not be accurate. They also include beliefs, assumptions, generalizations, and expectations, all of which seldom can be measured for accuracy. You also know that schemas tend to bias your attention, interpretations, and memory. So how can you determine if your schemas are legitimate? How can you be sure your schemas perceive reality at least to some reasonable degree?

Balance and Self Schemas

Recall that self schemas are schemas you have about different aspects of yourself. They develop automatically from your brain's recognition of patterns in your actions and reactions. Self schemas help you make sense of what you do and how you are treated. They allow you to make predictions about yourself—about how you will react, what you will think, what you are capable of doing, how you will feel, and so forth. Self schemas vary anywhere from being exclusively negative to exclusively hyperpositive. Hyperpositive means unrealistically positive. Exclusively negative or hyperpositive self schemas are polar extremes that are one-sided views of yourself.

Let's look at the self schemas in the domain of *Worthiness* to illustrate this. The *Unworthy* self schema is a negative view that sees the self as undeserving of having his or her needs met, and being less important and valuable than other people. The *Entitled* self schema is a hyperpositive view that sees the self as more deserving than other people, superior to others, and having a right to the best of everything. The *Worthy* self schema sees the self as worthwhile as others but not necessarily more so, and as deserving of having many of his or her needs met—but certainly not all. On the subject of worthiness, the *Worthy* self schema includes both positive content (seeing the self as worthwhile as others) and negative content (not deserving of having *all* needs met). The *Unworthy* and *Entitled* self schemas are extreme views, whereas the *Worthy* view is more moderate.

Since self schemas range from negative to hyperpositive, the self schemas in any domain can be placed on a continuum according to how negative or hyperpositive they are, in other words, according to their polarities. The most extreme self schemas would be at either end of the continuum. On the *Worthiness* continuum *Unworthy* would be a negative self schema, and *Entitled* would be a hyperpositive self schema, so *Unworthy* and *Entitled* would be at opposite poles of the continuum. *Worthy* would fall on the continuum between them. On any continuum, the more negative the self schema, the closer it will be to the negative pole, and the more hyperpositive the self schema, the closer it will be to the hyperpositive pole. The drawing depicts how the *Worthiness* schemas are distributed according to their polarities.

The Worthiness Continuum

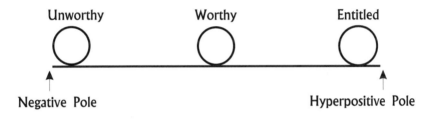

Understanding that self schemas vary in polarity can help you determine the validity of your own self schemas. The validity of a self schema is better viewed as a matter of balance rather than as a question of accuracy. Accuracy refers to whether something is right or wrong. Information in a self schema may be accurate but incomplete. This incomplete picture creates distortion by omission. Thus, your self schema may be very limited and present a lopsided picture of you to yourself. Balance refers to how comprehensive—how complete—the information in a schema is. The more balanced a self schema is, the more complete the picture it presents of you.

Self schemas can be balanced or unbalanced. Balanced self schemas integrate negative, neutral, and positive information on a subject. The *Worthy* self schema is a balanced self schema. Unbalanced self schemas contain either almost all negative or almost all hyperpositive content. *Unworthy* and *Entitled* self schemas are unbalanced self schemas. Whether tilted in a hyperpositive or negative direction, unbalanced self schemas are distorted views that give you incomplete pictures of yourself. The drawings below illustrate the principle of balance using the *Worthy, Unworthy,* and *Entitled* self schemas from the *Worthiness* continuum:

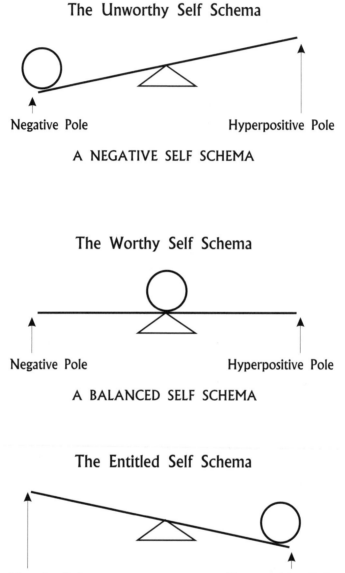

The Unworthy Self Schema

Negative Pole   Hyperpositive Pole

A NEGATIVE SELF SCHEMA

The Worthy Self Schema

Negative Pole   Hyperpositive Pole

A BALANCED SELF SCHEMA

The Entitled Self Schema

Negative Pole   Hyperpositive Pole

A HYPERPOSITIVE SELF SCHEMA

Because accuracy is often an elusive concept, thinking of schemas in terms of balance better addresses their validity. The more balanced a self schema is, the more complete the picture it presents. Unbalanced self schemas present incomplete pictures of you. A balanced schema does not have to have an equal amount of positive and negative information. In fact, in most cases, balanced self schemas tend to have somewhat more positive than negative information (Fiske and Taylor 1991). Having a somewhat more positive view of yourself seems to be adaptive for good functioning and emotional well-being.

What Hyperpositive Means

This somewhat more positive view of the self, typical of balanced self schemas, is why the positive end of the continuum is called *hyperpositive*, not just positive. *Hyperpositive is positive to excess, with no inclusion of any negative information.* Such hyperpositive self schemas are detrimental to one's functioning and frequently alienate others (Shedler, Mayman, and Manis 1993; Colvin and Block 1994; Colvin, Block, and Funder 1995). Therefore balanced self schemas are not neutral or zero in polarity. They are slightly positive, but on a continuum that ranges from negative to hyperpositive poles; balanced self schemas fall in the middle. Person and role schemas also can be viewed in terms of balance, and they can be either balanced or unbalanced. If they are unbalanced, they can be unbalanced in either a negative or hyperpositive way. Let's look at some person schemas.

Balance and Person Schemas

Remember Aaron? He is Jason's son from his first marriage. As Jason's second wife, Sarah is Aaron's stepmother and her person schema of him sees him as selfish, thoughtless, and lazy, among other negative attributes. Few if any positive attributes are included in Sarah's schema of Aaron, which is a negative person schema. In contrast to Sarah's schema, Jason's schema depicts Aaron as loving, playful, motivated, and intelligent. Jason's schema of his son is a hyperpositive person schema, which is devoid of any negative content. Both Jason and Sarah's person schemas of Aaron provide incomplete pictures of the young man.

Aaron's wife, Tracy, has a balanced person schema of Aaron. Tracy's schema views Aaron as loving, faithful, responsible, fun, and somewhat insecure, impatient, and overly competitive. Tracy's schema includes both positive and negative aspects about Aaron. Rather than a one-sided view, Tracy's person schema has integrated both positive and negative information about her husband. The drawings below illustrate the principle of balance with the person schemas for Aaron.

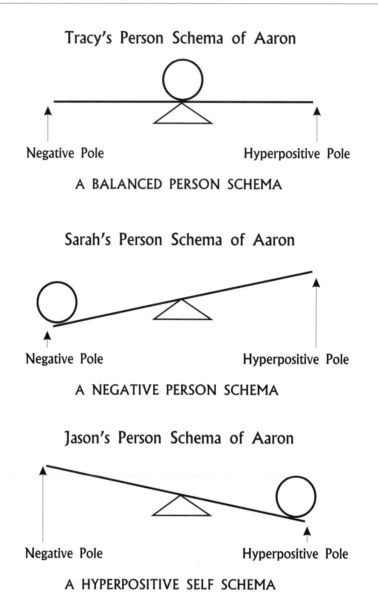

Tracy's Person Schema of Aaron

Negative Pole   Hyperpositive Pole

A BALANCED PERSON SCHEMA

Sarah's Person Schema of Aaron

Negative Pole   Hyperpositive Pole

A NEGATIVE PERSON SCHEMA

Jason's Person Schema of Aaron

Negative Pole   Hyperpositive Pole

A HYPERPOSITIVE SELF SCHEMA

Balance and Role Schemas

As with self schemas and person schemas, role schemas also can be either balanced or unbalanced. Remember Lindsay, the young woman whose divorced mother modeled a very miserable picture of motherhood? Lindsay's role schema of a mother is a woman who is relentlessly overworked, never satisfied, irritable, and unhappy with her children. Lindsay's role schema is clearly a negative role schema. A hyperpositive role schema might view a mother as someone who is always cheerful, tirelessly helpful, never critical, endlessly patient, playful yet hard-working, always emotionally accessible, an excellent cook, and an impeccable housekeeper. Such a role schema is just as unidimensional in a hyperpositive way as Lindsay's role schema was in a negative way.

An example of a balanced role schema for a mother is a one who is loving but occasionally moody, usually helpful, sets effective limits for her children, may or may not be a particularly good housekeeper or cook, doesn't enjoy sporting events even if her kids are participants, and tries to be fair in deciding sibling disagreements. This role schema includes both positive and negative content.

Similarly, a balanced role schema of a family might view family members as cooperative for the most part, argumentative at times but never to the point of vicious name calling or physical aggression, eating one meal together most days, going to church and school activities regularly, disagreeing at times on recreational interests, disagreeing about household responsibilities, being supportive of each other and not making disparaging comments about family members to other people. As with all balanced schemas, the balanced *family* schema contains both positive and negative information, thereby providing a more comprehensive picture of a family.

A hyperpositive role schema of a family might see the family as eating two meals together daily, agreeing on all family activities consensually, cheerfully accepting differences of opinion, never raising their voices in anger, eagerly pitching in to do household chores, volunteering to help each other with any odious task, and being unfailingly respectful of parental authority. A negative role schema of a family will be at the other end of the continuum, such as a schema that views family members as being detached and unconcerned about each other; parents being neglectful and/or abusive and drinking and using drugs frequently, children left to fend for themselves, and all family members constantly arguing and fighting, even to the point of physical aggression.

These examples illustrate how balance applies to all three types of schemas: self schemas, person schemas, and role schemas. Schemas on any subject, such as marriage, your grandmother, or your worthiness, can be placed on a continuum with opposite polarities at the ends. The schemas will fall on the continuum according to their polarities. Overly negative schemas will be closer to the negative end of the continuum, and overly positive schemas will be closer to the hyperpositive end of the continuum.

Unbalanced Schemas: More Than an Absence of Balance

Interestingly, unbalanced schemas at either end of the continuum are more similar to each other in many respects than they are to balanced schemas in the middle. How are negative schemas and hyperpositive schemas more similar to each other than they are to balanced schemas? They are incomplete, unidimensional views. They tend to be inflexible and have difficulty integrating contradictory information. They evoke more intense emotional reactions, and they can be an obstacle to developing more effective coping behavior.

For example, the last description of a negative *family* schema was produced by Jake, a twenty-five-year-old single man. When he understood that this was a negative schema, he said, "But that is my family schema. My family members are awful to each other. That is what my family and the families in my neighborhood were like. So even if I have a negative family schema, it's real. It's not inaccurate." And Jake is right. *Just because a schema is unbalanced does not mean that it is inaccurate.*

Unbalanced = Rigid Thinking

At the beginning of this chapter there is a quote from Susan Sontag, "The truth is balance, but the opposite of truth, which is unbalance, may not be a lie." Sontag was not referring to schemas, but she could have been. The content in an unbalanced schema is not necessarily inaccurate and is certainly not a lie, but an unbalanced schema is *incomplete*. Not only is the information primarily one-sided, the schema itself seems impermeable to accepting alternative content. Even though Jake's experience was consistent with the negative family schema described earlier, at various times Jake has also seen examples of other types of families. However, Jake's unbalanced schema will not allow that information to be absorbed or even considered as a possibility.

Remember the confirmatory bias process that was described earlier? Confirmatory bias causes you to interpret information in a way that is consistent with the knowledge you already have. In unbalanced schemas, the confirmatory bias process seems extreme. There is a very good explanation for that. *People develop extremely unbalanced schemas when there is little contradictory data available during the schema's development.* Once that extreme schema is in place, discrepant information simply seems unbelievable. Because much information is contradictory to an unbalanced schema, the confirmatory bias process is very busy interpreting this incompatible data to fit the existing extreme schema content.

Jake had many exposures to that negative type of family in his own family and among the families of his friends. Jake's negative *family* schema did not view concern or love as descriptive terms for family members. As he got older, he was exposed to other more balanced families, but his negative schema was already firmly in place. As a result, he believed those other families were a sham: He thought, "People are not concerned about each other. People are out for themselves. When family members act nice to each other, they are up to something."

Extremely unbalanced schemas tend to discount contradictory information automatically, because it is too different from the content already in the schema. This then produces a *closed* information processing system. Only information consistent with the schema is allowed into the system. In contrast, a balanced schema is open to considering all relevant information, because the content in that schema is already more varied. This is why balanced schemas are more flexible than unbalanced schemas. Flexibility refers to modifiability. Flexible schemas can adjust to new information.

For example, Bill has a balanced person schema of Sam, his employee. Initially, Bill's balanced schema saw Sam as hardworking, reliable, trustworthy, somewhat clumsy, and aloof. Over time, Bill realized that Sam is not really aloof but rather is shy. Once Sam gets to know people, he is friendly and talkative. After Bill saw Sam in various situations, Bill's schema dropped "aloof" and incorporated "shy" into its view of Sam. This illustrates the flexibility of a balanced schema. An unbalanced schema puts the schema's owner at a disadvantage. It automatically discounts information that might expand or alter the schema, thus maintaining a rigid one-dimensional perspective. Clearly then, balanced schemas differ from unbalanced schemas in several important ways.

Unbalanced schemas do not just interfere with our cognitive processes, they also disrupt our emotional systems as well. Unbalanced schemas are more readily associated with stronger and more frequent negative emotional reactions. Think about the examples of the different types of unbalanced schemas described earlier in this chapter. What kind of emotions would such schemas evoke? Apprehension, tension, anxiety, dread, anger, disappointment, sadness, depression, hopelessness, despair—all negative emotions.

Unbalanced = Intense Emotions

More extreme schemas evoke more extreme emotions. Balanced schemas evoke more moderate emotions. How do schemas do that? They do it primarily in two ways. One, they do it largely through the expectations they produce. For example, consider the negative *Unworthy* self schema described earlier: *I do not deserve to have my needs met; I am less important than other people are; I don't count as much as other people do; other people's needs are more important than mine.* What kind of expectations would that schema produce? You would expect to rarely get much of what you want and would expect that other people's needs will take precedence over yours. You also would expect to be mostly ignored and neglected by others. What kind of emotions would those expectations elicit? Disappointment, pessimism, and depression would be the most likely.

Now consider the hyperpositive polarity on the *Worthiness* continuum. The hyperpositive schema would be *Entitled*: *I am more important than other people; I deserve to have what I want regardless of the costs to others; all my needs should be met; I have a right to whatever I want.* Such expectations might suggest a happy, almost euphoric mood, and that may be true. But when such elevated expectations are not met, and at some point they most surely will not be, the *Entitled* person will react with shock, despair, and even rage. You can see how both hyperpositive and negative schemas are prone to evoke extreme emotions.

In contrast, think about the balanced schema of *Worthy* on the *Worthiness* continuum: *I am as important as other people but no more so; my needs are as important as those of other people; I deserve to have some of my needs met but not all; I am entitled to nice things but not necessarily the best of everything.* The *Worthy* schema produces more moderate expectations: *I will get some of my needs met, but not all of them.* Such expectations are unlikely to produce frequent or prolonged bouts of pessimism or despair. There will be occasional periods of disappointment, but nothing that will prevent an effective emotional rebound. Balanced schemas produce more tempered expectations and evoke more moderate emotional reactions. This does not mean that a *Worthy* schema will prevent you from experiencing joy or agony on various occasions, but a *Worthy* schema will not create expectations that typically produce extreme emotions. The expectations associated with schemas are critical to the emotions produced by schemas.

A second major way that schemas affect our emotional systems is through the memories associated with schemas. Schemas include a variety of memories related to the schema. For example, Jake's negatively unbalanced family schema has a thousand memories of his parents drinking, yelling, and cursing each other and the kids, of the kids being left alone for hours night and day while his parents were at the bars, of the kids always being hungry because there was seldom anything edible in the house, and of often being cold and frequently sick because alcohol and drugs used up any money the parents might have had for warm clothing or health care.

What emotions would be associated with such experiences? Fear, apprehension, anger, sadness, and helplessness are all likely candidates. Strong emotions that are present during our experiences attach to the memories of those experiences. When we recall memories that had intense emotional reactions connected with them, we often re-experience to some degree the emotions associated with those memories. Thus, when Jake's family schema is triggered, along with the memories for that schema come the negative emotions connected to those memories.

Negative schemas include numerous memories of emotionally unpleasant experiences, but hyperpositive schemas also include memories of unpleasant emotional experiences. Hyperpositive schemas will include memories of occasions when the schema's unrealistic expectations were not met. When those memories are activated, the despair or rage that might have accompanied such experiences also will be activated.

In contrast, balanced schemas will have more moderate emotions associated with most of the memories in them, but inevitably there will be some memories that are associated with strong emotions too. The difference is that strong negative emotions will have been attached to a small percentage of the balanced schema's memories, whereas a larger number of such intense emotional memories exist in unbalanced schemas. Moreover, the intensity and duration of the emotions associated with unbalanced schemas are likely to be much greater than the intensity or the duration of negative emotions associated with balanced schemas.

Unbalanced = Behavior Interference

Unbalanced schemas are more likely to evoke negative emotions through the expectations and memories such schemas evoke, thereby disrupting your emotional systems as well as your cognitive systems. Unbalanced schemas create problems in your thinking and your feelings, but they don't stop there. They also create problems in your behavior, in the actions you take and the actions you don't take. Let's take another look at Jake's negative family schema.

Would you be surprised to discover that Jake has never been in a serious relationship? Probably not. From his perspective, a family is something to avoid. He has no intention of ever creating another family in his life. So he keeps people at a distance. He does not want any close attachments, because according to his schema they bring only disappointment and pain. He dates occasionally, but never sees anyone more than two or three times. You can readily see how Jake's *family* schema has influenced his behavior.

Let's look at another example of the connection between schemas and behavior. Angela has been in a verbally abusive relationship with Frank for three years. He verbally berates her, ridicules anything she tries to do, embarrasses her in front of others, and swears at her whenever he is in a bad mood. Angela's *Unworthy* self schema makes such behavior seem reasonable: *I don't deserve to be treated nicely. I must deserve such behavior, or he wouldn't treat me like that. I must do things that upset him. I must be inadequate in meeting his needs, so no wonder he gets upset with me.* Unfortunately, the more of this abuse Angela receives, the more her *Unworthy* schema is reinforced. The abuse fits her schema: *I deserve it.* So Angela takes no action to change Frank's behavior or to leave the situation. Rather, she simply tries harder and harder to please Frank and to not upset him. Her *Unworthy* schema clearly affects the action she does take and the action she does not take. *Schemas have a powerful impact on your thoughts, feelings, and behavior.* When schemas are unbalanced, they create distress within you and impair the quality of your relationships.

Schema Characteristics

Balanced Schemas	Unbalanced Schemas
Multidimensional views	Unidimensional views
Can include positive, negative, and neutral information	Limited to negative or hyperpositive information
Flexible	Inflexible
Open to novel information	Closed to novel information
Evoke moderate emotions	Evoke intense emotions
Open to behavioral changes	Inhibit behavioral changes

Are Your Schemas of Others Balanced?

Now that you know what balanced and unbalanced schemas are, you can figure out whether your person and role schemas are balanced or unbalanced. Return to the person and role schemas you identified and described at the end of chapter 1. Reread what you wrote for each person or each role. Now, label whether all of the information you have written describes a balanced, negative, or hyperpositive schema.

Then, describe the typical emotions that each person and role schema evokes in you. How do you usually feel when you think about these people or roles? Describe specific emotions that these people evoke in you when you are around them. All of this information will be important later when you analyze your relationships. To illustrate what one of your exercise sheets would look like at this point, here is a continuation for Jack's person schema.

Jack

Is generous: always gives some kind of donation to any charity drive; paid for his mom to take a cruise on her seventy-fifth birthday; let me borrow his car when mine broke down and I had a job interview.

Is trustworthy: never told anyone what I told him about the way my dad treated me; has never been unfaithful to his wife.

Has a good sense of humor: is witty; enjoys jokes; can take a joke on himself.

Can be opinionated: when he thinks he is right, he will not give up in an argument; he seemed annoyed with me that I ended up buying the Chevy instead of the Ford he recommended.

Is judgmental: he has strong religious opinions and views people in black-or-white terms; when his seventeen-year-old niece got pregnant, he was angry with her and wouldn't speak to her for months.

Overall Balance of Person Schema: *balanced (includes both positive and negative attributes of Jack).*

Emotions Jack evokes in me: *laughter; calmness, when in trouble I seek his advice; fear at times when I disagree with him or do something which I know he would disapprove.*

3

To Bond or Not to Bond

The bonds that unite another person to ourself
exist only in our mind.

—Marcel Proust, *Remembrance of*
Things Past: The Sweet Cheat Gone

Unbalanced schemas disrupt your thinking, your emotions, and your behavior. They produce personal distress and disrupt your relationships. Their influence is so automatic and subtle that you don't even recognize that they are at work. For years your schemas have been directing your life even though you may never have heard the term until you picked up this book. The schema idea is not some new off-the-wall psychology fad. Sir Frederick Bartlett, an early experimental psychologist, identified the concept in the 1930s when he was investigating how people process information. Only in the past ten to twenty years have psychologists begun to appreciate the enormous influence schemas have. And even more recently has the effect schemas have on interpersonal functioning begun to be uncovered. This chapter will begin to illuminate how your self schemas are influencing your interpersonal life. In the last two chapters you began to identify the schemas you have for specific people and for different roles. Now you will identify your self schemas.

The Bonding Self Schemas

All self schemas have interpersonal implications, but certain self schemas seem to be particularly influential in the way you approach relationships. These are called the *bonding* self schemas, because of their role in how you develop bonds with other people. There are four bonding self schema areas, or domains, that are particularly important in relationships: Worthiness, Intimacy, Expressiveness, and Interdependency.

- *Worthiness* refers to how you value yourself, whether you think you are as deserving as most other people or more or less so.

- *Intimacy* is the schema domain that focuses on how comfortable you are being emotionally close to others.

- *Expressiveness* has to do with whether and how you express your thoughts and emotions.

- *Interdependency* refers to your views about relying on other people and on yourself.

All four of these bonding self schema domains have a major impact on the way you interact with other people. To understand your approach to relationships, you need to know what your bonding self schemas are.

Doing the Exercises

The following exercises will allow you to identify your bonding self schemas. A *negative self schema,* a *balanced self schema,* and a *hyperpositive self schema* will be described for each of the bonding areas of *Worthiness, Intimacy, Interdependency,* and *Expressiveness.* You can check one, two, or all three of the self schemas on any continuum as being descriptive of you. Follow these steps in doing this exercise:

1. There will be a general description for each self schema. If parts of it apply to you and parts don't, you will need to individualize each description to fit yourself. If part of the definition fits you and part of it doesn't, draw a line through the parts that do not describe you. If none of the description fits you, do nothing until step 2.

2. For each schema, check whether the self schema is *usually, sometimes,* or *never* descriptive of you. Put a check mark in the space provided.

3. For each schema that you check as *usually* or *sometimes* descriptive of you, give an example. Examples by other people with that self schema are provided for each schema.

The Worthiness Continuum

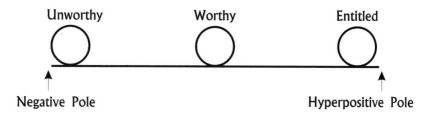

Unworthy   Worthy   Entitled

Negative Pole   Hyperpositive Pole

The *Worthiness* self schemas reflect your fundamental image of yourself, whether you see yourself as inferior, equal to, or superior to others in basic humanness. The *Worthiness* self schemas convey whether you think your needs matter. They determine how you treat yourself and what kind of treatment you expect and tolerate from others. They also influence how you treat others, whether with mutual respect, subservience, or condescension. The *Worthiness* self schemas indicate how you value yourself and others.

People with a balanced *Worthy* self schema are egalitarians, that is, they believe in human equality and they apply this belief toward themselves and others. They view others as deserving the same respect that they do. People with the negative *Unworthy* self schema view themselves as less deserving than others. Their needs and rights are less important than those of other people. Individuals with a hyperpositive *Entitled* self schema see themselves as superior to others. For various reasons, they feel they deserve special treatment. You can have one, two, or all three of these *Worthiness* self schemas.

The Unworthy Self Schema

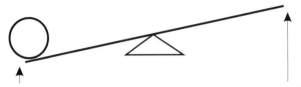

Negative Pole   Hyperpositive Pole

A NEGATIVE SELF SCHEMA

UNWORTHY: I often feel that somehow I am not as good as other people. My needs are not as important as the needs of other people. I don't deserve to be happy. The needs of other people should come before my own. I tend to feel guilty if I do nice things for myself. I also feel uncomfortable when other people do nice things for me.

Examples:

> At work when other people ask for time off, I always agree to cover for them even if it means that I miss out on things I want to do.

> My wife says I will spend money on whatever the kids want, but I won't buy myself a new sport coat to replace the worn one I have.

> I loaned my brother several hundred dollars that I had been saving to use to repair my truck, even though my brother has never repaid me any of the money he has borrowed.

> I am uncomfortable whenever someone gives me an expensive present . . . or any kind of present, actually. I am even uncomfortable receiving compliments.

The Unworthy self schema describes me:

_____ Usually _____ Sometimes _____ Never

My examples of my Unworthy self schema are:

_____

_____

_____

_____

The Worthy Self Schema

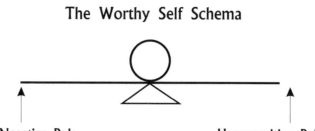

Negative Pole   Hyperpositive Pole

A BALANCED SELF SCHEMA

WORTHY: I am a worthwhile person. My needs are as important as the needs of other people, but not necessarily more so. I deserve to be as happy as everyone else. I deserve to have many of my needs met, but certainly not all of them. I can treat myself occasionally without feeling guilty. I am comfortable when other people do things for me. I like nice things, but I don't have to have the best of everything.

Examples*:*

I am comfortable taking my allotted vacation or sick time without feeling guilty, but I do appreciate how that may create a burden on others.

Sometimes I will spend money on myself for things I want, not just things I need, but I won't go into excessive debt for those things.

I enjoy receiving presents from other people, but not if those presents create a financial burden for them.

Occasionally I will do things for other people that may inconvenience me, but I don't do that all the time.

The Worthy self schema describes me:

_____ Usually   _____ Sometimes   _____ Never

My examples of my Worthy self schema are:

_____

_____

_____

_____

The Entitled Self Schema

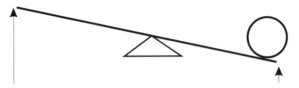

Negative Pole   Hyperpositive Pole

A HYPERPOSITIVE SELF SCHEMA

ENTITLED: I think I am as good as anyone else, if not better. I am entitled to have whatever I want. I deserve to have the best of everything. I have a right to have all my needs met. I don't think about what my needs may cost others. I am special. I think more about my own needs than how those needs may affect other people.

Examples:

When I can't have what I want, I feel cheated.

I have bought things that I couldn't afford, because I couldn't stand to get anything less than exactly what I wanted.

People don't ask me for favors, because they know I don't like to be inconvenienced.

I get very annoyed when I have to wait in line for anything.

I will express my disappointment when people give me presents that I don't care for.

The Entitled self schema describes me:

_____ Usually   _____ Sometimes   _____ Never

My examples of my Entitled self schema are:

_____

_____

_____

_____

The Intimacy Continuum

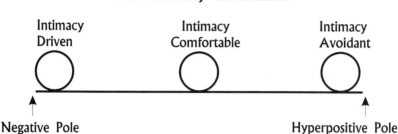

Intimacy
Driven

Intimacy
Comfortable

Intimacy
Avoidant

Negative Pole   **Hyperpositive Pole**

The self schemas on the *Intimacy* continuum indicate how you feel about emotional closeness. Do you enjoy emotional intimacy or try to avoid it? Do you like other people to get to know you, or do you prefer to remain aloof and unknown? Do you feel uncomfortable when others ask you personal questions, or do you appreciate their interest? Do you feel tense when others reveal personal information about themselves to you? Do you worry about losing the people close to you? Do you feel desperate if you are not in a relationship? Does a committed relationship feel more like a burden than a joy? Do you enjoy time alone, or do you feel uncomfortable if you are not doing something with someone else?

All of these questions relate to your *Intimacy* self schemas. The *Intimacy* self schemas reveal your comfort with emotional intimacy and how secure you feel in your relationships. These self schemas are integral to your approach to relationships. People with the balanced *Intimacy Comfortable* self schema enjoy emotional closeness and do not worry about being abandoned. People with the negative *Intimacy Driven* self schema crave emotional closeness but worry whether their relationships will last. Those with the hyperpositive *Intimacy Avoidant* self schema feel uncomfortable with emotional intimacy and keep people at a distance. As with all schemas, you can have one, two, or all three of the *Intimacy* self schemas at different times.

The Intimacy Driven Self Schema

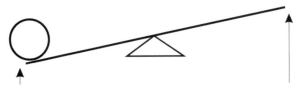

Negative Pole   Hyperpositive Pole

A NEGATIVE SELF SCHEMA

INTIMACY DRIVEN: I often want more closeness or greater intimacy than others give me. I seek repeated reassurance from others that I am loved. I feel lost if I am not in an intimate relationship. I have difficulty functioning if I am not involved with someone. I worry about losing people who are close to me. I worry about being abandoned. I am usually alert to any signs of rejection by others.

Examples:

I repeatedly ask my partner if he loves me.

Jealousy has often been a problem in my relationships.

I never end one relationship completely until I have begun another one.

I have stayed in unhealthy relationships, because I had not yet found someone else to be with.

Other people describe me as having my feelings easily hurt.

The Intimacy Driven self schema describes me:

_____ Usually _____ Sometimes _____ Never

My examples of the Intimacy Driven self schema are:

_____

_____

_____

_____

The Intimacy Comfortable Self Schema

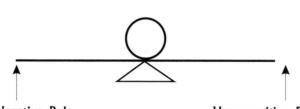

Negative Pole   Hyperpositive Pole

A BALANCED SELF SCHEMA

INTIMACY COMFORTABLE: I enjoy having close relationships, and I also enjoy my time by myself. I like emotional intimacy with certain people, but I don't like to be smothered. I am able to function fine when I am not in a close relationship even if I would prefer to be. It would be painful to lose someone close to me, but I think I could handle it. I don't like rejection, but it's not the end of the world when I get it. I seldom worry about being abandoned.

Examples:

I enjoy being in a close intimate relationship with my spouse, but I also enjoyed the time when I was single and not attached to anyone in particular.

I don't spend time wondering whether my spouse and close friends are loyal to me.

Jealousy has seldom been a problem in any of my close intimate relationships.

When people disagree with me, I don't think that means they don't like me.

I like having close friends in whom I can confide.

The Intimacy Comfortable self schema describes me:

_____ **Usually**   _____ **Sometimes**   _____ **Never**

My examples of my Intimacy Comfortable self schema are:

_____

_____

_____

_____

The Intimacy Avoidant Self Schema

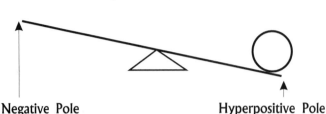

Negative Pole   Hyperpositive Pole

A HYPERPOSITIVE SELF SCHEMA

INTIMACY AVOIDANT: I prefer to keep most people at a distance. I am not comfortable being too close to other people. Relationships often seem like a burden to me. Emotional intimacy feels suffocating. Relationships aren't that important to me. I prefer not getting too attached to people.

Examples:

I am friendly with people, but I never have had a best friend.

I would rather spend my time alone than with other people.

Other people expect too much emotional intimacy from me in relationships.

I don't like it when other people try to get too close to me.

I have been described as a loner.

I always feel more relaxed alone than I do with other people.

The Intimacy Avoidant self schema describes me:

_____ Usually _____ Sometimes _____ Never

My examples of my Intimacy Avoidant self schema are:

_____

_____

_____

_____

The Expressiveness Continuum

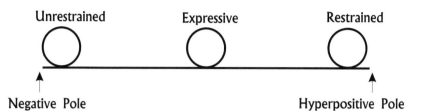

Unrestrained   Expressive   Restrained

Negative Pole   Hyperpositive Pole

The *Expressiveness* self schemas address how you feel about revealing your emotions. Do you think that showing emotions is a sign of weakness? Are you embarrassed about feeling strong emotions? Do you often feel overwhelmed by your emotions? Do you usually try to express intense negative emotions in a constructive manner? When you are angry, do you say mean and hateful things? Do you try to hide your feelings? Are you able to stand up for yourself without being abusive to others? Do you think feeling angry is a human flaw? Do you think you are unable to contain your emotional reactions?

The self schemas on the *Expressiveness* continuum reveal your thoughts about the need for emotional control and your ability to handle your emotional reactions. People with a balanced *Expressive* self schema view emotions as fundamental to being human and usually are able to express their positive and negative feelings to others constructively. Those with the negative *Unrestrained* self schema think they are unable to control their emotional reactions and, at times, feel taken over by their emotions. People with the *Restrained* self schema pride themselves on their emotional control to the point of denying the presence of any negative feelings. They are embarrassed to let others see them upset. *Expressiveness* self schemas vary in whether they allow you to be open with others about your personal thoughts and feelings, regardless of whether they are positive or negative.

The Unrestrained Self Schema

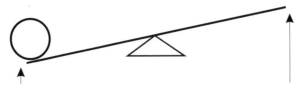

Negative Pole   Hyperpositive Pole

A NEGATIVE SELF SCHEMA

UNRESTRAINED: My emotions often are overwhelming. It is difficult for me to control them. People can easily tell how I am feeling. I cannot hide my emotions, they often seem out of control.

Examples:

People say that I wear my feelings on my sleeve.

People have told me that I am too emotional.

I get frustrated easily. I have trouble controlling my temper.

When I feel strong emotions, I often say or do things I regret later.

Some of my relationships have been strained because of how emotional I have been.

If I am upset, I often yell, curse, and, at times, throw things. I have even broken things.

On several occasions I have regretted what I disclosed to some people.

The Unrestrained self schema describes me:

_____ Usually _____ Sometimes _____ Never

My examples of my Unrestrained self schema are:

_____

_____

_____

_____

The Expressive Self Schema

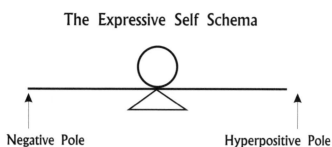

Negative Pole   Hyperpositive Pole

A BALANCED SELF SCHEMA

EXPRESSIVE: I am comfortable expressing my feelings. As a rule, I can control my feelings when I need to, but not always. Even if I am upset, I usually can express my thoughts calmly. I try to express my feelings constructively, so that I am not unnecessarily hurtful to others. I am not embarrassed about feeling strong emotions, but I am seldom totally unrestrained.

Examples:

I enjoy exchanging personal thoughts and feelings with those close to me, but I don't want to do that every minute we're together.

I am not embarrassed about having people see me when I am especially happy or sad.

I share my innermost thoughts only with some people, not with just anyone who will listen.

When I get angry, I still try to express my thoughts calmly or else I will wait until later to say something.

I don't usually try to hide my emotions, but there are occasions when I do.

The Expressive self schema describes me:

_____ Usually   _____ Sometimes   _____ Never

My examples of my Expressive self schema are:

_____

_____

_____

_____

The Restrained Self Schema

Negative Pole   Hyperpositive Pole

A HYPERPOSITIVE SELF SCHEMA

RESTRAINED: I seldom show my feelings. I am uncomfortable expressing my emotions. I don't let people see how I feel. I am almost always in control of my emotions. Other people usually can't tell how I feel. I don't like other people to know when I'm feeling bad. I hate to cry in front of other people.

Examples:

Even the people closest to me don't really know me.

I do not like to talk about my feelings.

When I get angry, I usually don't say anything. People are often surprised to find out I have been upset about something.

I usually try to hide my emotions.

I am uncomfortable having other people see me when I am upset.

I seldom let people know if they have hurt my feelings or offended me.

The Restrained self schema describes me:

_____ Usually _____ Sometimes _____ Never

My examples of my Restrained self schema are:

_____

_____

_____

_____

The Interdependency Continuum

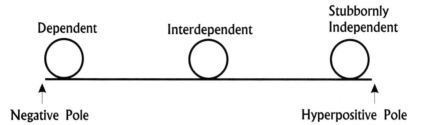

The self schemas on the *Interdependency* continuum reveal your thoughts and feelings about relying on yourself and others. Do you feel comfortable asking for help if you need it? Are you able to make most decisions on your own, or do you often feel anxious if you are unable to seek the advice of others first? Do you think that you cannot handle many things in life on your own? Do you think asking for assistance is a sign of weakness or incompetence? Do you think receiving help from others makes you obligated to them in some way? Do you think less of people who depend on you? Do you find it stressful working on projects with others rather than by yourself?

The *Interdependency* self schemas are your beliefs about being dependent on other people and handling things on your own. Individuals with the balanced *Interdependent* self schema are usually self-reliant but are comfortable depending on others for some things. People with the negative *Dependent* self schema think they are incapable of handling many things on their own and that they need the advice of others in making most decisions. Those with the hyperpositive *Stubbornly Independent* self schema view self-reliance as essential to their well-being and intensely avoid seeking or accepting support from others. The *Interdependency* self schemas relate to our willingness and comfort in dealing with the many challenges that life presents and, at times, in seeking help from others.

The Dependent Self Schema

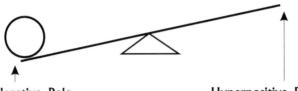

Negative Pole   Hyperpositive Pole

A NEGATIVE SELF SCHEMA

DEPENDENT: I tend to be dependent. I rely on other people to help me with most things. Life is too difficult for me to handle alone. I have a hard time making decisions by myself. I frequently seek assistance from others. I do not like being completely on my own. I need other people to take care of me.

Examples:

I usually need to talk to several people before I make any kind of decision, even minor ones.

My boyfriend complains that I need him to do too many things for me.

I usually ask for help before I try to solve something on my own.

My co-workers have complained that I depend on them too much.

I was offered a great promotion, but the thought of moving away from my parents was too scary for me to accept it.

The Dependent self schema describes me:

_____ **Usually** _____ **Sometimes** _____ **Never**

My examples of my Dependent self schema are:

_____

_____

_____

_____

The Interdependent Self Schema

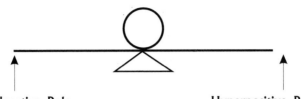

Negative Pole   Hyperpositive Pole

A BALANCED SELF SCHEMA

INTERDEPENDENT: I can handle most things on my own, but I will ask for help if I need it. I like to make my own decisions, but am comfortable seeking advice from others.

Examples:

I usually try to solve a problem on my own first, but if I can't figure it out, I will ask someone else for help.

My last evaluation said that I work well on my own and that I am also a good team player.

I borrowed money from my older brother to go to school. As soon as I got a job, I began paying him back with the interest he would have made as we had agreed. I only have three monthly payments left.

My parents helped me off and on over the years financially with my family, so now that they are retired and on a fixed income, I am glad that I am able to help them out.

The Interdependent self schema describes me:

_____ **Usually** _____ **Sometimes** _____ **Never**

My examples of my Interdependent self schema are:

_____

_____

_____

_____

The Stubbornly Independent Self Schema

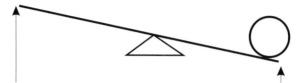

Negative Pole   Hyperpositive Pole

A HYPERPOSITIVE SELF SCHEMA

STUBBORNLY INDEPENDENT: I do not like to rely on anyone but myself. It is hard for me to ask for help. I don't like it when other people offer me advice or assistance. I feel irritated when someone tries to help me. I can't stand being dependent on anybody for anything. I prefer to do things on my own.

Examples:

There have been times when I have left a project unfinished rather than ask for help.

People hate to ride anywhere new with me because I never ask for directions, no matter how lost I am.

My supervisor has reprimanded me for not asking for his help when I needed it.

Several people would have loaned me money to finish school. I was too proud to ask.

I hate to admit that I can't figure something out.

The Stubbornly Independent self schema describes me:

_____ Usually _____ Sometimes _____ Never

My examples of my Stubbornly Independent self schema are:

_____

_____

_____

_____

My Bonding Self Schema Ratings

Indicate in the chart below how you rated yourself on the bonding self schemas. Review the chapter to find your responses and write them here.

WORTHINESS SELF SCHEMAS:

Unworthy	____ Usually	____ Sometimes	____ Never
Worthy	____ Usually	____ Sometimes	____ Never
Entitled	____ Usually	____ Sometimes	____ Never

INTIMACY SELF SCHEMAS:

Intimacy Driven	____ Usually	____ Sometimes	____ Never
Intimacy Comfortable	____ Usually	____ Sometimes	____ Never
Intimacy Avoidant	____ Usually	____ Sometimes	____ Never

EXPRESSIVENESS SELF SCHEMAS:

Unrestrained	____ Usually	____ Sometimes	____ Never
Expressive	____ Usually	____ Sometimes	____ Never
Restrained	____ Usually	____ Sometimes	____ Never

INTERDEPENDENCY SELF SCHEMAS:

Dependent	____ Usually	____ Sometimes	____ Never
Interdependent	____ Usually	____ Sometimes	____ Never
Stubbornly Independent	____ Usually	____ Sometimes	____ Never

You now have rated yourself on the bonding self schemas. You can see how the views of the self schemas vary by their polarity. The negative bonding schemas present negative views of the self: "I am not as good as others" (*Unworthy*); "I can't function without emotional intimacy" (*Intimacy Driven*); "I can't control my emotions" (*Unrestrained*); and "I can't handle things on my own" (*Dependent*). The hyperpositive bonding schemas are hyperpositive views of the self: "I am better than others" (*Entitled*); "I don't need emotional intimacy from others" (*Intimacy Avoidant*); "I am always in control of my emotions" (*Restrained*); and "I can handle anything by myself" (*Stubbornly Independent*). The balanced bonding schemas present balanced self views: "I am as worthwhile as others but not necessarily more so" (*Worthy*); I like emotional intimacy and I enjoy my own space too" (*Intimacy Comfortable*); "I usually can control my emotions but I am open about my thoughts and feelings" (*Expressive*); "I can handle most things on my own but I am comfortable asking for help when I need it" (*Interdependent*).

The Seeds of Schemas

By now, you have probably begun to speculate about how you got your self schemas. One powerful influence is your social environment. That has a powerful impact on the development of all your schemas, including your self schemas. For example, if you have the *Unworthy* self schema, you may have gotten feedback from your family that you were worthless. Maybe society conveyed to you that you were inferior in some way, perhaps you were raised in a religion that taught all human beings are unworthy, or you might have had all three influences.

If you have the *Entitled* self schema, you might have been a spoiled child who learned to expect to receive whatever you wanted. Perhaps you were taught that you were better than other people because you were especially bright, athletic, or attractive. You might have learned those attitudes and behaviors by observing your parents act as if they were superior to others and deserved special treatment. Or you might have been deprived, and over time came to believe that you were entitled because of the hardships or humiliation you had endured. Families, society, schools, religion, and cultural beliefs and practices all influence the schemas that you develop.

Biology also influences your schemas. From birth, people vary in a variety of ways that are biologically influenced, such as adaptability, sociability, temperament, and language skills. However, biology is always influenced by the environment. Thus, schemas are the result of interactions between biological tendencies and social experiences. The *Expressiveness* self schemas of *Unrestrained*, *Expressive*, and *Restrained* clearly demonstrate that. Language skills are biologically influenced, but social experiences play a powerful role in language development and expressiveness.

Consider how you might have developed a *Restrained* self schema. You might have learned not to show your emotions or express your opinions, because to do so resulted in ridicule or a slap across the face. You may have learned not to express your thoughts because no one responded to you when you did. Or you may have been told that your feelings were inappropriate or even invalid, that you had no right to feel the way you did. In that case, not only would you then be less inclined to express your emotions, you also might begin to question whether you could even interpret your emotions accurately. You also might have discovered that not talking and not displaying emotion was the only control you had with an intrusive parent. You discovered that by not expressing yourself you could maintain some separate space that could not be invaded.

Restrained schemas can develop from living with others who do not express personal thoughts and seldom show emotion. They may talk a great deal about impersonal topics, but personal thoughts and feelings go unexpressed. You even may have been explicitly taught that emotional displays of any kind are unseemly.

What about the *Unrestrained* self schema? If you identified yourself as having an *Unrestrained* self schema, you may have learned that you received attention only when you reacted intensely. Mild reactions drew no response. At home or in school perhaps you were heard only when you turned up the volume, otherwise, you were ignored. Or you may have grown up observing others who displayed little emotional control, so you never tried to manage your own emotions or behavior. You may have learned that when you are angry, it is alright to say mean and hateful things. Or you may have lived in a situation where your family's existence was always on the edge, and any minor trouble triggered major disasters. Such experiences would tend to make you apprehensive about any prospective problem and more easily distraught.

If you identified yourself as having an *Expressive* self schema, that could have developed from living in a family that encouraged conversation, listened to you, and responded to what you said. You might have observed others expressing personal thoughts and feelings honestly and constructively. They also could have modeled reasonable self-restraint, even when they were quite upset. You learned that your thoughts and feelings mattered to other people, and you learned how to express them in a constructive and direct manner. Other people expressed love and showed affection to you, and encouraged those expressions in return.

If you want to figure out where your self schemas originated, ask yourself the following questions about each of your schemas:

- Did someone model this self schema for me?
- Did this self schema serve some useful purpose for me?
- Did someone encourage this self schema in me?
- What influences in my life taught me this self schema?
- What biological factor might predispose me to have this self schema?

Answers to these questions can give you a fairly good idea of why you developed the self schemas you have. However, remember, you are only speculating. You cannot be fully aware of all the influences that resulted in your particular set of schemas. Regardless of how your schemas developed, you may want to change some of them. However, before you decide which schemas to change, you must have a clearer understanding of the effects your self schemas have on you and on other people. Chapter 4 will help you toward that understanding.

Others' Self Schemas

Now that you have identified your own bonding self schemas, try to determine which self schemas other people have. Go back to the exercises you began in chapter 1 where you listed the important people in your life. You began to identify your person schemas of those people by writing down generalizations and specific examples. Now that you know about the bonding self schemas, you can expand your person schemas. Review your sheet on each person. Under what you already have written, write "Self Schemas." Next, reread the bonding schemas descriptions in this chapter. For each schema, decide if that schema applies to the individuals in your life. If so, write the name of the self schema under "Self Schemas." By identifying each person's self schemas, you will develop a more complete picture of your person schema of that individual. This information will be used in later chapters when you analyze your relationships with these people.

To determine someone's self schema, think about their behavior and emotions. How do they react in different situations and with different people? Don't worry if they might disagree with whether they think they have a particular self schema. The question here is what you think. For example, your twenty-three-year-old sister might think she is quite independent. Yet you notice that she panics if she has to make a major decision on her own. She frequently calls your parents seeking advice on almost everything. She asks for the opinions of several people before making almost any decision. Regardless of what she might claim, you have substantial evidence to think that she has a *Dependent* self schema. So you would list that schema under her self schemas.

Here is a sample of what one of your pages will look like after you complete this exercise. This continues Jack's example from chapters 1 and 2.

Jack

Is generous: always gives some kind of donation to any charity drive; paid for his mom to take a cruise on her seventy-fifth birthday; let me borrow his car when mine broke down and I had a job interview.

Is trustworthy: never told anyone what I told him about the way my dad treated me; has never been unfaithful to his wife.

Has a good sense of humor: is witty; enjoys jokes; can take a joke on himself.

Can be opinionated: when he thinks he is right, he will not give up in an argument; he seemed annoyed with me that I ended up buying the Chevy instead of the Ford he recommended.

Is judgmental: he has strong religious opinions and views people in black-or-white terms; when his seventeen-year-old niece got pregnant, he was angry with her and wouldn't speak to her for months.

Overall Balance of Person Schema: *Balanced (includes both positive and negative attributes).*

Emotions Jack evokes in me: *laughter; calmness, when in trouble I seek his advice; fear at times when I disagree with him or do something which I know he would disapprove.*

Jack's Self Schemas: *Worthy, Intimacy Comfortable, both Expressive and Unrestrained, and Interdependent.*

The Importance of Bonding Schemas

The bonding self schemas direct our interactions with other people. By now you should understand the importance of the bonding self schemas in the areas of *Worthiness, Intimacy, Expressiveness,* and *Interdependency.* The *Worthiness* self schemas influence how you value yourself in comparison to other people. The *Intimacy* self schemas affect how comfortable you are being emotionally close to other people. The *Expressiveness* self schemas influence whether and how you express your thoughts and feelings to those around you. The *Interdependency* self schemas focus on how comfortable you are being dependent on yourself and on others.

In this chapter you were able to identify which of the various bonding self schemas you have. You may be surprised to discover that in several or all of the bonding self schema domains you have more than one schema on a continuum. Having more than one self schema on any continuum is *not* atypical, as you will learn in the next chapter. You will discover how that happens and what determines which schema is active in any situation. You also will learn why you switch from schema to schema in different circumstances, and how that may be confusing to you as well as to others.

The balanced, negatively unbalanced, and positively unbalanced self schemas in each domain can have very different effects on you and on the people in your life. These effects can enhance your relationships or strain them. Each of the self schemas have distinct effects on you, on the way you are with other people, and on the way others perceive you. In the next chapter you will identify the specific effects your self schemas have on you and on others.

4

Your Impact on Yourself
and Others

You can't change the way you were, but you can change the way you are.

In the last chapter you learned about the bonding self schemas in the areas of *Worthiness, Intimacy, Expressiveness,* and *Interdependency.* You identified which self schemas you have in each area. By now, you have developed a substantial picture of your self, person, and role schemas. You may also have accumulated some questions, like: What effects do your self schemas have on you and the people around you? Can people have more than one schema in an area, and if so, why do they switch between them? What causes one schema to be active at any time? This chapter addresses these questions. As you begin to understand the answers to these questions, you will become even more aware of the powerful impact that bonding schemas have on your relationships. You will see which of your self schemas may be hurting you and others.

The Impact of the Bonding Self Schemas

In the last chapter, the bonding self schemas were noted for their importance in your relationships and your interpersonal behavior. In this chapter you will identify the effects your self schemas have on you and others. You may be surprised at the impact of these self schemas. In the following pages some of the common effects of the bonding self schemas are listed. Different people who have the same bonding self schema may experience some of the effects listed and not others for that self schema. Remember how you personalized the definitions of the self schemas in the last chapter. Even though people may have the same schema, the specific schema content will vary from individual to individual, so the effects also will vary.

The effects listed for each self schema are typical effects that people with that schema have reported. For each self schema, read the effects that it can have on you and the people with whom you interact. For the self schemas that you checked on page 61 in chapter 3 as *sometimes* or *usually* descriptive of you, check the effects that seem descriptive of what you have experienced yourself and what you think others have experienced with you. When you think of other people, think specifically about the effects on your partners, your children, your parents, and other people with whom you interact frequently.

Write in any other effects you have noticed that your self schemas create for you or others in the spaces provided. Review the examples you listed for your self schemas in chapter 3 for ideas of how they have an impact on you and the people in your life. For example, under the *Unworthy* self schema, you might add the following examples to the effect this schema has on you: *I put myself down in front of my family and friends; I laugh at their ridicule but I am ashamed inside.* You might add these additional comments to the effect your schema has on others: *My spouse and children always interrupt me when I am talking; they make fun of me; they call me stupid; they never ask for my opinion about anything.* Add as many specific effects as you can identify for each schema that applies to you.

The Unworthy Self Schema

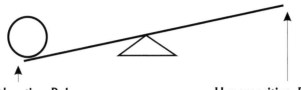

Negative Pole   Hyperpositive Pole

A NEGATIVE SELF SCHEMA

Effects on self:

_____ You ignore your own needs.

_____ You tolerate mistreatment from others and then feel bad about yourself and them.

_____ You feel depressed, resentful, or angry that your needs are not met.

_____ You feel uncomfortable around people with greater achievements or wealth.

Other effects:

_____

_____

_____

Effects on others:

_____ Others may intentionally and unintentionally take advantage of you.

_____ Others may disrespect or devalue you.

_____ Others may show a lack of regard for your opinions or your feelings.

_____ Others may be ashamed or feel angry with you for not standing up for yourself.

Other effects:

_____

_____

_____

The Worthy Self Schema

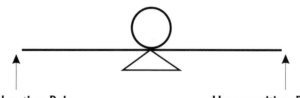

Negative Pole   Hyperpositive Pole

A BALANCED SELF SCHEMA

Effects on self:

____ You feel comfortable around others regardless of their achievements or wealth.

____ You treat yourself with the same respect and fairness you show to others.

____ You stand up for yourself.

____ You do special things for yourself sometimes.

Other effects:

_____

_____

_____

Effects on others:

____ Others feel respected and valued by you.

____ Others treat you with respect and regard.

____ Others usually don't try to take advantage of you.

____ Others view you as thoughtful and sincere.

Other effects:

_____

_____

_____

The Entitled Self Schema

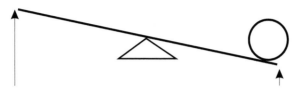

Negative Pole   Hyperpositive Pole

A HYPERPOSITIVE SELF SCHEMA

Effects on self:

____ You have difficulty feeling empathy.

____ You are easily offended, due to excessive expectations of how you ought to be treated.

____ You feel envious of others who have what you think you deserve.

____ You have a hard time denying yourself what you want.

Other effects:

_____

_____

_____

Effects on others:

____ Others feel hurt by your inconsiderate behavior and requests and resent you.

____ Others complain of being used by you and seek retaliation, directly or indirectly.

____ Others see you as a prima donna.

____ Others feel devalued by you.

Other effects:

_____

_____

_____

The Intimacy Driven Self Schema

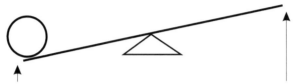

Negative Pole   Hyperpositive Pole

A NEGATIVE SELF SCHEMA

Effects on self:

____ You feel uncertain of the loyalty of others and frequently feel jealous.

____ You worry about being abandoned, either intentionally or not.

____ You have a hard time letting people have their space.

____ You are easily upset by any sign of rejection.

Other effects:

_____

_____

_____

Effects on others:

____ Others feel exhausted by your insatiable need for reassurance and attention.

____ Others are alienated by your jealousy when they are friendly or attentive to others.

____ Others feel suffocated by you and push you away, sometimes ending the relationship.

____ Others, including your children, feel emotionally responsible for you.

Other effects:

_____

_____

_____

The Intimacy Comfortable Self Schema

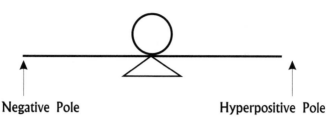

Negative Pole   Hyperpositive Pole

A BALANCED SELF SCHEMA

Effects on self:

____ You enjoy time with others and also enjoy time by yourself.

____ You feel secure in your relationships.

____ You love your children but encourage them to become independent.

____ You discriminate between what you tell close friends and casual ones.

Other effects:

_____

_____

_____

Effects on others:

____ Others feel comfortable expressing their feelings and thoughts to you.

____ Others feel that you allow them time alone to pursue their own interests.

____ Others feel your love or friendship is not conditional.

____ Others seldom express jealousy in their relationships with you.

Other effects:

_____

_____

_____

The Intimacy Avoidant Self Schema

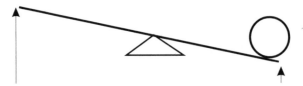

Negative Pole   Hyperpositive Pole

A HYPERPOSITIVE SELF SCHEMA

Effects on self:

____ You maintain distance and isolation from others.

____ You feel tense if people try to get too close to you or ask personal questions.

____ You are more comfortable by yourself than with others.

____ You may develop intimate relationships but have strong limits on how close or involved you will become.

Other effects:

_____

_____

_____

Effects on others:

____ Others feel rejected or alienated by your aloofness.

____ Others, even your family, question your regard for them.

____ Others seem uncomfortable around you.

____ Others are hesitant to reach out to you.

Other effects:

_____

_____

_____

The Unrestrained Self Schema

Negative Pole   Hyperpositive Pole

A NEGATIVE SELF SCHEMA

Effects on self:

____ You feel embarrassed by how emotional you can be.

____ You do and say things you feel ashamed about later.

____ You confide things in people you later regret.

____ You feel guilty about losing your temper.

Other effects:

_____

_____

_____

Effects on others:

____ Others feel fearful and tense around you because of your unpredictable behavior.

____ Others feel ashamed, hurt, and resentful from your attacks on them.

____ Others, even your own family, try to avoid being around you when you are upset.

____ Your children may have learned that self-control is not expected of them.

Other effects:

_____

_____

_____

The Expressive Self Schema

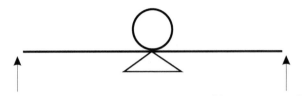

Negative Pole   Hyperpositive Pole

A BALANCED SELF SCHEMA

Effects on self:

____ You are comfortable expressing your thoughts and feelings directly to other people.

____ You are comfortable having others express their thoughts and feelings to you.

____ You are comfortable giving and receiving affection.

____ You seldom lose control of your temper.

Other effects:

_____

_____

_____

Effects on others:

____ Others feel comfortable sharing their thoughts and feelings with you.

____ Others feel that you listen to them.

____ Others feel that you are open with them and they know where they stand with you.

____ Others are comfortable being affectionate with you.

Other effects:

_____

_____

_____

The Restrained Self Schema

Negative Pole   Hyperpositive Pole

A HYPERPOSITIVE SELF SCHEMA

Effects on self:

____ You feel chronic tension from your constant need for self-control.

____ You feel anxious or embarrassed by strong emotions, especially anger, in yourself or others.

____ You express resentment in subtle, indirect ways.

____ You are uncomfortable having others express their thoughts or feelings to you.

Other effects:

_____

_____

_____

Effects on others:

____ Others view you as indifferent and uncaring.

____ Others feel you don't really understand them and don't want to either.

____ Others view you as emotionally dishonest with yourself and with them.

____ Others resent your passive-aggressive behavior when you aren't direct with them.

Other effects:

_____

_____

_____

The Dependent Self Schema

Negative Pole   Hyperpositive Pole

A NEGATIVE SELF SCHEMA

Effects on self:

____ You have little confidence in your ability to handle many situations.

____ You feel anxious when left on your own.

____ You are afraid to try to solve problems before consulting others.

____ You tend to obsess about decisions.

Other effects:

_____

_____

_____

Effects on others:

____ Others get tired of feeling responsible for you.

____ Others feel used by you.

____ Others don't respect you.

____ Others avoid you or don't return your calls because they assume you will want something from them.

Other effects:

_____

_____

_____

The Interdependent Self Schema

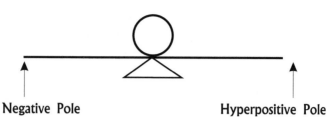

Negative Pole   Hyperpositive Pole

A BALANCED SELF SCHEMA

Effects on self:

_____ You have confidence in your ability to handle most situations.

_____ You ask for help after you have made some effort to solve a problem on your own.

_____ You make most of your own decisions but, at times, you ask others for advice.

_____ You offer to help others when they need it.

Other effects:

_____

_____

_____

Effects on others:

_____ Others feel they can rely on you if you say you will help them.

_____ Others respect your ability to handle your own problems for the most part.

_____ Others feel that you respect their opinions and abilities, but don't take advantage of them.

_____ Others view you as confident and reasonable, not stubborn or prideful.

Other effects:

_____

_____

_____

The Stubbornly Independent Self Schema

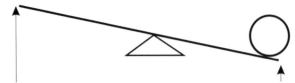

Negative Pole   Hyperpositive Pole

A HYPERPOSITIVE SELF SCHEMA

Effects on self:

____ You waste lots of time trying to solve things rather than asking for simple instructions or guidance, no matter how much you need it.

____ You feel irritated if someone offers you unsolicited advice or assistance.

____ You have inconvenienced yourself and your family by your stubbornness.

____ You can't accept help without feeling obligated.

Other effects:

_____

_____

_____

Effects on others:

____ Others, especially your family and co-workers, resent your stubbornness.

____ Others are reluctant to offer you help even when they see you need it.

____ Others hesitate asking you for help since you never ask them.

____ Others view you as obstinate and prideful.

Other effects:

_____

_____

_____

You now have identified the effects your bonding self schemas have on you and others. You may have noticed that some of the self schemas have similar effects. If you have self schemas with similar effects, their impact is even more powerful. You may feel good about some of the effects your schemas have and not so good about other effects. That is a pretty typical reaction. You may even feel quite sad to realize the unintended impact you are having on other people, as well as on yourself. Before you beat yourself up, you need to know a few more facts about schemas that might assuage your guilt.

Embrace Responsibility, Not Guilt

Schemas develop automatically, without requiring any conscious intent or planning on your part. Your brain is programmed to make sense of the world for you. Over time it connects similar information together into schemas. The brain spontaneously condenses and integrates information, updates information, and develops generalizations and expectations. Even though your brain is quite remarkable, it is not perfect. It is dependent upon the information it receives. The information it receives depends on the experiences you have had. Your experiences may have produced some unbalanced schemas. Moreover, information that is received earlier becomes more entrenched than newer contradictory information, as a result of the process of confirmatory bias (see chapter 2 for a discussion of confirmatory bias). This means that the experiences you had earlier in life tend to be more influential in your schema development than your later experiences.

For the most part, children and adolescents don't get to choose their experiences. Is it fair to blame yourself for schemas that developed automatically on the basis of experiences you did not even select? You might better ask how you could have had the experiences you have had and *not* have your schemas. Instead of dwelling on guilt, let's look at responsibility.

You can't change the way you were, but you can change the way you are. Until you picked up this book, you may have been only vaguely aware of what you now know are your schemas. Even now, you can never be completely aware of a schema, because parts of it simply remain outside the scope of conscious awareness. Nonetheless, you can get a fairly good picture of your schemas and the effects that they have. With that information, you can then consider whether you have a responsibility to yourself and others to change. If a schema is harmful to you or someone else, change certainly may be indicated. If you choose to change, you will know how to do that by the time you finish this book.

When you change a schema, do you eliminate the old one and create a new one, or do you just modify the schema that is already there? Frankly, psychologists are not sure. We do know that after someone has developed a balanced schema, sometimes the old unbalanced schema reappears. For example, you may have developed a *Worthy* self schema that has become more typical of you. However, when you run into an old high school classmate, you may feel your *Unworthy* self schema reappear temporarily.

Most likely, when consciously changing your schemas, you modify a moderately unbalanced schema to make it a balanced one. With extremely unbalanced schemas, you may simply create a new balanced schema or expand a previously weak balanced schema. This means that the old unbalanced schema can still be triggered by certain events, such as running into an old classmate.

Fortunately you don't have to wait to make schema changes until all of the neurological pathways of schemas have been mapped and charted. You can begin to make changes in your schemas now using the suggestions ahead.

Schema Principles

To understand bonding styles, you need to know five simple principles about schemas that will help you see how schemas work individually and with other schemas. You already know some of the principles and you probably already have guessed the others.

Principle One: Schemas May Be Balanced or Unbalanced

You already know this principle. All schemas can be either balanced or unbalanced in a negative or hyperpositive direction. Unbalanced schemas are incomplete pictures that present distorted images. They are less responsive to new information and less able to change themselves. They put you at a disadvantage in dealing with yourself and your world, interfering with your thinking, feelings, and behavior. Balanced schemas are not perfect pictures, but they tend to be relatively complete, including positive, neutral, and negative information. They are flexible and able to modify themselves, integrating and updating themselves with new information.

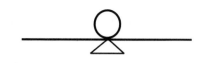

A Balanced Schema

A Negative Schema   A Hyperpositive Schema

Principle Two: Schemas on Any Subject Can Be Arranged on a Continuum

You also know this principle. Schemas can be arranged according to their balance on a continuum with negative and hyperpositive poles. Schemas that are more negative are closer to the negative pole. Schemas that are more hyperpositive are closer to the hyperpositive pole. Schemas that are balanced fall somewhere in the middle between the two poles, according to how balanced they are.

Negative Pole   Hyperpositive Pole

Principle Three: You Can Have More Than One Schema in Any Area

You may have been surprised to discover in the last chapter that you have different self schemas on the same continuum. Perhaps you recognized that on the *Interdependency* continuum you had all three of the schemas listed. You may have realized that you sometimes have a *Dependent* self schema, other times an *Interdependent* self schema, and on some occasions a *Stubbornly Independent* self schema, as shown in the diagram on the following page.

The Interdependency Continuum

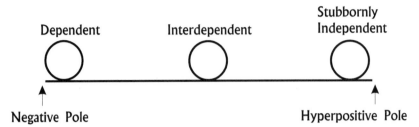

Dependent   Interdependent   Stubbornly
                                            Independent

Negative Pole   Hyperpositive Pole

Likewise, on the *Worthiness* continuum you might have discovered that occasionally you have an *Unworthy* self schema, at other times you have a *Worthy* self schema, and at still other times you have an *Entitled* self schema. You might have thought, "How can that be? Aren't people supposed to be just one way? If I'm not, does that mean I'm abnormal?" The answer is no, you're not abnormal. (Well, okay, you might be, but certainly not for this reason.) Having different schemas on the same continuum is common. Yet this idea may go against what you have probably read in the past.

Psychologists have often depicted people as possessing fixed, unvarying traits. You either are dependent or you're not. You either are stubbornly independent or you're not. Yet the data collected by personality psychologists does not support such a position. And neither does common sense. People behave differently in different situations. A person may behave dependently in some situations, and be stubbornly independent in others. People do not behave in fixed, robotic ways. They vary their behavior according to the particular circumstances. The ability to vary behavior depending on the situation is enormously adaptive. You wisely may choose to be more deferential to your boss than you are to your children. You will want to disclose more to your spouse than to the stranger you sit next to on a bus. How you react depends on what schemas are active at any time. Thus, the third schema principle is that you can have more than one schema on any one continuum. This principle applies to person and role schemas also.

You can have more than one person schema of the same individual. For example, nineteen-year-old Molly has been dating Ned for several weeks. Molly has two entirely different person schemas for Ned. She has a hyperpositive schema of Ned: *He is charming, irresistible, devastatingly handsome, unfailingly devoted to me, and clever and witty.* She also has a negative schema of Ned: *He has run around on all his other girlfriends in the past; in fact, he was in a relationship with another woman when he started dating me; he is incapable of being faithful;*

he will ultimately cheat on me with someone; he cannot be trusted; he flirts with every female he meets. Just as you can have more than one self schema on the same continuum, so can you have more than one person schema on the same continuum for a particular person as Molly does for Ned.

Similarly, you can have multiple schemas about the same role. For example, you could have a role schema of the ideal husband, a role schema of a balanced picture of a husband, and a role schema of the worst possible husband. You could have multiple schemas for all kinds of roles. This principle recognizes that you can have different schemas in the same area for the self, person, and role schemas, *but only one schema in any area can be active at a time.* For example, you couldn't have schemas of *Worthy* and *Unworthy* active at the same time, nor could Molly have her two person schemas of Ned active simultaneously.

Principle Four: You Can Switch from Schema to Schema in Any Schema Area

If you can have more than one schema on the same continuum and they can't be active at the same time, then you must be able to switch between them. Exactly. This principle simply recognizes that schema switching can occur on any continuum that has more than one schema. For example, Ramona has an *Unworthy* self schema that is very active and a less active *Entitled* self schema on the *Worthiness* continuum. She typically puts the desires of other people before her own. Whatever the kids or her partner want, she tries to accommodate. After doing that for long periods of time, her resentment at never having her own needs recognized builds, until one day someone unwittingly makes a request that pushes her resentment up one notch too far, and she voices that resentment. "I don't have to tolerate the selfishness of everyone around me. I shouldn't have to always go without. I deserve to get some of my needs met once in a while." Then she takes off for the mall and charges several hundred dollars worth of clothing for herself. Here, what Ramona is doing is switching from her *Unworthy* self schema to her *Entitled* self schema, as depicted in this drawing.

Schema Switching on the Worthiness Continuum

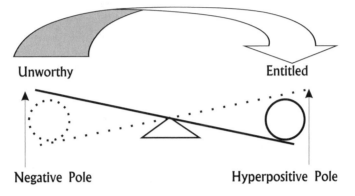

The schema that took Ramona to the mall was her *Entitled* self schema, which was triggered when her resentment finally reached a threshold level of intensity. After Ramona got back home from the mall and was sorting through her packages in the bedroom, she felt overwhelmed with guilt. "I don't deserve or need all of these things. There isn't enough money in the budget for me to get these items and meet the needs of the rest of the family. What's the matter with me? How could I behave so selfishly?" Being so indulgent retriggers Ramona's *Unworthy* self schema. Now, feeling ashamed and remorseful, she gathers her packages and returns them to the department store before anyone in the family returns home and discovers her extravagance. Ramona's *Unworthy* self schema is the force that takes her back to the mall. This example illustrates how people can switch from schema to schema within any schema area.

The principle of schema switching also applies to person schemas. Remember how Molly has two person schemas of Ned. She has a hyperpositive schema of Ned: *He is charming, irresistible, devastatingly handsome, unfailingly devoted to me, and clever and witty.* She also has a negative schema of Ned: *He has run around on all his other girlfriends in the past; in fact, he was in a relationship with another woman when he started dating me; he is incapable of being faithful; he will ultimately cheat on me with someone; he cannot be trusted; he flirts with every female he meets.* Molly switches back and forth between these two person schemas of Ned. However, switching between schemas makes your behavior confusing to others and, when other people do that, their behavior becomes confusing for you. You can imagine how confused Ned feels about Molly's different actions toward him, which unbeknownst to Ned depends on what person schema of him Molly currently has operating.

Principle Five: Schemas in Different Areas Can Be Active at the Same Time

Even though you can't have more than one schema within the same area active at one time, schemas on *different* continua can be active simultaneously. This principle simply recognizes the capacity of the mind to deal with multiple images or thoughts at a time. For example, you might be thinking about asking Keith, your boss, for a long overdue raise. In doing so, your person schema of Keith might be actively presenting images of what a gruff, harsh man he is; how he sets standards beyond what any of the salespeople can ever meet; and how he is always boasting about his previous great successes as a salesman. At the same time, your person schema of Keith is generating images of how he has ridiculed and belittled other salespeople when they made any kind of request. You may even have some memories activated of your own unpleasant interactions with him in the past.

As you review your sales figures, you also may have more than one self schema from different domains become active. For example, your *Unworthy* self schema from the *Worthiness* domain and your *Stubbornly Independent* self schema from the *Interdependency* domain may be simultaneously presenting images. Your *Unworthy* self schema may be producing thoughts of how your sales probably are not as good, much less any better, than the other salespeople who aren't asking for raises. Your *Stubbornly Independent* self schema may be creating thoughts of how asking for a raise is like asking for a favor and then somehow being obligated to someone. Although you couldn't have two schemas from the *Worthiness* continuum active simultaneously, nor two from the *Interdependency* continuum active at the same time, you can have schemas from different continua active at the same time. This example illustrates how schemas from *different* areas can be active simultaneously in your thought processes. In this example, you had your *person schema of Keith* active at the same time that you had two *self schemas* active, *Unworthy* from the *Worthiness* domain and *Stubbornly Independent* from the *Interdependency* domain. Your mind routinely has several schemas active at any moment.

Triggers: The Power Buttons

If you can have different schemas on the same continuum, what determines which schema is active at any moment? *Triggers* are the power buttons or the cues that activate different schemas. Triggers can be either *external* or *internal*. External triggers are cues that are outside of you. For example, the odor of a perfume or the sound of a song may trigger a person schema of an old girlfriend. The appearance and gait of an elderly man may trigger a person schema of your grandfather. A mere gesture can trigger a person schema. Watching someone in a movie being scolded can trigger an *Unworthy* self schema by cueing an old memory of a similar personal experience.

Remember how Molly has two different person schemas of Ned, one hyperpositive and one negative? When Ned is attentive to Molly, her hyperpositive person schema of Ned is active. Yet whenever they are around other people and she notices Ned interacting with another woman, whether a friend or a stranger, her negative schema of Ned is triggered and she views him very differently. So Molly flips between her two extreme person schemas of Ned, depending on external triggers: Ned's behavior and the other people present. Molly's behavior corresponds to whatever schema is active at the moment. When her hyperpositive *Ned* schema is active, she is warm and loving toward Ned. When her negative *Ned* schema is active, she is cold and indifferent. Ned complains of Molly being unpredictable. Yet Molly's behavior is quite predictable if you know which of her schemas is active at the moment, but that is certainly not always obvious to the observer.

Internal cues refer to events within you, such as a feeling, a memory, a thought, or even a schema. For example, Inga did not receive the promotion for which she had applied. She felt disappointed, as she was hoping to use the salary increase to move to a larger apartment. Her disappointment triggered another memory associated with the feeling of disappointment. Inga suddenly found herself thinking about the time she ran unsuccessfully for her high school student council. This memory triggered her *Unworthy* self schema. Feelings generated by a present situation can trigger memories associated with previous experiences when you felt the same way. That is why when you are angry about a current situation, you may find that your thoughts have drifted to another memory of when you were angry. The schemas that are associated with these memories then can be triggered, as happened to Inga.

Schemas can serve as internal triggers for other schemas. Molly's negative *Ned* schema triggered her *Intimacy Avoidant* self schema. When Molly's negative person schema of Ned was active, she would think about how unfaithful he had been in previous relationships. Her negative *Ned* schema then activated her *Intimacy Avoidant* self schema, which influenced her to avoid or pull back from a committed relationship with him.

Schemas can be triggered by a variety of external and internal cues. Any schema has multiple triggers, which can include both external and internal cues. For example, Inga's *Unworthy* self schema can be activated by external cues, such as a failure or being criticized, and by internal cues, such as feelings or memories. The more often a schema is active, the more frequently situations and memories will be associated with that schema. This in turn means that more cues become available to trigger that schema. Just as one schema can have many cues, the same cue can trigger several schemas simultaneously. In the example of Molly, her negative *Ned* schema triggered her *Unworthy* self schema at the same time it triggered her *Intimacy Avoidant* self schema. In the next chapter you will discover how your bonding styles result from repeatedly having a trigger activate certain clusters of your schemas at the same time.

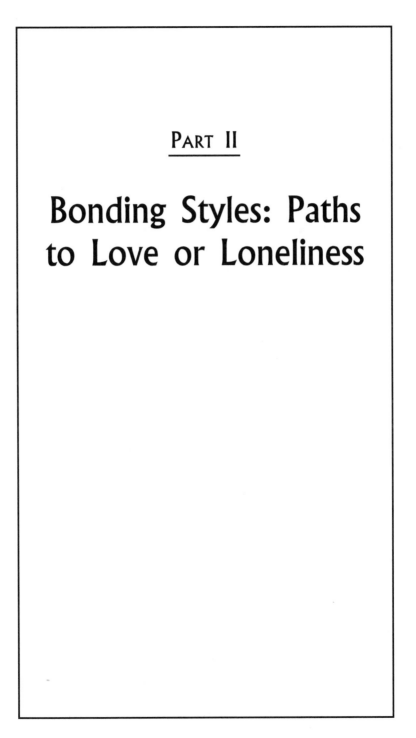

PART II

Bonding Styles: Paths to Love or Loneliness

5

Bonding Styles: How We Are with Others

Without wearing any mask we are conscious of, we have a special face for each friend.

——Oliver Wendell Holmes, *The Professor at the Breakfast Table*

By now, you are aware of which bonding schemas you have and how they affect you and the people around you. The bonding self schemas in the areas of *Worthiness*, *Intimacy*, *Expressiveness*, and *Interdependency* are enormously influential in how you interact with people. But as influential as the bonding schemas are alone, their impact is greatly magnified when they occur together. In this chapter you will learn how bonding schemas occur together in clusters to create bonding styles. By identifying your own bonding styles and the bonding styles of the people in your life, you will more easily understand why some of your relationships are so much more comfortable than other ones.

Bonding Styles

Bonding styles refer to the way we approach and interact with other people. Each style is associated with certain bonding schemas, which will be discussed later. First, you will be asked to identify your bonding styles. Three bonding styles are presented. The names of the bonding styles and the schemas that comprise them will be presented *after* you complete this initial exercise, in order for your ratings not to be subtly influenced by the style names. Read each description. After the description, put a checkmark next to the phrase that best applies to you for each paragraph: "a lot like me," "sometimes like me," or "not like me." Don't allow what you check for one style to influence what you choose for another style. The styles are independent of each other. In other words, you can choose the same descriptive phrases for different styles.

Style One

I am a worthwhile person. My needs are as important as the needs of other people, but not necessarily more so. I enjoy having close relationships. I also enjoy my time by myself. I seldom worry about being abandoned. I am comfortable expressing my feelings. I don't mind showing my feelings, but I don't like to fall apart. I handle most things on my own, but I am comfortable asking for help. I don't mind depending on other people or having them depend on me.

____ A lot like me   ____ Sometimes like me   ____ Not like me

Style Two

I often feel that somehow I am not as good as other people. My needs are not as important as the needs of other people. I often want more closeness or intimacy than I get. I need a lot of reassurance that I am loved or valued. I feel lost if I am not in a close relationship. I worry about being abandoned or being alone. My feelings often overwhelm me. I seldom feel in control of my emotions. I tend to be dependent. I rely on other people to help me with most things.

____ A lot like me   ____ Sometimes like me   ____ Not like me

Style Three

I think I am as good as anyone else, if not better. I think more about my own needs than the needs of other people. I keep most people at a distance. I am not comfortable being especially close to people. I seldom show my feelings. I am uncomfortable expressing my emotions. I don't like other people to know when I am feeling bad. I do not like to rely on anyone but myself. I don't like to ask for help.

____ A lot like me   ____ Sometimes like me   ____ Not like me

Characteristic Bonding Style

Now, pick the bonding style that you think is *most* descriptive of you. From among the three bonding styles, select the style that you feel is the *best* description of you in your relationships. Ignore your earlier ratings and just select the one style that you think best captures you. Reread the three bonding style descriptions and then write below the number of the bonding style that you think is most characteristic of you.

My Characteristic Bonding Style is _____

Bonding Styles and Their Self Schemas

Previously, a schema was described as a constellation of information on a particular subject. A bonding style then can be viewed as a galaxy of constellations, because each bonding style consists of four self schemas. The schemas are from the bonding continua: *Worthiness, Intimacy, Expressiveness,* and *Interdependency.* The first style is the **Easy Bonding Style**, which consists of the balanced self schemas of *Worthy, Intimacy Comfortable, Expressive,* and *Interdependent.* The second style is the **Anxious Bonding Style**, which consists of the negatively unbalanced self schemas on these continua: *Unworthy, Intimacy Driven, Unrestrained,* and *Dependent.* The hyperpositive unbalanced self schemas on these continua comprise the third style, the **Distant Bonding Style**: *Entitled, Intimacy Avoidant, Restrained,* and *Stubbornly Independent.* Above by the style number you recorded, write the name of the style, either (1) Easy, (2) Anxious, or (3) Distant.

The descriptions that follow for each bonding style include the names of their schemas. As you read the descriptions, you will see how the schemas fit together for each bonding style. After each paragraph, write in the phrase that you selected earlier as most applicable to you for that style: "a lot like me," "sometimes like me," "not like me."

Style One: The Easy Bonder

The Balanced Bonding Self Schemas

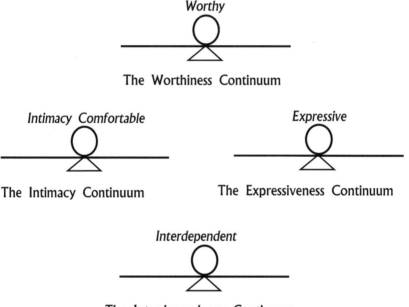

(*Worthy*) I am a worthwhile person. My needs are as important as the needs of other people, but not necessarily more so. (*Intimacy Comfortable*) I enjoy having close relationships. I also enjoy my time by myself. I seldom worry about being abandoned. (*Expressive*) I am comfortable expressing my feelings. I don't mind showing my feelings, but I don't like to fall apart. (*Interdependent*) I handle most things on my own, but I am comfortable asking for help. I don't mind depending on other people or having them depend on me.

How descriptive this style is of me: _____

Style Two: The Anxious Bonder

The Negative Bonding Self Schemas

Unworthy

The Worthiness Continuum

Intimacy Driven

The Intimacy Continuum

Unrestrained

The Expressiveness Continuum

Dependent

The Interdependency Continuum

(*Unworthy*) I often feel that somehow I am not as good as other people. My needs are not as important as the needs of other people. (*Intimacy Driven*) I often want more closeness or intimacy than I get. I need a lot of reassurance that I am loved or valued. I feel lost if I am not in a close relationship. I worry about being abandoned or being alone. (*Unrestrained*) My feelings often overwhelm me. I seldom feel in control of my emotions. (*Dependent*) I tend to be dependent. I rely on other people to help me with most things.

How descriptive this style is of me: _____

Style Three: The Distant Bonder

The Hyperpositive Bonding Self Schemas

Entitled

The Worthiness Continuum

Intimacy Avoidant

The Intimacy Continuum

Restrained

The Expressiveness Continuum

Stubbornly Independent

The Interdependency Continuum

(*Entitled*) I think I am as good as anyone else, if not better. I think more about my own needs than the needs of other people. (*Intimacy Avoidant*) I keep most people at a distance. I am not comfortable being especially close to people. (*Restrained*) I seldom show my feelings. I am uncomfortable expressing my emotions. I don't like other people to know when I'm feeling bad. (*Stubbornly Independent*) I do not like to rely on anyone but myself. I don't like to ask for help.

How descriptive this style is of me: _____

Bonding Style Descriptions

You may have felt that all three styles describe you to some extent. If so, you are not alone. Almost a third of all people say that they have two styles that are equal in strength. The majority describe themselves as having *three* bonding styles at different times. Nine out of ten people say that *at least two* styles describe them sometimes. Less than ten percent of people report that just one style describes them all the time (Baldwin, Keelan, Fehr, et al. 1996; Diehl, Elnick, Bourbeau, et al. 1998).

Your Characteristic Bonding Style

You may have found that more than one of the bonding styles is descriptive of you at times, as most people do. However, people usually can identify one style that best fits them. You already did that earlier. Go back and see which bonding style you selected as most characteristic of you. Write the name of that bonding style below.

My Characteristic Bonding Style is _____

When asked to select their most characteristic style, about 60 percent of people pick the Easy Bonding Style, about 25 percent pick the Distant Bonding Style, and about 15 percent pick the Anxious Bonding Style. Although 90 percent of all people report that they have more than one bonding style, these are the results when they are asked which style is most characteristic of them (Hazan and Shaver 1987; Baldwin, Keelan, Fehr, et al. 1996 ; Mickelson, Kessler, and Shaver 1997; Diehl, Elnick, Bourbeau, et al. 1998). Although these three bonding styles have been the most studied, you can have bonding styles other than these. Any combination of schemas from each bonding style continuum can constitute a bonding style.

Characteristic Bonding Styles of Others

Everyone has a characteristic bonding style. Read the bonding style descriptions below. They have been revised to apply to others, not to yourself. For everyone for whom you have been developing a person schema in the previous exercises, select the style that best describes how you think each person was in their relationship with you. You may feel that some of those individuals had more than one bonding style with you during the relationship with you. That is possible. On the pages where you are developing person schemas, write the names of all the styles that apply to each person during their relationship with you.

The Easy Bonding Style

They balance their own needs with the needs of others. They enjoy having close relationships. They also enjoy their time alone. They seldom worry about being abandoned. They are comfortable expressing their feelings. They don't mind showing their feelings, but they don't like to fall apart. They handle most things on their own, but are comfortable asking for help. They don't mind depending on other people or having others depend on them.

The Anxious Bonding Style

They tend to focus on the needs of others and neglect their own needs. They often want more closeness or intimacy than they get. They need a lot of reassurance that they are loved or valued. They seem lost if they are not in a relationship. They worry about being abandoned or being alone. Their feelings often overwhelm them. They seldom feel in control of their emotions. They tend to be dependent. They rely on other people to help them with most things.

The Distant Bonding Style

They tend to focus more on their own needs than on the needs of others. They keep most people at a distance. They are not comfortable being especially close to people. They seldom show their feelings. They are uncomfortable expressing their emotions. They don't like other people to know when they are feeling bad. They do not like to rely on other people. They don't like to ask for help.

Bonding Style Triggers

Triggers were described earlier as cues that could activate different schemas and different bonding styles. There are three primary triggers for the bonding styles. One trigger is an external cue: *the other person in the interaction*. The other two triggers are internal cues: your *role schemas* and your *person schemas*. Let's look at these triggers more closely and see how they work together to elicit a bonding style.

The Other Person

The appearance and behavior of the other person are major triggers for the role and person schemas you have about people. Other people can trigger role schemas about certain kinds of people, such as older men, attractive women, adolescents, grandmothers, or people of different nationalities and races. For example, the appearance of a longhaired teenage boy might trigger a role schema of a drug user in someone else.

> *Longhaired Teenage Boy → Role Schema of a Drug User*

In another person that teenager might trigger a more benign role schema of an adolescent male.

> *Longhaired Teenage Boy → Role Schema of an Adolescent Male*

The behavior of other people also can trigger person schemas about specific individuals. Remember how Molly has two person schemas of Ned? When Ned is flirtatious with other women, his behavior triggers Molly's negative *Ned* schema.

> *Ned's Flirtatious Behavior → Molly's Negative Person Schema of Ned*

In contrast, when Ned's attention is focused on Molly, that triggers her hyperpositive *Ned* schema.

> *Ned's Attention to Molly → Molly's Hyperpositive*
> *Person Schema of Ned*

Ned's behavior is the critical factor in activating Molly's different person schemas of him.

Another person can trigger both person and role schemas simultaneously. Ned's flirtatious behavior triggers Molly's negative person schema of Ned. It also triggers Molly's negative male role schema, which depicts men as calculating philanderers.

Your Person and Role Schemas

The person and role schemas that are activated include certain expectations of how that person might be, such as whether he or she is trustworthy, intelligent, gentle, or reliable. These person and role schemas then trigger a bonding style. An elderly white-haired female stranger may elicit someone's role schema of elderly women as warm, accepting, and lovable. In turn, this role schema could trigger an Easy Bonding Style, because the woman would be viewed as friendly and approachable.

> *Elderly White-haired Female Stranger → Role Schema of Elderly*
> *Women as Lovable*
> *Role Schema of Elderly Women as Lovable →*
> *Easy Bonding Style*

A person schema could produce the same results. Seeing the elderly woman might elicit your person schema of your Grandmother Ella, who is a friendly, loving person. Your Grandmother Ella schema then could elicit your Easy Bonding Style, because this stranger reminds you of your grandmother and you expect she will be similar to her.

Elderly White-haired Female Stranger → Person Schema of Ella
Person Schema of Ella → Your Easy Bonding Style

Both person and role schemas can elicit bonding styles.

Can two bonding styles be triggered at the same moment? No, two styles cannot be active simultaneously, but they can be sequentially. You can flip from style to style with different people or with the same person at different times, but only one style can be active at any moment.

A Chain Reaction in Your Brain

The three types of triggers work like a simple chain reaction in your brain. The other person's appearance and behavior trigger person and role schemas, which in turn trigger bonding styles. The diagram below illustrates the chain reaction of the triggers and the bonding styles:

Other Person → Person and/or Role Schemas → Bonding Styles

Although this looks like a simple one-way process, your mind is never simply a passive receptacle of what is being observed. As explained in chapter 2, your existing schemas influence what information engages your attention, how you interpret what you experience, and what information you remember. Your mind has an active role in this chain reaction of triggers. Your person and role schemas do not treat the data objectively. In other words, your existing person and role schemas influence how you *interpret* the appearance and behavior of other people, whether you know them or not. This confirmatory bias in your interpretations is illustrated by how the same longhaired teenage boy triggers different role schemas in different people. What you "observe" always is influenced by your current schemas to some extent.

In analyzing your relationships, identifying the triggers for your bonding styles will be illuminating. As you will see later, once you understand your triggers, you can gain more control over your bonding style reactions. Your person and role schemas include expectations of how other people will view you and how they will act in different circumstances. These expectations influence which bonding style is activated in you.

We all have models of people in general, as well as having general models of women, men, different ethnic and racial groups, and all the other categories into which we can place people. These models are examples of role schemas. When you meet another person, one of these role schemas will be triggered. The different bonding styles are associated with different role schemas for the *typical* human being. The Easy Bonding Style is associated with a role schema of people as trustworthy, accepting, dependable, and altruistic. The Anxious Bonding Style is associated with a role schema of people as complex, hard to understand, and likely to be rejecting as familiarity increases. The Distant Bonding Style is associated with a role schema of people that has a negative view of human nature, viewing people as hurtful, not trustworthy or dependable, and having ulterior motives behind their behavior.

Until you get to know a stranger, your general role schemas will be more dominant when assessing that stranger. Over time you will develop a more specific person schema of that person. Then that person will trigger your new specific person schema rather than your role schema of people in general.

For example, Edie has a characteristic Anxious Bonding Style. Edie has a role schema of people as likely to be unaccepting and disapproving. This role schema is triggered at her new job when she first meets her colleague, Jana. Edie's role schema of people as overly critical triggers her Anxious Bonding Style, which influences how she acts around Jana.

Initial Chain of Events

Jana as a Stranger → *Edie's Role Schema of People in General as critical* → *Edie's Anxious Bonding Style*

However, over time Edie develops a trustworthy, accepting person schema of Jana, as Jana is consistently accepting and supportive of Edie in different situations, even when Edie makes mistakes. Eventually when Edie encounters Jana, Edie's specific person schema of Jana is triggered. As Edie's Jana schema becomes more powerful than Edie's general role schema in Jana's presence, Edie's Easy Bonding Style is activated by Jana, not her Anxious Bonding Style. The chain reactions for Edie's process are shown below:

Later Chain of Events

Jana, over time → *Edie's new Person Schema of Jana as accepting* → *Edie's Easy Bonding Style*

Now, Debra joins Edie's department. Again, initially, as with all strangers, Debra triggers Edie's Anxious Bonding Style. Debra and Edie gradually get to know each other. At times, when Edie makes mistakes, Debra is critical of Edie's competence. Over time Edie develops a person schema of Debra as critical, unaccepting, and perhaps unpredictable. In this case, Edie's new Debra schema still triggers Edie's Anxious Bonding Style. The chain of events for Edie's schemas regarding Debra are shown below:

Initial Chain of Events

Debra as a Stranger → *Edie's Role Schema of People in General as critical* → *Edie's Anxious Bonding Style*

Later Chain of Events

Debra, over time → *Edie's new Person Schema of Debra as critical* → *Edie's Anxious Bonding Style*

In this case, both the person schema of Debra and the role schema of people in general trigger Edie's Anxious Bonding Style. These examples illustrate how person and role schemas trigger bonding styles.

Bonding Style Descriptors

Your characteristic bonding style influences how you view yourself and others, how others view you, and the quality of your relationships (Hazan and Shaver 1987; Kobak and Sceery 1988; Bartholomew and Horowitz 1991; Baldwin 1992; Bartholomew 1993; Colvin and Block 1994; Colvin, Block, and Funder 1995; Mikulincer 1995; Mikulincer 1998a; Mikulincer 1998b; Baldwin, Keelan, Fehr, et al. 1996; Collins 1996). Your style also affects the way you manage your emotions and how you experience and express anger. You will see that the Easy Bonding Style is associated with much greater personal and interpersonal satisfaction than are the Anxious and Distant styles.

Self-Views

The influence of the balanced bonding self schemas can be seen in what we know about the Easy bonders. They have a positive self-view but can acknowledge their shortcomings or flaws. They are able to integrate their strengths and weaknesses into a coherent and primarily positive view of themselves. This positive self-view enables them to confront problems and challenges confidently and optimistically. Their awareness of their strengths and weaknesses also allows them to set realistic goals and develop reasonable plans, which may prevent them from experiencing excessive emotional distress when their expectations are not met.

Descriptions of people with the Anxious Bonding Style are consistent with what one would predict for the negative bonding self schemas. Anxious bonders have more self-doubt and describe themselves in more negative terms. They seem unable to accept or integrate their positive attributes into their self-images, which are overly negative. They experience more negative emotions and are less able to control the intensity of their emotions. Their self-image is neither what they want to be nor what they think others want them to be, which can create great emotional distress and fear of disapproval. They are excessively dependent on reassurance from others to validate their worth.

Those with the Distant Bonding Style describe themselves in positive terms but seem out of touch with their weaknesses or unwilling to acknowledge them. Their self-awareness seems markedly biased in a hyperpositive direction, which is consistent with the hyperpositive schemas that comprise the Distant Bonding Style. Distant bonders deny feelings of insecurity, minimize hurtful experiences, and suppress negative emotions and memories. They maintain an idealized self-image by ignoring negative attributes and by appearing to be impervious to negative feedback, either by ignoring or rationalizing it away.

This discounting ability may have developed during childhood in an effort to emotionally survive in a painful, rejecting environment, which is consistent with the parental rejection that Distant bonders sometimes experience. By becoming detached and unresponsive to hurtful experiences, they were able to function and survive psychologically. This detachment and minimization of negative feedback may have been essential for them to survive but, as adults, Distant bonders are out of touch with themselves, their emotions, and the people around them.

Relationships

People with the Easy Bonding Style describe themselves as likable, sociable, and having few problems with most other people. Easy bonders report warm parental relationships, are optimistic about their romantic relationships, and view others as generally well-meaning and good-hearted. Acquaintances describe Easy bonders as socially skillful, engaging, likable, and cheerful.

Anxious bonders report having interpersonal problems related to their being overly demanding of support and attention in their relationships. They feel others misunderstand and underappreciate them. Other people see Anxious bonders as more self-conscious, more obsessed with relationship issues, and less socially sensitive than Easy or Distant bonders.

Distant bonders are uncomfortable with intimacy and view others as untrustworthy and undependable. Others describe Distant bonders as hostile, defensive, and less socially skilled than Easy bonders.

People with the different bonding styles also differ in the quality of their love relationships. Easy bonders report more positive relationship experiences than do Distant or Anxious bonders. Easy bonders describe their relationships as intimate, stable, and satisfying. In resolving conflicts, they are more inclined to consider both their own and their partners' interests and to compromise. Anxious bonders describe their romantic relationships as marked by jealousy, conflict, and emotional highs and lows. They see other people as being less willing to commit to relationships with them than they are. Distant bonders report low levels of intimacy, commitment, and satisfaction in relationships.

Distress Management

The Anxious and Distant Bonding Styles are more likely to report anxiety, depressive, and antisocial disorders than the Easy Bonding Style. Alcohol abuse and drug dependence are more common in the Distant style than in the Easy or Anxious styles (Mickelson, Kessler, and Shaver 1997). Because the Distant style is uncomfortable with closeness, self-disclosure, and the expression of emotions, alcohol and drugs may be an effective albeit destructive way that those who have the Distant Bonding Style use to numb their feelings and to shut out other people.

Differences in styles become more obvious when people are distressed, as in situations involving conflict, requests for greater intimacy and support, and stressful circumstances (Mikulincer 1998a). Easy bonders acknowledge distress, seek support from others, use effective coping strategies to manage their emotions, and employ constructive problem-solving to resolve dilemmas.

In contrast, Anxious bonders tend to become overly focused on their emotions, which increases their distress and interferes with their problem-solving skills. They desperately seek support from others and become clinging and controlling. When under stress, Distant bonders tend to suppress negative thoughts and feelings, avoid acknowledging personal weaknesses, withdraw from others, and try to increase their self-reliance and control.

Bonding styles differ in how susceptible they are to anger, how they express anger, how they interpret another person's motives, and how they attempt to resolve anger (Mikulincer, 1998b). Easy bonders are not easily angered and less apt to attribute hostile motives to the other person. They engage in more constructive strategies to resolve problems and maintain the relationship, such as talking with the other person. Easy bonders also expect positive outcomes when they express anger, which they do without animosity or hatefulness.

Anxious bonders are more easily angered, tend to ruminate about angry incidents, and have more difficulty controlling their anger. Distant bonders do not report any more intense anger or more frequent loss of control than do Easy bonders, but they show more intense physiological signs of anger and greater hostility. They also try to escape from conflict situations rather than attempt to resolve the problem. Both Anxious and Distant bonders expect more negative outcomes when they express anger, such as a partner attacking or leaving them. Both Anxious and Distant bonders also attribute more hostile motives to other people, but Distant bonders do so more than Anxious bonders. Note that there are no gender differences in these patterns of anger. Men and women with similar bonding styles have similar patterns of anger.

The Development of Bonding Styles

How do people get their bonding styles? Schemas related to the bonding process begin to develop during infancy. Infants begin to form impressions of themselves and others based on how their parents and other caregivers respond to their needs. These impressions continue during the toddler years, childhood, and thereafter. Children with warm and responsive parents develop schemas of themselves as lovable and worthy (*Worthy, Intimacy Comfortable*). They develop role and person schemas of others as trustworthy and caring. Children who have parents who are inconsistent in their responsiveness and caretaking develop schemas of others as unpredictable and confusing and schemas of themselves as possibly undeserving of attention or as doing things that alienate others (*Unworthy, Intimacy Driven*).

Children with unresponsive and rejecting parents tend to develop schemas of others as unreliable and rejecting and schemas of themselves as unworthy. If, over time, these children learn that they need to meet their own needs and are able to do so, they also might develop self schemas that emphasize the necessity to focus on their own needs (*Entitled*) and to view themselves as not needing others (*Intimacy Avoidant, Stubbornly Independent*). How a child responds in that particular situation could very well depend on the child's innate temperament and dispositions, which illustrates how social experiences and biological tendencies interact.

Since schemas related to the bonding process begin to emerge during infancy, clearly parents play a major role in the schemas that evolve. But parents are by no means the only influence on bonding schemas. Not only do parents often have different caregiving styles, the child is exposed to multiple models of other people during childhood, including other children, daycare workers, teachers, relatives, and the parents of their friends. Television and videos expand the models children observe even further.

Not only are children exposed to different bonding styles, they also have different interpersonal experiences. Children may experience a rejecting, critical environment if they are of the "wrong" social class, gender, appearance, ethnic group, or race. Rejection can come from any perceivable difference in oneself or one's family. Even the fear of rejection can influence bonding styles. Fear of rejection can result from any characteristic about oneself or one's family that the individual thinks could be viewed as shameful by others, for example, having divorced parents or a handicapped sibling. Anything that can stigmatize a person can influence bonding schemas and how one expects others to act. So a child is exposed to a variety of bonding experiences, which generate different bonding schemas in the child. Indeed, as already noted, almost all adults claim to have at least two bonding styles that involve different schemas.

If a child is repeatedly exposed to consistent models and experiences, eventually the bonding schemas that develop will be triggered simultaneously and become enduring bonding styles. These bonding styles then are elicited automatically without awareness on the part of the person. As explained in the last chapter, role and person schemas trigger different bonding styles. For example, if one has a mother who is cold and rejecting, all women or perhaps women with a similar personality or appearance to the mother may trigger a role schema that is associated with mothers or with women in general. This schema in turn will trigger the bonding style that has come to be associated with that type of person.

If people consistently experience discrimination for any reason, they may develop a role schema of people in general as hurtful and rejecting or perhaps a role schema of certain types of people as hurtful and rejecting. However, as illustrated by the example of Edie and Jana above, if you come to know a stranger over time, a specific person schema may develop that is inconsistent with your original more general role schema of people. Ultimately, then, that person who is no longer a stranger might trigger a different bonding style.

Recall that your schemas interact with how you perceive and react to others. If your role schemas of other people depict them as undependable and hurtful, you will keep them at a distance and never give them a chance to disconfirm your schema expectations. The risk is perceived as too great. The bonding style that would be activated in that case, the Distant style, will then *seem* to work for you by maintaining your independence, avoiding intimacy, and being self-protective. You will have avoided being hurt. You also will have strengthened all the schemas in the Distant Bonding Style. Thus, bonding styles can be self-perpetuating, because they can preclude you from taking risks from your style. Not taking risks in turn prevents you from discovering that your corresponding schema expectations are not valid. For example, a role schema that depicts others as rejecting may generate too much fear to take a chance to see if someone might be accepting.

Hence, our experiences from infancy through adulthood with our families and other people are critical in the bonding styles that we develop. However, all social experiences apparently are not equal. Psychologist Mark Baldwin and his colleagues (1996) asked people to describe their bonding styles in their ten most important relationships. The participants in the study described having an Easy style in the majority of their relationships. Yet when they were asked to select the bonding style that was *most* descriptive of them, some selected the Distant style and others picked the Anxious style.

An analysis of the participants' relationship lists provided some insight into their responses. The people who picked Distant had more relationships with the Distant style than did the people who picked the Easy or the Anxious style as most characteristic. Still, the people in the Distant group listed a *majority* of their relationships as having the Easy style. Likewise, the people who picked the Anxious style had more relationships with the Anxious style than did the people who had chosen the Easy or the Distant style as most characteristic. But again, the Anxious style group had a *majority* of relationships where they described themselves as having the Easy style.

Dr. Baldwin and his colleagues concluded that particularly painful relationship experiences can have a bigger impact on people than pleasant interpersonal experiences. In other words, all relationships do not have equal impact. Certain painful relationships may have more impact than pleasant or less painful relationships. Even occasional experiences of being painfully abandoned or rejected may strengthen the Distant or Anxious styles, making those styles more easily triggered and making those styles feel more descriptive of you. This analysis makes a lot of sense. A painful rejection by a parent or a heartbreaking experience with a deeply loved partner can be much more prominent in your schema system than several other loving successful relationships might be.

6

The Easy Bonding Style

There is no hope of joy except in human relations.

—Saint-Exupery, *Flight to Arras*

The last chapter described three bonding styles: Easy, Anxious, and Distant. People with the Easy Bonding Style find it easy to be close to others and believe others will be available in times of need. Those with the Anxious Bonding Style intensely desire closeness but are anxious about being rejected and they worry that others do not really care about them. People with the Distant Bonding Style are uncomfortable with closeness, prefer to keep people at a distance, and find it difficult to trust other people.

Bonding styles consist of self schemas. Different people and different situations trigger different styles. Nine out of ten people say that they have at least two bonding styles. However, people usually are able to identify a characteristic bonding style, because they think that one particular style is more descriptive of them.

In this and the following chapters each bonding style will be described in more detail. You will find out what past experiences tend to be associated with these styles. You will learn what triggers each style. You also will discover how bonding styles exert enormous influence on our attitudes and actions toward other people. Nowhere are schema expectations more influential than they are in the bonding styles. These expectations, which can be productive or counterproductive, will be described for each style. You will be able to determine if your bonding style expectations are having a constructive or destructive impact on your relationships. Now let's take a closer look at the Easy Bonding Style and the schemas relevant to that style.

The Balanced Bonding Self Schemas

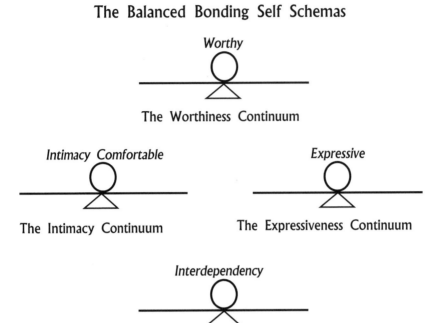

Worthy

The Worthiness Continuum

Intimacy Comfortable

The Intimacy Continuum

Expressive

The Expressiveness Continuum

Interdependency

The Interdependency Continuum

(*Worthy*) I am a worthwhile person. My needs are as important as the needs of other people, but not necessarily more so. (*Intimacy Comfortable*) I enjoy having close relationships. I also enjoy my time by myself. I seldom worry about being abandoned. (*Expressive*) I am comfortable expressing my feelings. I don't mind showing my feelings, but I don't like to fall apart. (*Interdependency*) I handle most things on my own, but I am comfortable asking for help. I don't mind depending on other people or having them depend on me.

Easy Bonders

Research studies repeatedly find that Easy bonders experience less personal distress and more relationship satisfaction than do Anxious or Distant bonders. Who are these good-natured folks with the Easy Bonding Style? Let's look at an example of someone who has this characteristic bonding style.

Dan

Dan is a thirty-seven-year-old high school math teacher who married his college sweetheart, Becky. They have three children, a son, eleven, and two daughters, thirteen and nine. Dan is the sponsor of the senior high Youth Fellowship at his church, has coached all his children in their athletic activities, and is an assistant baseball coach at the junior high school.

Dan is an outgoing, friendly man. Many parents want their kids on his teams because he takes a personal interest in their children, especially kids from single-parent homes. He makes sure every child participates in each game and is more concerned about developing self-confidence than with winning conference titles. Some parents who want their kids to become league champs have expressed anger at Dan for his approach. Dan told those parents that they have the option of changing teams. With some of the nastier parents Dan insisted they do so. Most adults like Dan just as well as children do. He remembers people's names, makes them feel comfortable, and speaks to everyone, regardless of their background or social standing. He has several close friends and still is best friends with a childhood friend.

Dan, the first of five children, grew up in a Denver suburb. His father was an insurance agent and his mom stayed home with the children and did most of his dad's office work out of their house. A "B" student, Dan participated in both sports and drama during high school. Popular with his classmates, he was elected captain of several of his sports teams, not because he was a great athlete but because he treated his teammates fairly and always praised their efforts. After graduation, he attended a local community college and continued working part-time. He finished his last two years at a small college and played second string positions on the football and baseball teams. Dan describes his childhood as happy though money was tight at times. Although his parents' financial support was limited, they had tried to help as much as they could with his college expenses. Both parents expressed great pride that he was the first child from either family to graduate from college.

After their youngest daughter entered first grade three years ago, Becky took a job with an insurance company. During the following year Dan felt that Becky had become increasingly short-tempered with him and the kids. She complained of always being tired, and their sex lives almost disappeared. In the past they had been sensitive to each other's feelings and could talk easily with each other. When they had differences, they usually were able to work them out amicably. Their arguments had increased in both frequency and intensity. They had begun to yell at each other and act resentful. They could tell the children sensed the growing tension between them. Because of that, Dan asked Becky if she would go to counseling with him. She agreed.

At the psychologist's office, Becky expressed her frustration that Dan seemed overcommitted and unavailable for the extra help she needed with the household tasks. She also complained that they never had any time together alone and Dan seemed less interested in her. Dan acknowledged that he had a hard time turning down requests from others, but he said that he enjoyed his extracurricular activities, especially those that involved his kids and Becky. He also felt frustrated that since Becky had started her job they had less time together and he no longer had time to continue his evening college courses to become a CPA.

Both had viewed Becky's return to full-time employment as a positive move for Becky personally and for them financially. Unfortunately, neither had realized how significantly her job would influence the family's routines. Dan had not readjusted his obligations when Becky went back to work, though he had not signed up for an accounting class that semester. With his current obligations Dan didn't see how he could take over any more household tasks. Becky suggested that after they paid off their credit card balance, they use that monthly payment for a housekeeper one-half day a week. Dan agreed. They also agreed that Dan would limit his future coaching responsibilities, so he could return to his CPA classes next semester. Until they can hire a housekeeper, they worked out an arrangement that prioritized tasks and split them up more equitably. After about eight therapy sessions, they agreed that their relationship had moved back to their original comfort level and further counseling was no longer needed.

Schema Analysis

Dan exemplifies someone with a characteristic Easy Bonding Style. To understand how this style influences Dan and others, you need to analyze the influence of his self schemas. You also need to identify what triggers his person and role schemas, which in turn trigger his self schemas for the Easy Bonding Style.

The Balanced Self Schemas

Let's now go back and identify some examples of how balanced self schemas of the Easy Bonding Style have influenced Dan and the people in his life.

Worthy: **My needs are as important as the needs of other people, but not necessarily more so. I deserve to be as happy as** everyone else. **I deserve to have many of my needs met, but certainly not all of them. I can treat myself occasionally without feeling guilty. I am comfortable when other people do things for me. I like nice things, but I don't have to have the best of everything.**

Dan tries to balance his needs with the needs of others. In high school he was able to recognize the achievements of his teammates without feeling inadequate. He shows an interest in other people by remembering their names and making sure they have a chance to participate. He feels good about himself and makes other people feel good about themselves. He feels comfortable around people regardless of their social standing or wealth. Dan coached and assumed other extracurricular activities because he enjoyed the activities and because others appreciated his ability and compassion. He was willing to continue coaching but not by sacrificing his own individual goal of becoming a CPA. He was able to stand up respectfully but firmly to angry parents for what he believed to be in the best interests of the children he coached.

Intimacy Comfortable: **I enjoy having close relationships, and I also enjoy my time by myself. I like emotional intimacy with certain people, but I don't like to be smothered. I am able to function fine when I am not in a close relationship even if I would prefer to be. It would be painful to lose someone close to me, but I think I could handle such an experience. I don't like rejection, but it's not the end of the world when I get it. I seldom worry about being abandoned.**

Dan's description includes several examples of the influence of this self schema. He has several close friends in Arizona and has maintained a relationship with a childhood friend. He enjoys people, but also has individual pursuits, such as his CPA studies. Although he was upset about what was happening between Becky and him, he did not panic about a possible divorce. Rather he sought the option of counseling to resolve their impasse.

Expressive: **I am comfortable expressing my feelings. I usually can control my feelings when I need to, but not always. Even if I am upset, I usually can express my thoughts calmly. I try to express my feelings constructively, so that I am not unnecessarily hurtful to others. I am not embarrassed about feeling strong emotions, but I am seldom totally unrestrained.**

Examples of the *Expressive* schema are numerous. Dan has close friends to whom he expresses his private thoughts. Dan and Becky have a long history of sharing their intimate feelings and thoughts. Dan is able to express his feelings to angry parents without becoming abusive. He seldom yells but had begun to do so as his relationship with Becky deteriorated. With this self schema people are not *always* in control, but they are not comfortable being verbally abusive or yelling at people. He was willing to openly discuss his thoughts and feelings to a psychologist to improve his marriage.

Interdependent: I can handle most things on my own, but I will ask for help if I need it. I like to make my own decisions, but am comfortable seeking advice from others.

The Interdependency schema is evident in the partnership Dan and Becky had. Dan is comfortable relying on her and having her rely on him. He is willing to be an assistant coach and take direction from head coaches. When he and Becky were unable to resolve their problems, he was willing to seek professional advice.

The impact of the balanced bonding schemas shows up in a variety of examples in Dan's behavior and the reactions of other people toward him. Dan's example also reveals how having a characteristic Easy Bonding Style does not require perfect people. Dan loses his temper on occasion. He isn't always able to say "no" when necessary. He has problems that sometimes overwhelm him, as evident in his relationship with Becky. Having the balanced bonding schemas does not mean that someone cannot have other problematic self schemas, such as perfectionism, or other troublesome behaviors. However, having the Easy Bonding Style has a positive impact on how one feels about oneself and how others feel toward that person as well.

Easy Bonding Style Triggers

Individuals with the Easy style have a role schema of people in general as being trustworthy, well-meaning, and reliable. This positive view of human beings triggers the Easy style, a bonding style that makes it possible to approach others more readily and to accept their overtures in return. Dan's description reveals that he usually views other people positively. He also has numerous long-term relationships with people about whom he has developed specific person schemas that primarily are positive. Dan also has a strong self schema of his own worthiness. This makes it easier to trigger his Easy Bonding Style, because in Dan the self schemas of Intimacy Comfortable, Expressive, and Interdependent are closely associated with his Worthy schema. Thus, in any situation that would trigger a bonding schema, the Easy Bonding Style is more likely to occur in Dan because his Worthy schema is usually already active.

However, the Easy Bonding Style does not mean that others are viewed indiscriminately. If someone acts in a way that triggers a role schema of an untrustworthy person, the Easy bonder is able to consciously be more cautious, less revealing, and less engaging with that person. When something specific about that other person triggers an untrustworthy role schema of others, Easy bonders are able to shift their typical responses. This shift does not require switching to the more rigid Anxious or Distant styles. Remember, the schemas of the Easy Bonding Style are balanced. Balanced schemas are able to incorporate more different types of information. In this situation, the balanced role schemas include knowledge on how to behave with possibly untrustworthy or unsavory people. People with balanced bonding schemas have much more flexibility in their reactions and actions than do people with a characteristic Anxious or Distant style, who tend to react to most people with rigidity and inflexibility.

Other Easy Bonders

Although Dan is an outgoing, high energy person, who enjoys community involvement, everyone with a characteristic Easy Bonding Style does not have to be outgoing and engaged in many group projects. Dan's wife Becky also is an Easy bonder. She is friendly but not as extroverted as Dan. She also participates in community activities but prefers more time alone than Dan does.

Ebony is another Easy bonder. She is a twenty-eight-year-old lawyer in her first year of practice in a small firm. She dated a moderate amount as an undergraduate, but much less during law school. Then her focus was on doing well to earn scholarship money for tuition. During law school she clerked part-time in various law firms for the experience and the additional income. Ebony is close to her family and several friends. She dates a few different men occasionally, but does not have a steady boyfriend. She would like to marry eventually, but says she has not met the right guy yet. She admits she is not in a hurry to find him. She enjoyed her educational experiences and wants some time for herself before she settles down to a major relationship.

Dan, Becky, and Ebony illustrate that Easy bonders are not clones. Everyone who is an Easy bonder is not necessarily the life of the party or in a committed relationship. Some Easy bonders are more outgoing than others, some are more talkative than others, some have many close friends, and others have only a few. What Easy bonders have in common are the four balanced bonding schemas. Yet they can differ from each other in those schemas to some extent and do.

Bonding Style Trends

About 60 percent of people pick the Easy Bonding Style as most characteristic of them, about 25 percent pick the Distant Bonding Style, and about 15 percent pick the Anxious Bonding Style (Hazan and Shaver 1987; Baldwin, Keelan, Fehr, Enns, et al. 1996; Mickelson, Kessler and Shaver 1997; Diehl, Elnick, Bourbeau, and Labouvie-Vief 1998). Are these styles associated with any particular demographics of people, such as sex, race, age, education, or income? Let's see what the studies listed above have found.

Gender

Do men and women differ in the bonding styles they pick as most characteristic of them? Not very much. Men and women both choose the Easy style as being most characteristic of them, the Distant style is the next most chosen, and the Anxious style is the least chosen. However, women have a slightly higher rate of the Easy style than do men. Likewise, men have a slightly higher rate of the Distant style than do women, but for both sexes the Easy style is chosen twice as often as the Distant style. In any case, the rates for men and women for most characteristic bonding styles are very similar to the percentages reported for the general population.

Race

Is race associated with characteristic bonding styles? The styles chosen are more similar than different among Whites, African-Americans, and Hispanics in the United States. All three groups select the Easy style most often, the Distant style second, and the Anxious style least often. However, a larger percentage of African-Americans and Hispanics picked the Anxious style than did Whites. Compared to Whites and Hispanics, a larger percentage of African-Americans chose the Distant style as most characteristic. The Anxious and Distant styles are associated with being distrusting of other people's actions. A minority group in any society might be expected to be less sure about how others will treat them, particularly if their race has experienced discrimination in that society.

Still, the point remains: the distribution of styles for Whites, African-Americans, and Hispanics is much more similar than different. However, these statistics are from the United States. Different cultures and ethnic groups may have very different expectations of appropriate behavior between people. Different expectations could produce different bonding styles in various groups. The statistics presented here are for the United States and may not apply to different countries or even to different ethnic groups within the United States.

Age

Age has an interesting impact on the most characteristic bonding style selected. The majority of all adults regardless of age select the Easy style as most characteristic of them, the second most chosen is the Distant style, and the Anxious style is the least chosen. However, among adolescents, the Anxious style is twice as high as it is among middle-aged adults. The Anxious style is highest among adolescents and lowest among people aged seventy or older. This higher frequency of the Anxious style among adolescents makes sense. This age group is the most unsettled, with uncertain futures and fluctuating relationships, and with the least experience in dealing with life's constant changes.

In contrast, by the age of seventy, there is a striking shift in both the Anxious and Distant styles. In seventy-year-old adults, the Anxious style is selected by less than 5 percent whereas almost 40 percent pick the Distant style as most characteristic. This age shift in characteristic styles suggests that as individuals grow older, a significant number of people with a characteristic Anxious style change to the Distant style. With aging, people experience more losses of relationships through death, divorce, and perhaps physical moves. These experiences might cause them to be less invested in other relationships, to focus more on meeting their own needs, and to be less fearful of being abandoned, having discovered that they can survive on their own.

Education

Are other demographic factors, such as urbanism, education, and income, associated with bonding styles? Some are, some are not. Bonding styles are not influenced by whether people live in large metropolitan areas, suburbs, or rural settings. However, education and income levels are related to bonding style frequencies. The higher the levels of education, the higher are the frequencies of the Easy style. The reverse is true for the Anxious style. The lower the levels of education, the higher are the frequencies of the Anxious style. However, the frequency of the Distant style remains the same across different levels of education.

Income

Income also has an effect on bonding styles. People with incomes below $20,000 a year are more likely to have a higher frequency of the Anxious style than those with greater incomes. As income level rises in the population, frequency of the Anxious style decreases. In contrast, people with incomes below $20,000 report an Easy style less often than do people with incomes greater than that. However, once yearly income exceeds $20,000, there is no greater incidence of the Easy style at any income level. Thus, the Anxious style frequency is affected across income levels, but the Easy style frequency is only affected by low income levels. The Distant style remains fairly stable across income levels, suggesting that this style is not particularly influenced by financial circumstances, just as it is not influenced by education level.

What Does This All Mean?

This data indicates that some demographic variables have an impact on the incidence of the bonding styles. Sex, race, age, income, and education all can influence the way we view others and ourselves in some manner. Yet a critical point remains. Although bonding style percentages change with these factors, the *order* of the distribution of the bonding styles remains the same. *Regardless of sex, race, age, income, or education, the majority of people in any of the subcategories still selects the Easy Bonding Style as their most characteristic style, the Distant style is the second most chosen, and the Anxious style is the least chosen.* In other words, this is the frequency order of the styles for males and females, for rich and poor, for the uneducated and the well educated, for young and old, and for African-Americans, White, and Hispanic.

The fact that the order does not change indicates that while some people in any category are affected by these factors, the bonding styles of the majority of the people in any of the categories are not changed. How can this finding be explained? Perhaps some individuals are more vulnerable to these variables than others. Perhaps having a combination of these variables has a bigger impact on bonding styles. What seems clear is that the majority of people in any category are quite resistant to any effect from these variables on their characteristic bonding styles.

While the *order* of styles chosen did not change, the *percentages* of the styles did change with the different demographic variables. The style showing the greatest change with the different variables was the Anxious style. The percentage of people with this style was higher at lower income levels, lower education levels, younger ages, with women, and with minority populations. All of these categories in our society carry increased vulnerabilities and correspondingly decreased empowerment to varying degrees. These results suggest that the Anxious style increases as the vulnerabilities of the individual increase and that this style is particularly sensitive to environmental and social influences. Among the three styles, the Anxious style is clearly the most unstable style.

Bonding Styles Can Shift

The fact that older adults describe a shift in bonding styles illustrates that characteristic bonding styles can change. Research has shown that even with other age groups over time, about one out of three people change what they report as their most characteristic style. People report changing from all three styles, but the Easy Bonding Style is the most stable. People switch between the Anxious and Distant Bonding Styles more often than they do between the Easy style and the other two styles. However, the Anxious style is the least stable style (Baldwin and Fehr 1995; Baldwin, Keelan, Fehr, Enns, et al. 1996; Davila, Burge, and Hammen 1997; Diehl, et al. 1998).

What produces changes in characteristic bonding styles? Major life transitions, such as graduation, job changes, or leaving home, have been associated with style changes. Stress in romantic relationships and overall interpersonal distress also can lead to bonding style changes. Emotional distress, such as anxiety or depression, and other psychological problems, such as eating disorders and substance abuse, also have been associated with style shifts (Davila, Burge, and Hammen 1997). Further, experiences that change the way you view other people and yourself can result in changes in styles. For example, people have been found to change their characteristic bonding styles after participating in psychotherapy, which typically focuses on how we think about others and ourselves (Fonagy, Leigh, Steele, et al. 1996).

Not only can people change their characteristic styles across time, they also can change styles in the same relationship and have different styles in different relationships. Although vacillating between styles can be problematic and confusing, the fact that characteristic bonding styles can change is *good* news. Since the Easy Bonding Style is related to less stressful relationships and less personal distress than the Anxious and Distant styles, enhancing an Easy style can be quite beneficial. Ways to modify schemas to strengthen or develop an Easy Bonding Style will be presented throughout this book.

Bonding Style Influences

If almost everyone reports having at least two bonding styles, then bonding styles cannot be fixed character traits. If they were, people would report having the same type of bonding style over time and in all of their relationships. If bonding styles didn't change over time or in different circumstances, that also would mean that you are stuck with whatever bonding style you inherited, which is not the case. You don't inherit a particular bonding style. As explained earlier, you develop your bonding styles as a result of your personal dispositions and temperament and experiences with other people. For example, emotional regulation problems seem more common with the Anxious Bonding Style. The temperaments and dispositions present at birth influence our emotional and behavioral reactions and make us more or less sensitive to certain experiences. The development of the brain itself is influenced by one's experiences, especially during infancy and childhood.

Parental Warmth

Psychologists have discovered certain events or experiences occur more frequently in the history of certain styles. However, simply having such an experience in one's history does not mean that you *inevitably* will have that style. Rather, these events or experiences might better be viewed as *incidence factors*: the more of the factors you have, the more likely you are to have a certain style. For example, parental warmth, both from fathers and mothers, is related to the development of an Easy style. The absence of parental warmth is associated with the other two styles. So the presence of parental warmth is an incidence factor for the Easy style, and the absence of parental warmth is an incidence factor for the Anxious and Distant styles.

Parental Treatment of Each Other

What can we learn about bonding styles by looking at events that occur in a person's life during childhood and adolescence? Drs. Kristin Mickelson, Ronald Kessler, and Philip Shaver (1997) discovered a great deal by doing exactly that. The quality of the relationship between the parents has a significant impact on the bonding styles of the offspring. Both Anxious and Distant styles are more frequent in people with parents who had a poor marital relationship and especially with parents who were physically abusive to each other. Physical violence between parents is a powerful incidence factor for both the Anxious and Distant styles. Abusive behavior between parents conveys a message to the child that people—even those who might act loving toward each other at other times—can be hurtful, untrustworthy, and unpredictable, the very characteristics that the Anxious and Distant styles attribute to other people.

Divorce

Parental divorce seems more related to the Anxious style. This finding suggests that the divorce of one's parents may contribute to the view of others as not being available consistently. Since children rarely continue to live with both parents after a divorce, one parent inevitably is somewhat less available after a divorce, and in some cases, absent altogether. However, parental divorce is not associated with the Distant style, which suggests that divorce per se does not create the impression of parents as cold and rejecting. Parental divorce can increase the likelihood of the Anxious style, but witnessing parental violence has a stronger impact on the development of both the Anxious and Distant styles. Parents staying together in a hostile, destructive marriage presents a greater risk than divorce for Anxious and Distant Bonding Styles in their children.

Psychological Problems of Parents

Are your bonding styles influenced by whether or not your parents had psychological problems? Apparently so. People with the Easy style are less likely to have parents who had anxiety, depression, suicidal, or antisocial behavior. People with the Anxious style are more apt to describe anxiety or depression problems in their parents or a suicidal parent, especially a suicidal mother, and antisocial mothers. Individuals with the Distant style are similar to those with the Anxious style in being more likely to describe anxiety and depression problems in their parents, a suicidal father, and an antisocial mother. People with untreated psychological problems and antisocial behavior can create a stressful and unpredictable environment for their children, making it difficult for those children to learn to trust or rely on others, even people whom they know love them. These experiences are a blueprint for a role schema of other people as untrustworthy.

People with the Distant style are more likely to report a depressed mother and parental drug and alcohol abuse than the other styles. Depression and substance abuse have similar effects. They both make people less responsive and less able to focus on other people's needs. In essence, people suffering from depression or engaged in substance abuse are less able to care for their children. Their children often are forced to take care of themselves, which could explain how the Entitled self schema in the Distant Bonding Style develops in these children. They are forced to focus more on their own needs than the needs of other people because no one is focusing on them.

Interpersonal Traumas

Interpersonal traumas refer to events in which someone directly harms a child or adolescent. These traumas include being physically abused, seriously neglected, threatened with a weapon, raped, molested, and becoming pregnant. Such traumas during childhood and adolescence have a powerful effect on bonding styles. All of these interpersonal traumas are strongly related to the presence of Anxious and Distant styles in adulthood. Any of these traumas provide evidence that other people are not trustworthy. Although neglect may seem less traumatic than the other interpersonal traumas listed, serious neglect is strongly correlated with the Anxious and Distant styles. Being neglected by their parents puts children and adolescents at physical and emotional risk, just as do the other interpersonal traumas. Serious neglect is not an uncommon experience for those with the Anxious and Distant styles. All of these interpersonal traumas are much less likely to be found in the histories of people with the Easy style. The table below summarizes the kind of experiences Dr. Mickelson and her colleagues found associated with the different bonding styles. "Yes" indicates that the event is more likely to have occurred in the history of people with that style.

Childhood and Adolescent Experiences Associated with Bonding Styles

Event	Easy	Anxious	Distant
Absence of Parental Warmth		Yes	Yes
Poor Relationship between Parents		Yes	Yes
Violence between Parents		Yes	Yes
Parental Divorce		Yes	
Anxious Parents		Yes	Yes
Depressed Father		Yes	Yes
Depressed Mother		Yes	Especially
Suicidal Father		Yes	Yes
Suicidal Mother		Especially	
Antisocial Mothers		Yes	Yes

Parental Drug and Alcohol Abuse		Yes
Physical Abuse	Yes	Yes
Neglect	Yes	Yes
Threatened with a Weapon	Yes	Yes
Raped	Yes	Yes
Molested	Yes	Yes
Becoming Pregnant	Yes	Yes
Being in a Life-Threatening Accident	Yes	
Experiencing Financial Hardship	Yes	Yes

Check which of the above events you have experienced. You can see what events have made you more vulnerable to certain styles, whether you have them or not. If you have an Easy style instead of an Anxious or Distant style even though you have several vulnerability factors, what influences contributed to you developing that Easy style?

Betrayal of Trust

The summary table shows that adults with the Anxious and Distant styles are far more likely to have experienced harmful and upsetting experiences in their pasts than have adults with the Easy style. Personally experiencing neglect, physical violence, and sexual abuse, and witnessing physical violence between parents are strongly associated with the Anxious and Distant styles. The experiences listed in the table have a powerful impact on how children and adolescents come to see themselves and others, thus influencing the development of the self, person, and role schemas associated with their bonding styles. Experiences that involve the betrayal of trust in both the care and protection of a child and adolescent are the most likely to affect adult bonding styles. Positive views of the self and others become less likely after damaging experiences in the early years.

Clearly, certain events that occur during childhood and adolescence are powerful incidence factors for bonding styles. Remember, though, that having one or even several of these incidence factors in your past does not guarantee that you will have a certain style. For example, everyone who has been molested or has parents who divorced does not necessarily end up with a characteristic Distant or Anxious style. The data also mean that people with a Distant or Anxious style are more likely to report the presence of these experiences than people with the Easy style, but certainly not everyone with a Distant or Anxious style reports having these experiences.

For example, many people describe themselves as characteristically Distant, yet have none of the items listed under the Distant column. What the data mean is that among the people who report Distant as a characteristic style, these experiences occur more often than they do among people who do not claim Distant as a characteristic style. However, that does not mean that everyone with a Distant style has those experiences. This is true, too, for the other styles. Even those with the Easy Bonding Style may have divorced parents and may have been molested, but those experiences are less frequent with this style than for other styles.

There are four conclusions to be drawn from the research on bonding styles.

1. Individuals respond differently to similar experiences. This can be due to individual dispositions, to differences in support systems, and to differences in the experiences themselves.

2. Experiences that are similar in name may be quite different in reality. For example, all divorces are most assuredly not the same. Divorces vary greatly in the surrounding circumstances and how the parents handle the process, which means that those experiences will have different impacts on the children.

3. Certain experiences seem to increase our vulnerability to certain styles but do not guarantee those styles will emerge.

4. We don't know *exactly* what causes people to develop different styles, because some people may have a style and not have any of the corresponding experiences listed above. However, if we know which schemas are associated with the different styles, that information can guide us in learning how to modify bonding styles.

Enhancing the Easy Bonding Style

Since the Easy Bonding Style is associated with fewer interpersonal conflicts and happier relationships, you might be interested in strengthening or developing your own Easy style. First, reread the four bonding schemas of this style in Appendix B. Whom do you know who fits this style? Who are the people that almost everybody seems to like and trust? Begin to keep a list of people you think have this style. Watch how they treat others, how they react to bad news, how they express their feelings, how they handle stress, how they act around strangers. Consider whether you could use them as models to imitate. Chapters 9, 10, 11, 12, and 13 will provide additional suggestions on how to enhance the Easy style.

Encouraging the Easy Bonding Style in Children

Since the Easy Bonding Style is associated with the least personal and interpersonal distress, can you learn from this data how to help children develop the Easy style? Yes, you can. There are several guidelines listed below that can be drawn from this research that will aid you in this endeavor.

- Provide a warm, loving relationship for your children. Listen to them. Hug them. Be affectionate. Tell them that you love them, and show it. Say "I love you" on many occasions. Let them know that they are important, worthwhile people. Invest your time in them. Play with them. Go to their activities, no matter how boring you think they might be. You are not going to be entertained. You're going because your presence matters to your kids. Be there for them.

- Maintain a respectful, nonhostile, nonsarcastic atmosphere among the people in your family. Eliminate name calling, ridicule, or hateful teasing. Treat your children with respect. Never say mean and vicious things to them, no matter how upset you are. If you feel that much anger toward your children, *you* need to get counseling.

- Seek professional help for psychological problems.

- If you drink alcohol, model how to drink responsibly, which means never being intoxicated.

- Stop any drug abuse, whether with prescription or illegal drugs. If you can't stop, get help. Now.

- Provide a safe, secure environment where your child is not in danger from people you don't know. Develop a set of safety procedures for your children when you aren't with them.

- Explain to your children what sexual abuse is and how another person is wrong to ever improperly touch them. Tell them what to do if they ever find themselves in a threatening situation. Tell them to always come to you if anyone, family member or stranger, has been inappropriate with them and even if the other person has threatened to hurt them, their family, or their pets if the child tells. If you suspect your child has been sexually abused, seek help immediately. You can call a crisis number, the Child Protective Services in your area, or any mental health professional for guidance.

- Eliminate any physical abuse in the family toward *any* family member or pets. Exposing your children to the sight of physical violence is as abusive as subjecting the child to it. Watching a parent, sibling, or pet being abused is absolutely terrorizing to a child. Seeing a loved one beaten and being unable to stop it creates enormous shame, fear, and helplessness in the observer. These experiences can reprogram a child's nervous system in ways that may never be reparable.

- You can teach children nurturing behavior by showing them how to care for animals. If you have pets, model responsible, caring behavior. Feed and exercise your pets regularly. Spend time every day with your pets. Never curse, strike, or kick an animal. Teach your children that animals have feelings too. Cruelty to animals has repeatedly been found to be a first step toward cruelty toward people.

- If you are in an abusive relationship, seek guidance from a domestic shelter in your area. You are not safe, and neither are your children. Do not do anything impulsively. You need guidance from experts to extricate yourself safely from the situation.

- If your child has a friend from a dysfunctional family, do what you can to include that child in your family's activities. You can give that child a model of people who care about each other in a loving atmosphere. If you can help the child experience the benefits of a loving family, you can provide an alternative schema of a functional family for that child. Many well-functioning adults come out of dysfunctional families and identify nonfamily role models who showed them how functional families exist.

- If you know of a child who is being neglected or abused, do something, whether it is reaching out to the child directly or getting other responsible parties involved. If you are unsure about what to do, seek guidance from a mental health professional. When adults ignore the abuse or neglect of a child, it is inevitable that those children feel disconnected from a society that does not protect them. One caring, concerned adult can change a child's destiny.

These guidelines are not complicated, but simple does not mean easy. If you think any guideline would be hard for you to implement, get help. Your children and your children's friends deserve help, and so do you.

7

The Anxious Bonding Style

Jealousy and anger shorten life, and anxiety brings on old age too soon.

—*Apocrypha*, Ecclesiasticus 30:24

People with a characteristic Anxious Bonding Style experience doubt about themselves and their relationships. They are overly negative about themselves and unable to maintain a positive self-image without repeated reassurance from others. They experience frequent emotional distress, either anxiety, anger, depression, or all three. Their relationships are turbulent. The Anxious bonders tend to idealize others at first and then experience disappointment when those idealized people do not meet their elevated expectations. Ever alert to any sign of rejection, they worry about being abandoned and often feel jealous. They think they need to depend on others but worry that others will not be there for them. Life is not easy for Anxious bonders and the people connected to them.

This chapter will focus on the Anxious Bonding Style and its negative schemas. Different examples of people with this style will be described. Although there is considerable variability among those who claim the Anxious style to be most characteristic of them, emotional distress plays a prominent role in the life of any Anxious bonder. We will look at why emotional control is difficult for this style and how that problem emerged. This chapter also will provide insights into how this problematic bonding style disrupts relationships and how to modify it.

The Negative Bonding Self Schemas

Unworthy

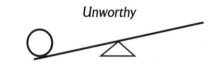

The Worthiness Continuum

Intimacy Driven   *Unrestrained*

The Intimacy Continuum   The Expressiveness Continuum

Dependent

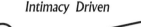

The Interdependency Continuum

(*Unworthy*) I often feel that somehow I am not as good as other people. My needs are not as important as the needs of other people. (*Intimacy Driven*) I often want more closeness or intimacy than I get. I need a lot of reassurance that I am loved or valued. I feel lost if I am not in a close relationship. I worry about being abandoned or being alone. (*Unrestrained*) My feelings often overwhelm me. I seldom feel in control of my emotions. (*Dependent*) I tend to be dependent. I rely on other people to help me with most things.

An Anxious Bonder

People with a characteristic Anxious Bonding Style experience uncertainty about themselves and the people in their lives. Their quest for intimacy is usually insatiable and frequently disappointing. Their expectations of others are usually excessive and ultimately not met. Their lives are filled with chronic bouts of intense anxiety, hence the name the Anxious bonder.

Camille

Camille is a twenty-nine-year-old single woman who has been a paralegal for the last three years with a small law firm. She has been living with her current boyfriend, Alex, for a year after dating steadily for about two months. Alex is an electronics technician with the same large company that hired him seven years ago after he earned his associate degree. Camille and Alex's relationship has been stormy for most of the time they have been together. They met when Alex was hired as a consultant by Camille's law firm. After the case was over, they began dating, hit it off immediately, and started seeing each other daily. When Alex's apartment lease expired, Camille invited him to move into her townhouse with her. Alex expressed some hesitancy because of the newness of the relationship. Camille acted hurt and disappointed at his reluctance and continued to press him until he relented and put most of his own furniture in storage.

About a month after Alex moved in, Camille became more critical of his habits and his cat, which he had had for four years and which, before he moved, Camille had assured him she adored. She complained that Alex was messy, that his clothes were not stylish, that he loved his cat more than he did her, and that he spent all his time on his computer or watching sports shows on television. She accused him of not being interested in her and only using her to have a cheaper place to live.

In response, Alex pointed out that they spent virtually all their time outside of work together; that he fixed dinner for both of them almost every night; that he thought she liked his cat and sports as much as he did; and that he didn't spend any more time on the computer than she did on her paralegal work in the evening. Although Alex's reassurances helped, the effect was always short-lived.

When they did go out to parties, Camille would often accuse him of being too friendly with the other women who were there. When Alex tried to reason with her, she would be inconsolable, often saying hurtful things and calling him names. Attempts to reassure her of his devotion to her were met with scorn. Camille's accusations would intensify after she had been drinking.

One Saturday night after a party, Camille became so enraged that she struck Alex, who responded by shoving her onto the bed and storming out of the townhouse. The next morning he returned and said that he couldn't continue in the relationship this way. He had never had these kinds of arguments in previous relationships, had never been abusive to anyone, and had never been angry enough to even consider striking a partner. Alex said that Camille either needed to see a counselor for her mood swings or he was leaving. He said he was willing to see a counselor with her if the counselor thought that would help, but he couldn't take it anymore if she didn't change.

Camille has never been without a boyfriend since junior high and she never ended one relationship until she had another on the horizon. All of her romantic relationships have been turbulent, with accusations from her and sometimes from them of flirtatious behavior with others. Her longest relationship lasted three years. It began when she was a sophomore. The boy was a year older and hung out with the drug crowd, much to the chagrin of her parents and sister. Her family's efforts to prevent the relationship only seemed to intensify Camille's devotion to him, in spite of repeated rumors of his encounters with girls at other high schools.

In looking back, Camille thinks that she always has been attracted to men who seemed to need her. She envisioned herself as the one who finally understood them and could rescue them from their lost lives, for which they would be forever devoted to her. Many of her relationships began when these men were still involved with other women, and most of the men had alcohol or drug abuse problems. The relationships usually were like roller-coaster rides. She experienced great panic and hysteria if the current boyfriend left her, at times being barely able to function. Those feelings of desperation would subside once she had found someone new.

Camille thinks Alex is the most stable man she has ever dated. He drinks very little and never to excess. He doesn't run around on her. He calls her daily at work. He is supportive of her professionally and proud of her achievements. He has a good job, insists on paying two-thirds of her monthly mortgage, and shares all the other expenses. She doesn't know why he has stayed this long, because she thinks he doesn't really need her and she knows that she makes his life miserable at times. The closer she gets to him, the more frightened she becomes that he will leave. She told her therapist that sometimes she thinks she precipitates the arguments so he will leave, because she views his departure as inevitable once he realizes that she doesn't deserve him.

Camille and her older sister, Pamela, were raised by her parents in the Los Angeles area. Her father was a stern, critical man with an explosive temper. Her mother was a loving, submissive woman who developed a significant drinking problem by the time Camille was in early grade school. Camille and Pamela became reluctant to bring any of their friends home, because they never knew whether their mother would be sober or drunk. When their mother was intoxicated, Pamela would be disgusted and go to her room or out to play with friends, but Camille would try to get her mother to lie down and would hide her bottles. These efforts were met with varying degrees of success, but often resulted in Camille being cursed and pushed aside. Later, her mother would express remorse to Camille and promise never to drink again, which Camille longed to hear but eventually learned to not believe.

Most evenings and weekends were punctuated with arguments between her parents about her mother's drinking, with her father threatening to take the children away and file for divorce. Time after time in the late evening Camille would hear her mother sobbing and pleading for one more chance. Sometimes her mother would go for a few weeks without a drink, but inevitably Camille and Pamela would come home from school one day and find her glassy-eyed and slurring her words, yet denying she had had a drop.

Both her father and Pamela treated her mother with increasing disrespect and coldness. Camille would ache with sadness at their contempt and would try to console her mother. Finally, when Camille was a junior in high school, her mother agreed to enroll in an inpatient alcohol treatment program. She has been able to remain sober since then, but the tension between Camille's parents has never diminished. They co-exist in a stony silence, essentially leading separate lives with only their children as a common interest.

Pamela and Camille have never been close. Camille feels that Pamela treats her in the same contemptuous manner as she does her mother. Both girls competed for their father's attention while growing up, and still do. Camille calls her father for guidance before making any decision that isn't routine. Pamela was a gifted student, but Camille struggled in school; she had a hard time staying focused. Although she was never diagnosed with an attention deficit disorder, she remembers a school psychologist telling her parents that her attention problems were caused by anxiety and encouraged them to seek help for her. They never did.

Schema Analysis

Camille's story is a good illustration of the Anxious Bonding Style. Let's analyze Camille's self, person, and role schemas to see how they maintain and support this style for her.

The Negative Self Schemas

The impact of the negative schemas of the Anxious Bonding Style permeates Camille's entire description. You can see how these schemas produce distress for Camille and her boyfriend, Alex.

Unworthy: I often feel that somehow I am not as good as other people. My needs are not as important as the needs of other people. I don't deserve to be happy. The needs of other people should come before my own. I tend to feel guilty if I do nice things for myself. I also feel uncomfortable when other people do nice things for me.

The influence of the *Unworthy* schema is obvious in the men Camille typically has chosen. Her boyfriends have been alcohol or drug abusers whom she has tried to rescue and nurture, whether they wanted that or not. Camille thinks if she can rescue them, she will make herself worthy of their love. She does not view herself as worthy of Alex's affections. She continues to question why Alex would love her and cannot believe him when he says he does, since he really doesn't need anything from her.

Intimacy Driven: I often want more closeness or greater intimacy than others give me. I seek repeated reassurance from others that I am loved. I feel lost if I am not in an intimate relationship. I have difficulty functioning if I am not involved with someone. I worry about losing people who are close to me. I worry about being abandoned. I am usually alert to any signs of rejection by others.

Camille has never been without a boyfriend for any length of time. In the past, she always waited to break off a relationship until she had a new man in sight. In spite of spending almost all their time away from work together, Camille complains that she still does not have enough of Alex's attention. She is jealous of Alex's affection for his cat and his other interests. Alex's reassurances about his love for Camille never keep Camille's doubts from re-emerging for very long. Camille is constantly alert for any signs of abandonment. She interprets any interest Alex shows in another woman as a sign that he is on the verge of leaving her. Camille's behavior also illustrates how her Intimacy Driven self schema makes her so desperate to have a relationship that initially she acted more interested in Alex's activities than she genuinely was. After the relationship became established, she became more critical of his interest in sports. This particular fluctuating pattern of supposedly shared interests is typical of the Anxious bonder. Such change can create great confusion and resentment in the partner.

Unrestrained: My emotions often are overwhelming. It is difficult for me to control my emotions. People can easily tell how I am feeling. I cannot hide my emotions. My emotions often seem out of control.

Camille describes emotional turbulence as characteristic of all of her romantic relationships. She experienced surges of panic whenever her partners ended their relationships, no matter how unfulfilling those relationships had been for her. She has suffered chronic feelings of anxiety and depression since childhood.

Dependent: **I tend to be dependent. I rely on other people to help me with most things. Life is too difficult for me to handle alone. I have a hard time making decisions by myself. I frequently seek assistance from others. I do not like being completely on my own. I need other people to take care of me.**

Although in the past Camille took care of her boyfriends in mostly lopsided relationships, she always felt dependent upon them. She is terrified of being alone and has always lined up someone to replace whomever she plans to discard. Even at twenty-nine, Camille seeks her father's advice before making any decision that is out of the ordinary.

Anxious Bonding Style Triggers

Camille tends to view everyone as being more worthwhile than she is, even after she gets to know them and their flaws. Both her role schemas of people in general and the person schemas she develops for specific individuals are overly positive and seemingly blind to any shortcomings. This perceived discrepancy between her own worth and the worth of others makes her fear eventual rejection or disapproval when other people get to know her. She expects that eventually they will be disappointed in who she really is. Although she desperately wants intimacy and total acceptance, she cannot convince herself that others will ever be able to give her that. Any criticism is seen as rejection and a sign of impending abandonment.

In Camille's case, her *Unworthy* schema is very strong and easily activated by any threatening or anxiety-arousing situation. Since Camille views almost everyone else as superior to her, other people are usually perceived as threatening to some degree and can easily trigger her *Unworthy* schema if it is not already active. Consequently, her Anxious Bonding Style is readily triggered because of the close association between her *Unworthy* schema and her other negative schemas of *Intimacy Driven*, *Unrestrained*, and *Dependent*.

Social situations that are perceived to be threatening can trigger any or all of the Anxious Bonding Style schemas. For example, when Alex is friendly with other women, Camille's *Unworthy* schema makes her believe that he will find them more appealing than she is. This interpretation then triggers her *Intimacy Driven* schema, which convinces Camille that Alex will abandon her. In turn, this conclusion generates an overwhelming emotional reaction in Camille. Her intense emotions trigger her *Unrestrained* schema and the belief that she cannot contain her emotions and must confront Alex immediately with her fears.

In spite of her schemas, Camille doesn't *want* to believe that Alex will leave, so her attacks intensify, hoping for a reaction from him that will be strong enough to reassure her that he won't leave. If Camille gets the reassurance she is seeking, her verbally abusive or hysterical outbursts are unintentionally reinforced. Unfortunately, her attacks often push Alex further away, causing Camille more dismay, reinforcing the schemas in her Anxious Bonding Style, and often escalating her emotional behavior. Either result is destructive. The following diagram shows how these events trigger her negative schemas, creating a destructive cycle:

Alex being friendly with other women →
Camille's *Unworthy* schema →
Belief that other women are more appealing than she is →
Camille's *Intimacy Driven* schema →
Conclusion that Alex will abandon her for someone else →
Intense emotional reaction in Camille →
Camille's *Unrestrained* schema →
Belief that Camille needs to express her fears to
Alex immediately →
Alex's reassurance or withdrawal from Camille.

Any perceived relationship threat can trigger Camille's Anxious Bonding Style. However, threats of any nature seem to make the Anxious Bonding Style more easily triggered. Threatening situations raise the overall level of arousal in everyone, which makes one more vigilant and more apt to misinterpret innocuous events or behaviors as dangerous. Any threat to our security, whether in our personal or professional lives, can have this effect. People with a characteristic Anxious Bonding Style usually have a higher baseline tension level, because their negative schemas have them primed to expect negative outcomes. Because they already tend to be more apprehensive, they often feel flooded with anxiety when any event threatens their security.

For example, Camille had been under increased pressure at her law firm. She was involved in preparing a complicated and important case and was fearful that her preparation might not be complete by the time the trial began. She had been staying up late and getting to work early. Increased stress and less sleep tend to make people less hopeful and more easily discouraged but especially more emotionally reactive. Think of the times when you have been stressed and not sleeping well. Didn't little things that you might not even notice at other times more easily irritate you? The combination of increased stress and less sleep is hard on anyone's emotional state, but for someone with the Anxious Bonding Style it's deadly.

Camille's fear of losing her job made her feel more dependent on her relationship. If she lost her job, she had to have someone take care of her. That possibility made her seek more reassurance from Alex, whom she already feared would leave her when he realized how unworthy she was. If she lost her job or was demoted, that would be further evidence of her unworthiness. All of these fears made her more prone to misinterpret situations related to Alex's commitment to her, increasing the tension between them. The increased strain made her even more fearful that he would leave and she increased her demands for more reassurance that he would not. You can see how Camille's negative schemas fed on each other, increasing her tension and her expectations that something awful was imminent.

An increase in stress from any source inevitably affects our closest relationships, if not our more casual ones. However, Anxious bonders already put a lot of pressure on their relationships because of their vigilance about being abandoned or rejected. When stress increases in their lives, the pressure on their relationships can escalate to even more destructive levels of intensity, which further increases the stress the Anxious bonders experience. The distressing effect of the negative schemas is pervasive in the lives of Anxious bonders and those around them.

All Anxious Bonders Are Not Alike

When Camille's Anxious style is active, she sees herself as unworthy, likely to be abandoned, and unable to cope on her own. She cannot see what attracts Alex to her. On the other hand, Alex can't see how she could even wonder about that. Camille is attractive, funny, thoughtful, and kind. She is a conscientious worker and is self-motivated, never needing to be reminded to meet her responsibilities. She is supportive of Alex and tells him and others how proud she is of him. This is Camille when her Easy Bonding Style is active. However, that Camille disappears when her Anxious style is activated. Many people with the Anxious style also have an Easy style, as Camille does. Most of the people around them may be totally unaware of their Anxious styles, which may be revealed only to their closest intimates. Most of the time Camille is a highly functional person, but her Anxious style has repeatedly disrupted her life.

Matt

However, all those with an Anxious style are not necessarily highly functional people, and they don't always have an alternative Easy style. For example, Matt, who is in his early thirties and was raised in an abusive family with an alcoholic father, has been involved in several sequential relationships with different women. These relationships have always followed the same pattern as a result of his Anxious Bonding Style.

When a woman shows interest in him, he responds eagerly, showering her with attention and gifts. He wants to spend every free moment with her and is completely accommodating. Once the relationship is established, he becomes increasingly possessive, disparaging her family and friends and discouraging contact with them, especially if he is not with her. Any unexpected change in his girlfriends' schedules precipitates angry accusations and jealous rages. In each case, the woman finally breaks off the relationship.

Breakups are followed by desperate calls from Matt, threatening to hurt himself if she does not change her mind. Some women responded to these threats the first few times he made them, but eventually they saw that they were being emotionally blackmailed. They told him he was responsible for his own choices and permanently severed contact, some even obtaining restraining orders against him. Matt has been hospitalized on one occasion and has sought counseling after several other experiences, but he disdains the therapists who told him that it is his behavior that precipitates these disastrous endings. He refuses to consider that. He believes that the women should be more understanding, less flirtatious with others, more devoted to him. He cannot see his role in these events. And he does not change. Matt also has difficulty holding down a job because when his relationships begin to deteriorate, his emotional turmoil increases his obsession about them. Losing jobs means frequent moves to avoid eviction. The severity of his Anxious Bonding Style makes his life chaotic.

Is there something wrong with the women who are attracted to Matt? Not necessarily. In fact, most of them have characteristic Easy Bonding Styles. Matt has a good appearance and sophisticated computer skills that make finding new jobs easy. When women first meet him, he always is employed and presents an optimistic future for himself. This illustrates how the Easy Bonding Style will not prevent you from becoming entangled with Anxious bonders who may be quite dysfunctional but are able to appear normal to those who do not know them well. If you become involved in a situation similar to that of the women who dated Matt, extricating yourself is your best option. People can be deceptive, and Matt is one of those people. There are many highly functional people with the Anxious Bonding Style who are well worth the effort it will take to help them change. No amount of effort will work with Matt because he will not accept that *he* needs to change, not the women he has known.

Barbara

Barbara is in her late thirties, works in a management position for an insurance company, and lives with her fifteen-year-old son, Ryan. Barbara divorced her husband three years ago after she discovered he was having an affair. The affair was a shock to her. She and her ex-husband had never really argued, although he was not very expressive. Barbara says that she has always had an Anxious Bonding Style, but it became much stronger after she found out about her husband's affair. She had known him since high school and had never been in love with anyone else. She was devastated by the betrayal, and became clinically depressed for several months after the discovery. During that time she became increasingly dependent on her son, who was then twelve, and began treating him as a confidant. Over time Barbara has become more possessive of Ryan's time and attention. She feels threatened and resentful when he spends time with his friends.

Bonding Styles in Children and Adolescents

Bonding styles can be identified in children and adolescents also. Stevie is an eight-year-old third grader. His parents both work and don't get home until about six o'clock every night. He gets out of school at 3:00 P.M. and walks the half mile home from school alone. He has his own key and lets himself into the house, relocks the door, has a snack, watches television for a while, and then does his homework before his parents get home. He has been told to not answer the phone unless he hears the voice of one of his parents on the speaker. He is to keep the drapes drawn and not go outside. This has been Stevie's routine since second grade. Stevie stays at school until the teacher leaves, and then walks home as slowly as he possibly can, kicking every rock he can find on the sidewalk. He is terrified to be home alone, but he is even more afraid to tell his parents of his fears.

He knows that daycare costs them more than they want to pay, and his parents argue about money a lot. His mother gets angry with him for being too dependent. She complains that he cries about everything, and she has threatened that if he doesn't stop wetting the bed, he will have to sleep on the floor.

One day Stevie forgot his key and had to sit outside until his folks got home after dark. He was terrified, and after headlights started flashing at him on the steps, he hid in the bushes in front of the house. His mother scolded him for being so irresponsible. Stevie is an average student, but his teachers say that he is an underachiever with little self-confidence. He bites his nails to the quick and seems unkempt.

Essentially, since the age of seven Stevie has been instructed to rear himself. His parents are too busy with their own lives to be bothered. Occasionally, his parents show some concern for him, but usually they act disgusted and impatient with him. Stevie already has a powerful Anxious Bonding Style, and there is no reason to expect that it won't become more powerful in the years ahead. The Anxious style has been shown to be related to unpredictability in a child's life. That unpredictability can be the result of inconsistent parenting, as in Stevie's case, or from other disruptive influences, such as family health problems, parental financial instability, and many other uncontrollable influences.

Domineering parents often produce Anxious bonders in emotionally susceptible kids. Consider Tiffany's example. She is a seventeen-year-old high school senior, an excellent student, and a skilled clarinet player. She has always been well liked by her teachers. However, her social relationships have been more problematic. Her relationships with her girlfriends seem somewhat turbulent, with close friendships seldom surviving a school year. Each friendship begins with great intensity, then shows signs of tension, and then suddenly disappears. Tiffany complains that her friends do not give her enough attention, and expresses jealousy over their friendships with other students. She has never dated and feels uncomfortable around most boys of her age. Her father is a domineering person and her mother is rather submissive. All of Tiffany's decisions are strongly influenced by her father, who selected her private out-of-state college, indicated which classes he deemed acceptable for her, and arranged her first semester class schedule for college. Tiffany exhibits a great deal of tension, is a fitful sleeper, and worries about pleasing her parents, especially her dad. Already, she has developed a strong Anxious Bonding Style.

As you can see from these examples, people with an Anxious Bonding Style vary from individuals who are high functioning most of the time to people who have difficulty functioning at all. Some people with an Anxious style may have Easy or Avoidant styles too, or both, or neither. People with a characteristic Anxious style can vary greatly from each other, but they all have the negative bonding self schemas that comprise the Anxious style: *Unworthy*, *Intimacy Driven*, *Unrestrained*, and *Dependent*. Furthermore, emotional distress is the keynote of their lives.

The Emotional Lives of Anxious Bonders

Emotional distress plays a prominent role in the life of anyone who has the Anxious Bonding Style. Anxiety, panic, anger, guilt, and shame can all be frequent visitors. Let's see how this happens.

Anxiety

Anxious bonders are called that because of the major role anxiety plays in their lives. Unfortunately, the experience of anxiety generates even more anxiety for them, making it difficult for them to stop the escalation of their emotions and their frightening expectations. Camille recalled that as a little girl she constantly worried about her mother's drinking, the fights between her parents, and losing her mother if her dad followed through on his threats to divorce her mother and take the children. She didn't want to lose her mother, and she also worried about what would happen to her mother if no one was there to pick her up off the floor and put her into bed after her binges.

Every day, during the last hour of school, Camille worried about whether her mother had found the bottles she had hidden. At dinner, she worried whether her mother would say or do something that would trigger rebukes from her father or sister. At night, when Camille lay in her bed with the lights out, she strained to hear her parents, worried that an argument between them would break out at any moment. Camille's anxiety never stopped and sometimes it got even worse, but always she felt helpless about being able to influence the events about which she worried.

Fear of Fear

After her mother finished the alcohol treatment program, Camille's chronic anxiety gradually subsided to some extent. Eventually, she developed a new pattern. Whenever Camille experienced an increase in arousal or tension, that would trigger even more anxiety. Camille became fearful of feeling fearful. In the past, her anxiety had been a constant reminder of how little control she had in preventing awful things from happening. So her anxiety became a cue that things were completely out of control or soon to become so. She began to respond to any increased arousal with the same sense of apprehension and helplessness that she had felt as a little girl.

This anxiety about being anxious is a common reaction in people who have endured frightening experiences with little if any control of the outcomes. Increased arousal triggers the thought that things are about to blow up, which triggers a surge in anxiety or even activates panic. Anxious bonders learn to be fearful of arousal because they believe panic and chaos are right around the corner.

Often Anxious bonders have predictable reactions to increased tension. One reaction is to panic and seek help from others immediately, which is encouraged by their *Dependent* schemas. If they are unable to get hold of people to help, Anxious bonders become even more desperate, with their emotions rapidly escalating. They are still operating on their old beliefs that they are helpless and incapable of dealing with the impending doom, whatever that doom might be.

Their efforts to obtain help are often very demanding, with Anxious bonders oblivious to the strain that they place on others. In response to these demands, other people may pull away to create greater distance in the relationship. These actions are perceived by the Anxious bonder as abandonment and fulfill their expectations that others will not be there for them. They seem unaware of how their own demanding behavior produces withdrawal in others and generates further anxiety in themselves.

The Need for Control

Another strategy used by Anxious bonders is to minimize anxiety by trying to control everything as much as possible, so that nothing unexpected can occur. Consequently, those with the Anxious Bonding Style are often domineering. For example, Camille tried to control the way Alex dressed. As her boyfriend, she viewed him as an extension of herself. She wanted him to dress in a way that others would find acceptable. Otherwise, this might reflect on how worthwhile they considered her to be. She also tried to control Alex's interactions at social events, steering him away from other attractive women. To keep Alex from abandoning her, she believed that she had to prevent him from meeting other more appealing women.

Control tactics can be overt, as Camille's were, or they can be covert. Examples of covert control tactics are pouting, not speaking, and withholding sex or money until the person does what the Anxious bonder wants. Attempts to confront Anxious bonders about their covert tactics are usually met with protests of innocence and claims of being falsely accused, which lead only to further frustration and anger in their family and friends. Control tactics are common with the Anxious Bonding Style. Unfortunately, the control tactics of the Anxious bonder produce the opposite effects of what they are seeking. Their domineering, controlling behavior tends to cause others to either push back or withdraw, further straining the relationship.

Anger and Rage

When the controlling behavior of the Anxious bonder is frustrated, in addition to an increase in anxiety, anger also appears. The Anxious bonder becomes angry that others are unwilling to cooperate. When other people push back or withdraw, the Anxious bonder becomes angry and tries to enforce greater control. If this fails, rage may result with increasingly desperate attempts to gain control or to impede the other's withdrawal, actions that further alienate the other person. Anxious bonders may make vindictive threats to harm themselves or others. If threats are ineffective, Anxious bonders may escalate to actions that are hurtful to themselves or to others, including suicidal acts or acts of violence against others. In these enraged states, the Anxious bonder can say and do things that can result in police involvement. Ultimately these vitriolic actions often cause others to sever their relationships, which is, of course, the Anxious bonder's ultimate nightmare.

Despair, Guilt, and Shame

Increased dependency, controlling tactics, and anger are all products of the Anxious bonders' attempts to reduce their anxiety, particularly anxiety about being abandoned. All such efforts eventually backfire. People become exhausted by their demands, frustrated with their need for control, and alienated by their anger and manipulations. Anxious bonders frequently destroy the very relationships they desperately want to maintain, and thus flood themselves with despair, guilt, and shame. Why do obviously intelligent people seem so oblivious to the consequences of their own behavior? The answer has to do mostly with the interaction between thinking and intense emotional reactions.

Tunnel Vision

No matter how bright you are, intense emotions interfere with clear thinking. It is true that some increase in tension can actually increase your alertness and decrease your reaction times, improving your performance on various kinds of mental tasks. Unfortunately, elevated emotions impair problem-solving. High levels of emotion, such as anxiety or anger, disrupt the ability to sort through problems and identify different options. Intense emotions seem to produce tunnel vision, which limits creativity and impairs judgment. Tunnel vision makes it harder to generate multiple solutions and tends to increase fixation on one or two solutions, regardless of their short- or long-term effects.

For example, when people are extremely depressed or anxious, suicide may seem like a reasonable option to them. They think suicide will terminate the distress they are currently experiencing. That is not an illogical conclusion. However, suicide also preempts any other options to improve the situation and has devastating effects on everyone else. Yet very bright people have chosen the route of suicide under extreme emotional duress, and those who have been unsuccessful at suicide are typically greatly relieved at their failure once their emotions have subsided. Tunnel vision is a frequent visitor of Anxious bonders. As their emotions soar, their judgment plummets, producing badly thought-out plans and impulsive reactions. Their behavior strains their relationships and increases their emotional distress even further.

Modifying the Anxious Bonding Style

This style can be changed. As you have learned, the frequency of the Anxious style is lower among older people. If this is your characteristic style, you could wait for age to make the change for you, hoping that you will be one of those who will change your style naturally. But most Anxious bonders find this style distressing enough to merit a conscious effort to move toward the Easy style. If you have someone in your life who is an Anxious bonder, you may want to encourage him or her to try shifting away from this style for the sake of both of you.

The chapters in Part III, "Interactions, Changes, and Choices" have many specific suggestions to aid you in modifying your negative bonding schemas. When implementing schema changes, someone with the Anxious Bonding Style is encouraged to start with the

Unrestrained schema. Until you have a better handle on your emotional reactions, maintaining a focus on changing the other negatively unbalanced self schemas of *Unworthy*, *Intimacy Driven*, and *Dependent* will be a struggle. Your emotional turmoil will sabotage your other efforts at change, repeatedly throwing you into a state of chaos. The *Unrestrained* schema creates so many personal and interpersonal problems that all of chapter 12 is devoted to ways to shift from this distressing schema to an *Expressive* schema.

Although everyone who has an Anxious Bonding Style has the four negative bonding schemas, the strength of those schemas differs among people. Some have a highly intense and active *Unrestrained* schema, while others have a milder and less frequently active *Unrestrained* schema. The same can be true for the other negative bonding schemas of this style. The relative strengths of your schemas can guide where you should make your greatest effort in modifying this style. Become aware of which of your negative schemas in the Anxious style are the most predominant. This information will be essential when you tailor the schema change procedures described in Part III to your own needs.

Helping the Youthful Anxious Bonder

You may have noticed some signs of the Anxious Bonding Style in children or adolescents in your own family. Can you help them change styles? Yes, you can. Depending on their age, you might ask them to read this chapter and other parts of the book. However, if reading this book is not an option for them, there are many other things you can do on your own. You also can use several of the suggestions presented here when interacting with adults who exhibit the Anxious Bonding Style. Your reactions may allow Anxious bonders to modify their own style, but even if they don't change, your reactions may improve the quality of the relationship for you.

- When a child becomes emotional, try to remain calm but concerned. When you react emotionally, you accelerate the child's emotions. Just listen and try to summarize what is said and what the expressed concerns seem to be. Acknowledge the child's emotions by saying something like, "I can see that you are really upset about this." Acknowledging emotions does not mean that you would feel the same way or that you even understand why the child feels so strongly about a situation. Acknowledging emotions simply means that you recognize the intensity of the emotions without judging them. Often, this simple acknowledgment is very calming to someone who is upset.

- After they have told you their story, together try to identify what they are most upset about, what they think is going to happen, how they plan to handle that, and what they think the outcome will be. Here, you just try to get their perspective, you are not offering an alternative perspective. If they get angry, try to remain focused on what you are asking. Don't let them sidetrack you or upset you with their anger.

- After going through all of the questions above, ask if there are other possibilities. Could a situation be interpreted differently? Are there different possible outcomes? Are there different ways they could handle this? If they can't think of alternatives, you might be able to pose other alternatives by gently inquiring, "Is it possible that . . . ?" Ask that question as a question. Don't pose it as a fact that they have foolishly missed.

- Have them identify the worst case outcome and what that would mean for them. Ask them to apply the situation to someone else, such as one of their friends whom they admire, and ask what that other person might do if he or she experienced this worst case situation. Offer other possibilities by asking, "Is it possible that . . . ?"

- The use of gentle questioning helps people who are upset to expand their tunnel vision without becoming defensive. They don't experience gentle questioning as challenging their reactions, but rather as an effort by the questioner to understand the situation and their perspective.

- The above process will help a young Anxious bonder develop problem-solving skills, which is what you are trying to teach. By not overreacting emotionally, you will also teach that crises can be handled more effectively calmly than emotionally. Your reactions also convey that they do not have to be distraught to get your attention.

- Help them to expand their support system beyond you. Help them to identify other competent people, both adults and peers, with whom they can discuss their problems. If you are their only support person, not being able to contact you can precipitate a sense of desperation and panic, exacerbating whatever dilemma already exists.

- Don't rescue children from all the dilemmas they encounter. They need to discover that they can solve some of their problems on their own, and some problems simply need to be endured, such as a teacher whom they dislike. Learning how to endure less than ideal situations is an essential part of successful living, just as is surviving difficult relationships that they cannot change, such as a hostile boss or colleague. This involves increasing their tolerance for others who are different from them.

- Whenever possible, let children make their own choices. Let them pursue their own interests rather than imposing your interests on them.

- Don't make your approval depend on their acceptance of all your opinions and desires. If they disagree with you, don't punish them by getting mad or withdrawing.

- Give children responsibility for age-appropriate tasks. Don't overwhelm them with responsibilities beyond their ages, such as happened to Ryan and Stevie.

- Don't impose perfectionistic standards on children or be overly critical of them. Encourage their *efforts* in mastering a task. Praise them for trying.

- See chapter 12 for further suggestions to help children develop more effective ways to manage their emotions, especially the breathing procedures and the calming self-talk.

Assessing Your Anxious Bonding Strategies

Even if the Anxious style is not characteristic of you, you may have some of the strategies associated with it. In this section of this chapter you will have a chance to assess that. Knowing which of these strategies is a problem for you can help you to be more selective with the schema change suggestions in Part III. You also might gain some insights as to why you are not getting what you want. Are you using any of the emotional management strategies common to the Anxious style to control your emotions or to control others? Read the following questions and think about how you would answer them. Then, in a separate notebook, write down your answers to all of the questions. Your responses will help you to determine whether you employ some of the strategies associated with the Anxious Bonding Style.

- How do you try to control the behavior of other people? In other words, how do you try to get people to do what you want?

- Do you try to influence or restrict others' choices, in regard to their friends, activities, interests, religion, professional choices, dress, or in any other way? If so, how?

- List the rules you expect the people in your life to follow. Do some of these rules seem intrusive and disrespectful of their rights?

- Do you get angry when others disregard what you want them to do or say?

- How do you treat other people when you are disappointed in them?

- Do you pout or sulk when things don't go your way?

- Do you go for hours, days, weeks, or longer not speaking to someone you are mad at? If so, for how long?

- What typically brings this silence to an end?

- Do others always have to apologize, or do you?

- Do you withhold sex, money, or help until someone does what you want? Think of examples and describe them.

- Are you vindictive? If so, describe examples of how you have been vindictive and what the circumstances were.

- Have you ever been physically aggressive to people, animals, or inanimate objects (e.g., breaking things)? If so, describe how and what the circumstances were.

- Have you ever been suicidal? If so, describe how and what the circumstances were.

- When do you use overt and covert strategies of control? Examples could be when your child shows any independence, when your kids want to spend more time with their other parent, when you am feeling alone and fearful of the future. List your examples.

- How would you feel about someone who treated you the way you treat others?

- What would you do if someone treated you the way you do others?

- Think of the people you identified in the last chapter who have the Easy Bonding Style. How do they manage their emotions?

- How do they express their thoughts?

- How do they ask for help without seeming to be desperate?

- How do they deal with frustration and anger?

- How do you try to achieve intimacy now in your relationships?

- How effective is that? Describe the reactions of others to your efforts.

- How do the people in your current close relationships show you intimacy?

- What do you want from those people?

- What will you settle for from each of them?

8

The Distant Bonding Style

*The main motive for "non-attachment" is a desire to escape
from the pain of living, and above all from love, which,
sexual or non-sexual, is hard work.*

—George Orwell, "Reflections on
Ghandi," *Shooting an Elephant*

The Distant Bonding Style is a hyperpositive view of oneself: "I am
better than other people, I don't need emotional intimacy with others,
I can handle everything on my own, and I am always in control of
my emotions." Those with the Distant Bonding Style view others as
untrustworthy and potentially hurtful. Their style keeps them wary
of close relationships and explains why they have a history of fewer
committed relationships than do the other styles. In spite of their
hyperpositive self-view, the Distant bonder is at greater risk for substance abuse problems and emotional distress than is the Easy bonder
with a more moderate self-view. Distant bonders are unable to
acknowledge hurtful experiences or personal weaknesses. They seem
caught in a web of denial, suppressing their feelings and unwilling to
expose their thoughts. Their denial increases their vulnerability to
other harmful ways of escaping from their feelings.

As with the other styles, you will see that there is a great deal of
variability among people with this characteristic style. Nonetheless,
all Distant bonders maintain a distance between themselves and
other people. They may form bonds with people, but they will set
limits on just how close they will allow those people to be with them.
Not only does this distance create a sense of loneliness and isolation
in others, it traps the Distant bonder in the same loneliness. This
chapter looks at what purpose holding others at bay serves, and
makes suggestions on how the Distant bonder can begin to take
down some of the barriers that create distance.

The Hyperpositive Bonding Self Schemas

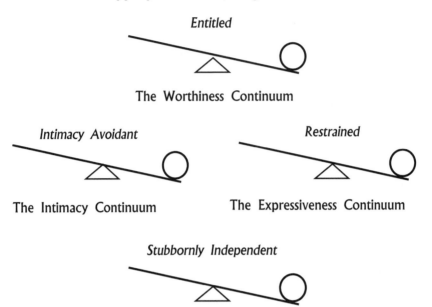

Entitled

The Worthiness Continuum

Intimacy Avoidant

The Intimacy Continuum

Restrained

The Expressiveness Continuum

Stubbornly Independent

The Interdependency Continuum

(*Entitled*) I think more about my own needs than the needs of other people. (*Intimacy Avoidant*) I keep most people at a distance. I am not comfortable being especially close to people. (*Restrained*) I seldom show my feelings. I am uncomfortable expressing my emotions. I don't like other people to know when I'm feeling bad. (*Stubbornly Independent*) I do not like to rely on anyone but myself. I don't like to ask for help.

A Distant Bonder

Distant bonders seem detached from themselves, others, and their emotions. They are uncomfortable with emotional closeness and reluctant to agree to committed relationships. Their partners complain of emotional distance and of feeling alone in the relationship.

Doug

Doug is forty-six years old and soon to be divorced for the third time. Although he had been unfaithful to his wife, Nancy, throughout their seven-year marriage, she first discovered his infidelity about a year ago. He expressed remorse and broke off the affair, promising to change but not revealing any of his other affairs. Several months later Nancy informed him that she had been seeing another man for about six weeks and was not sure that she wanted to continue the marriage. Although Doug was surprised and angry initially, he was also not certain that he wanted the marriage to continue. Consequently, they decided to divorce.

Doug had developed a relationship with Nancy while still married to his second wife, Shari. His second marriage had lasted about three years. Doug had married Shari shortly after his first divorce although they had little in common. Certain patterns repeated themselves in all three of Doug's marriages. Each wife had opted for marriage in spite of his reluctance to marry. During each of his marriages he saw other women, usually briefly, but a few extramarital relationships lasted for several years. He says the longer relationships were with women who were fun and did not want any commitment from him. His three wives all knew that he had been unfaithful in his previous relationships. All three marriages ended after his wives discovered his current affairs.

Doug admits, "I have had a sense of entitlement most of my life. I was an outstanding athlete since grade school. I always was the center of attention. I got out of a lot of class requirements because of sports. Girls were easy to get. I've always felt entitled to other women. My dad was unfaithful to my mother throughout their marriage. My mom never said much to my dad about it. I've just assumed men have a right to sex with other women. The other athletes seemed to think so too." Doug received an athletic scholarship to his state university. He had a string of girlfriends before he started dating his first wife in the spring semester of his senior year. He was unsure of what he was going to do after graduation, but his girlfriend wanted to marry him and her dad offered him a promising career track in his company. Doug agreed to both. He acknowledges that he was not in love with her, adding, "I don't think I have ever been in love with anyone."

Doug's dad was a salesman and on the road most of the time. He never spent much time with Doug, but he did try to go to his games. Doug thinks his dad came to see him play to bask in Doug's glory. He and his dad have never been close. His mother seemed overwhelmed with Doug's two older sisters, whom he describes as "wild and always into trouble. I was ashamed of who they hung around with. We were never close." His mother was proud of Doug but she never set any limits for him. She almost seemed relieved not to have to bother about him. With his dad out of town most of the time, Doug learned early that he could do what he wanted with little monitoring or interference from his parents. He never got into any trouble, but starting with junior high he essentially came and went as he pleased.

Doug has never spent much time with his kids from his first marriage, and they are not close to him. Even before his first divorce Doug was seldom at home. He was either at the office, the gym, or seeing other women. Working out was his primary form of recreation, and he was dedicated to maintaining his athletic build even if it meant hours at the gym. His son and daughter are now in their last years of high school. They live in another state with their mom and spend a week or two in the summers with him. He calls them occasionally, but he usually doesn't know what to talk about with them. His son once asked to live with him. Doug discouraged him, saying that his constant traveling would be a problem, but Doug admits he doesn't travel that much. He just didn't want the responsibility.

Doug is determined to make enough money to own his own business, so he won't have to work for someone else, which he points out he could have done a few years ago with two fewer marriages. He hates being dependent on anyone for anything. He has played tennis for decades, but won't take lessons to improve his game because "I don't want anyone else to get credit for my skills. I just don't ask for help. I even got a slipped disc because I wouldn't ask for help to move a file cabinet. I don't want to depend on anyone else. If you depend on people, they just let you down." Doug laughed when he said that his first wife once described him as "so stubborn he could be on fire in the middle of the street and he wouldn't ask anyone to pour water on him."

Doug has avoided emotional closeness by marrying women who allowed him a lot of freedom, which was a calculated decision on his part. "My first wife was more into her social groups and the children, and she pretty much let me have a separate life. My second wife was a workaholic like me, and she did not want me to put any demands on her for more closeness. My third wife spent most of her time with her ten-year-old daughter when she was not working. We spent very little time together and had few interests in common." Why did Doug get married if he didn't like being accountable or close? "Well, I liked all three of my wives. They also took care of all my basic needs, like the laundry, shopping, handling the bills, that kind of stuff. They made my life easier in a lot of ways."

All three of Doug's wives complained that they never could tell how he was feeling. Doug agrees that he doesn't like to talk about feelings. When his wives would get angry with him, he "would just take off until they had cooled down." Doug admits that he has always avoided women who expect much attention or intimacy. He says, "I don't like to get close to people. Then I won't be hurt if they do something I don't like. This last divorce kind of threw me when

Nancy said she had found someone else. I've never had that happen before. I've always been the one who was unfaithful. And I had stopped running around after she caught me."

Schema Analysis

The schemas associated with the Distant Bonding Style are evident in the description of Doug. His self, person, and role schemas have maintained this style throughout his three marriages and even with his children.

The Hyperpositive Self Schemas

Doug's hyperpositive self schemas have produced a trail of unhappy, disappointing relationships for him and the people with whom he has been involved. There were few emotional connections within his family when Doug was growing up, a pattern that has continued to the present. Let's examine Doug's self schemas to understand this pattern.

Entitled: **I think I am as good as anyone else, if not better. I am entitled to have whatever I want. I deserve to have the best of everything. I have a right to have all my needs met. I don't think about what my needs may cost others. I am special. I think more about my own needs than how those needs may affect other people.**

Doug's *Entitlement* self schema is impossible to miss. He sees himself as entitled to any women who seem interested in him. He married his first wife because the arrangement seemed like a good deal for him, not because he loved her. He shows little empathy for the impact his infidelity has had on his three wives. His interests are all clearly self-focused: his work, his body, his sexual pleasure. His needs come before anyone else's. He has invested little effort or interest in his kids. His freedom would have been considerably curtailed had his son come to live with him. He views marriage as a way to have someone else take care of his daily needs and handle mundane tasks.

Intimacy Avoidant: **I prefer to keep most people at a distance. I am not comfortable being too close to other people. Relationships often seem like a burden to me. Emotional intimacy feels suffocating. Relationships aren't that important to me. I prefer not getting too attached to people.**

Doug had not been close to his parents or his sisters. He has chosen not to be close to his own children. He viewed the prospect of a closer relationship with his son as a burden he did not want to assume. He married women who did not strive for emotional intimacy either. They seemed content for the most part to live separate lives within the marriages. His affairs are with women who seek no commitments. If they do want closeness, he disappears.

Restrained: I seldom show my feelings. I am uncomfortable expressing my emotions. I don't let people see how I feel. I am almost always in control of my emotions. Other people usually can't tell how I feel. I don't like other people to know when I'm feeling bad. I hate to cry in front of other people.

Doug readily admits that he does not like to talk about his feelings. He avoids confrontations by running away. None of his wives ever felt they understood him emotionally. They all complained that they could never tell what he was feeling or thinking.

Stubbornly Independent: I do not like to rely on anyone but myself. It is hard for me to ask for help. I don't like it when other people offer me advice or assistance. I feel irritated when someone tries to help me. I can't stand being dependent on anybody for anything. I prefer to do things on my own.

Doug is compulsively independent, often to his own disadvantage and even to the point of injury. He refuses to ask for help with anything and is determined to remain independent of other people. He is driven to acquire his own business, so that he can be his own boss and not be subject to anyone else's demands.

Distant Bonding Style Triggers

In general, other people seem to trigger Doug's Distant Bonding Style. He views other people as undependable and potentially disappointing. Becoming close to other people increases the possibility that they will place demands on him or desire emotional intimacy. His social contacts are all distant. He keeps his business relationships professional and limits his personal relationships to people who will accept the distance he imposes. He is most comfortable with women who want to avoid emotional intimacy too. He picked wives who did not demand closeness and his favorite girlfriends are those who do not want any more than a good time with him.

Doug's Distant style is activated by any other human being, even his own children. However, some people with the characteristic Distant Bonding Style react only to certain types of people with this style. For example, Andy views women who are about his age as potentially hurtful and disappointing, but he is able to have emotionally intimate relationships with much older and much younger women. The triggers for Andy's Distant style are women close to his age.

Women near Andy's age → Andy's Distant style

Martha views all men warily, but has numerous emotionally intimate relationships with other women. Martha's Distant style is triggered by any male, regardless of his age.

All men → Martha's Distant style

For Andy and Martha, only certain types of people trigger the Distant Bonding Style. However, with Doug everyone triggers his Distant style.

All people → Doug's Distant style

Doug has never had an emotionally intimate relationship in his life. Both of his parents were too preoccupied to invest much attention in him except to recognize his athletic prowess. No one in his family modeled how to have emotional intimacy or how to express feelings and thoughts. His mother ignored his father's hurtful infidelity, leaving Doug with the impression that such behavior wasn't that bad. There was no emotional honesty in his family. Conflicts were avoided and hurt was ignored. How could Doug have been any different than he was?

Distant Bonding Style Varieties

As with the other bonding styles, there can be quite a lot of variability among people with the Distant Bonding Style. Different bonding styles can be observed in children and adolescents just as they are in adults. Doug's Distant style was already obvious when he was a child. He thought he was special because of his athletic skills. Since he couldn't count on his parents to take much interest in him, he learned to take care of himself. He did what he wanted for the most part, ignoring the rules but not breaking them enough to get into any real trouble. He wasn't close to anyone. He hung around with other kids who were in sports, but the connections were superficial and limited to athletic encounters. Doug discovered early on that girls were impressed with his athletic achievements. He had a series of girlfriends from the time he was in late elementary school. He liked the attention each girl gave him, but he moved on to another at the first sign of any demands or expectations. Commitments from him were not part of the deal. Emotional involvement was absent. Women were interchangeable.

Pamela

Remember Camille's sister, Pamela, from the last chapter? As a little girl, Pamela began to show the Distant Bonding Style just as Camille displayed the Anxious Bonding Style. The fact that two sisters exhibit different bonding styles illustrates two points: no two children in the same family are treated exactly the same, and different children may respond differently to the same environment. From infancy, Pamela was cautious and reserved. She was a daddy's girl, which frustrated her mother at times. As she grew older, Pamela became irritated with her mother when her father expressed anger about her mother's drinking. She hated her parents' constant arguing. She hated her mother's slobbery unsteadiness after she was drunk. She hated the crying and embarrassment her mother displayed during a hangover.

Pamela retreated by spending lots of time in her room playing alone or in her treehouse in the backyard. As she got older, she spent as much time as possible at school or studying in her room. She was a gifted student and liked the recognition she got for her academic achievements. The attention motivated her to study even harder. Academics became the sole source of her self-esteem. She was accepted by an Ivy League college on the East Coast, which allowed her to move as far away as she could from the chaos of her California home. After finishing law school, Pamela got a position with the federal government in Washington, D.C., and has been there ever since. She feels resentful that her work has not received more recognition and thinks that some of her co-workers are jealous of her academic history.

Pamela lives alone with her two dogs. She has occasional telephone contact with her father by calling him at his office, but her relationship with her mother remains icy, in spite of her mother's efforts to reach out to her. Pamela and Camille have never been close. Unlike Pamela, Camille often struggled in school. Pamela sees a lot of similarity between Camille and her mother and treats them both with considerable contempt. Pamela has dated occasionally since high school, but has never had a long-term serious relationship. She is respected at her job, but seems aloof to her colleagues. She has no close friends. Most of her time is spent working, even at home. Although disgusted with her mother's alcoholism, Pamela has developed a drinking problem herself, which began in college. While she seldom drinks in public, over the years she has steadily increased her alcohol intake at home. Many nights, after too many glasses of wine, she falls asleep on the couch fully dressed. Feeling lonely, angry, and depressed, Pamela discovered long ago that alcohol could shut out all those feelings . . . at least for a little while.

As Pamela demonstrates, alcohol and drugs are ways to numb unwanted feelings, whether anxiety, depression, or anger. Ironically, many people often get together to engage in drinking or substance abuse, which simply tunes them out to each other and causes them to be oblivious to any meaningful interactions. Such people may appear to be gregarious, for they are always at the bar or at a party, but if you pay close attention to them, they are there for a single purpose: to get drunk or wasted. They are not seeking close relationships. They are looking for momentary exits from life.

Lilith

Ironically, for many people sexual relationships offer another way to avoid emotional intimacy. Lilith is a thirty-five-year-old realtor who has been divorced for nine years after two years of marriage. She is a former high school cheerleader who was raised by a successful banker and a wealthy socialite mother. They gave her whatever she wanted except their attention. Since her divorce, Lilith has been involved in several short-term relationships, three with married men. She has had a relationship with one married man for more than three years. She has no desire to marry him, nor does he have any intention of leaving his wife, but he treats Lilith well in many ways. Recently, Lilith has been seeing one of her single clients, who purchased a home with her assistance. At first, he invited her to dinner to celebrate the purchase of his new home. They had a lot of fun and discovered a shared interest in golf. They became physically intimate soon after she began dating him.

As they spent more time together, he became more affectionate and began giving her romantic presents. After about two weeks of daily calls from him and frequent dates, Lilith began feeling quite anxious about his ardor. She began to return his calls later in the day or the following day. She turned down invitations for dinner and golf. She expressed concern to him that their relationship was escalating too fast for her. She needed things to slow down. He was surprised and confused by her reactions.

What he didn't know is that Lilith always has used physical intimacy to avoid emotional intimacy. She picks men who are interested only in the moment, or married men who have a history of infidelity and will never ask for commitment. Lilith would rather share her body than her emotions or her thoughts. With most of the men she selects, this works. She is able to obtain some limited connection with another human being and can reinforce her long held view of herself as an extremely desirable woman. However, this man wanted more from her. He was not just interested in a quick, uninvolved sexual rendezvous. He seemed to genuinely care about her. Although she felt very attracted to him as a person, the strength of her emotions for him frightened her. She needed to pull back. Both Distant bonders, Lilith and Doug illustrate how sexual intimacy can be completely devoid of emotional intimacy; indeed, sexual intimacy can serve as a buffer from emotional closeness.

Sonja

People often think that emotional avoidance is more descriptive of men than of women. Men are frequently castigated for not being more emotionally vulnerable and self-disclosing. Yet in twenty-five years of practice I have seen innumerable couples where the wife's message was very clear: "I married you because you were strong and powerful. Your job is to take care of me. Don't tell me about your business problems. Don't tell me when you're worried. Don't tell me if you're afraid. Don't tell me when things go wrong. And don't ever let me see you cry."

Sonja is such a woman. When her first husband was fired from his job, she became disgusted and took their six-year-old daughter and left. Six months later she was working as a receptionist when she met Frank. Frank, recently widowed, was eager to take care of Sonja and her daughter. He had been devoted to his first wife and felt a painful void after her death. Several years Sonja's senior, Frank was financially well off, belonged to the country club, and had his own business. Sonja was charming. She acted awestruck by his devotion and infinitely grateful for every kindness. She seemed determined to meet all of his needs as well ... until they were married.

After the wedding Sonja became more demanding. She quit her job because she claimed it was inappropriate for Frank to have a working wife. She arranged for a substantial monthly allowance, which unbeknownst to Frank she put into a separate savings account. Sonja had no intention of ever being financially dependent again, in case the relationship soured. She complained of the demands her daughter made on her until Frank agreed to a live-in nanny. She joined his country club and began to spend most of her days there. She spent more of his money in a week than his late wife spent in a year. Her interest in sex depended on whether she wanted anything from Frank. Frank's coupled friends, who had warmly welcomed Sonja in the beginning, began to be less available. They were offended by the cutting remarks that Sonja made about Frank's supposedly small-minded ways, remarks she made in his presence and behind his back.

Then, Frank's small business ran into tough times because a national chain was undercutting his prices. Frank, worried about being forced into bankruptcy, needed Sonja to cut back on her spending. The nanny would have to go, too. He tried to express his concerns to Sonja, but she never let him finish expressing his fears about his company's viability. She didn't want to hear about his financial problems. Those were his responsibility. She shouldn't have to deal with them. She let him know she was uncomfortable discussing his concerns. Frank quickly got the message: "Don't bother me with this. Just fix it."

Sonja wanted a husband made of steel. She was not interested in any emotional connections. While Frank was doing well and giving her whatever she wanted, Frank felt strong, competent, and loved. He discounted his friends' concerns about his wife as their jealousy of her youth and beauty. But when the scenario changed, when his business ran into trouble, what he received from Sonja was contempt—not compassion. The more he reached out, the more she withdrew. The more desperate he became, the colder she grew. Compassion was not part of Sonja's unspoken agenda. Frank was supposed to be emotionally invulnerable. He was there to meet her needs and take care of his own. Failure to do so would prompt her quick exit to someone who could take care of her.

Sonja's example illustrates how people with the Distant Bonding Style can vary in the strength of their various hyperpositive schemas. In this case, Sonja's *Entitled* self schema is glaring. She expects to be supported in the style she desires, regardless of the cost to others. Although I have seen variations of this behavior in many women who married for money, I also have seen the same pattern in men who married their wives because of their striking good looks. When those looks begin to fade, these men look for a younger wife to replace the old one. Emotional connections don't hinder them. Marrying someone with the deadly combination of the *Entitled* and *Intimacy Avoidant* schemas is a grave emotional risk. If you stop meeting that person's needs for whatever reason, don't count on any latent emotional commitment to keep them with you.

All of these Distant bonders display the hyperpositive schemas of this style. All feel entitled. They see themselves as superior to others, whether for athletics, intelligence, appearance, or social-class membership. As a rule, people can develop a sense of entitlement from excessive attention for a particular attribute or from simply being overindulged. In other cases, however, people sometimes develop a sense of entitlement because of the *disadvantages* they have experienced. They feel that their previous abuse, pain, or deprivation makes them more deserving. They believe they have a right to special treatment to make up for what they have endured. Sarah, who was discussed in chapter 1, illustrates this. Sarah developed an *Entitled* schema after enduring a deprived childhood and then suffering further deprivation as a young woman after her divorce. Her *Entitled* schema made her resentful of any attention or gifts that her husband gave her stepson, Jason. This sense of entitlement is present in any Distant bonder, although it can vary in strength.

Distant Bonders' Hidden Agendas

Distant bonders may be dependent on people, but they hate it, as illustrated by both Doug and Sonja. Doug did not want to be dependent on his first wife's father. He single-mindedly pursued financial success to develop his own business. Sonja was financially dependent on Frank, but she surreptitiously planned to become financially independent over time. Although dreading emotional intimacy, many Distant bonders also are quite charming in social situations. But there is often a particular purpose to their behavior. Their social interactions are designed to further their own agendas.

Sonja was so charming to Frank and his friends early in their relationship because of her desire to acquire his lifestyle. Her charm waxed and waned with her needs. Doug was funny and endearing to obtain sexual gratification, but once that was met, he disappeared. Distant bonders do not invest emotionally in other people. Their social interactions often are intended to create a certain impression to help them achieve their desired results.

As with all Distant bonders, Doug, Pamela, Lilith, and Sonja see themselves as entitled, avoid close emotional bonds, suppress their emotions, keep personal commitments to a minimum, and dread being dependent. Other people are viewed in terms of the benefits they can provide to the Distant bonder. If those benefits are substantial, Distant bonders sometimes can adjust their behavior to achieve those benefits, but even then their underlying schemas remain unchanged. Other Distant bonders, however, would never adjust their behavior, because there are no benefits to be gained from anyone that would make the increased social engagement worth it for them. These hyperpositive views do not come without costs for the Distant bonders and especially for those connected to them.

The Costs of Hyperpositive Schemas

Over the years I have listened to many patients, both male and female, describe how their parents ridiculed them for crying or for showing any emotional reaction. If they indicated that they cared about anybody or anything, that parent was likely to hurt or destroy the object of their affection, even going so far as to kill their children's pets in front of them. No wonder these people don't show their emotions. Even more common are those who describe being tormented by peers. I have seen children with cancer who were teased by classmates about how their hair would fall out from chemotherapy, or the cancer would kill them. There seems to be no limit to how cruel some children and teenagers can be. They taunt each other mercilessly, hoping for a reaction. Few such experiences are necessary to teach you that other people are hurtful, and that the disclosure of any vulnerability can lead to torment.

Nevertheless, horrific experiences are not descriptive of all Distant bonders. Doug, Pamela, Lilith, and Sonja did not have such experiences, but they still developed a dim view of other people as a result of their own histories. One striking difference between the Anxious bonder and the Distant bonder is the element of hope regarding other people. Anxious bonders always continue to hope that other people will come through for them, but worry they will not. Distant bonders seem to have abandoned hope. They believe that other people deliver only pain and disappointment. They won't be there for you. Don't expect it. Distant bonders may have a hostile attitude toward others, or they may simply be indifferent. In either case, other people are not held in high regard.

Distant bonders prefer to remain insulated from emotional connections to other people and even to themselves. When in distress, they tend to withdraw, neither seeking nor desiring emotional support from others. Rather than reaching out during times of duress, they push others away. They are not comfortable expressing their own emotions, nor are they inclined to encourage others to disclose personal thoughts to them. Their *Intimacy Avoidant* and *Restrained* self schemas keep them well hidden from being truly known and provide them with what they perceive to be emotional safety. Unfortunately, Distant bonders are not as safe as they think.

The Distant Bonding Style and Health

Suppressing your thoughts and feelings can pose potential health risks. Emotional suppression has been implicated in increased cardiovascular reactivity, impaired immune system response, decreased blood monocytes and lymphocytes, elevated serum glucose levels, and cancer (Levy, Herberman, Maluish, et al. 1985; Jamner, Schwartz, and Leigh 1988; Shea, Burton, and Girgis 1993; Gross and Levenson 1997). In contrast, emotional expression can produce immunological changes that are associated with positive health outcomes (Futterman, Kemeny, Shapiro, et al. 1992; Knapp, Levy, Giorgi, et al. 1992; Petrie, Booth, and Pennebacker 1998).

If you have the *Restrained* self schema, you may have been quite smug as you read about the emotional struggles of those with the *Unrestrained* self schema. You can see that you shouldn't be. The Distant bonder is hardly the healthy alternative to the Anxious bonder. Don't let your *Restrained* self schema convince you that you are the only person in the universe whose nerve endings don't fire. Suppressing your emotions requires enormous effort on your part. You may have health problems that are exacerbated by your tension from hiding your emotional reactions. Chronic tension headaches or grinding your teeth together so hard that they have cracks in them are not good signs. Neither is exercising so much self-control that you suppress your immune system's ability to fight diseases and infections. Your body is not only revealing the cost of your emotionless charade, it's also trying to tell you something: "You are wearing me out with this need to stifle our thoughts and feelings. We need a different plan." Unfortunately, Distant bonders have suppressed their feelings for so long that they often can't even recognize their emotions. Every once in a while Distant bonders might explode, but they quickly retreat into their caverns of control.

Avoidance Strategies

In chapter 7 you read about the control tactics of the Anxious bonder. Compared to the Distant bonder, the Anxious bonder is a novice at control. The Distant bonder is a master. To suppress their emotions and to maintain their isolation, Distant bonders use a variety of strategies. Although these strategies can cut across styles, they are often found with the Distant style. The preferred strategy of control is avoidance. Avoidance behavior permeates the Distant bonding style. They avoid obligations by never asking for help. They avoid emotional closeness by never revealing their internal thoughts and feelings. They avoid their emotions by investing all their time in work, sports, the Internet, yard work, or even some social activities that keep the focus away from personal disclosure, such as golf or biking. These are activities that Distant bonders may enjoy but that allow them to avoid emotional engagement. They avoid caring about others by not paying much attention to them, not inquiring about their feelings, and not encouraging personal disclosures.

Dissociation

Some Distant bonders who as children repeatedly experienced vicious verbal attacks or abusive treatment have developed a particular avoidance strategy psychologists call *dissociation*. Dissociation refers to how you can *mentally* disengage or disassociate from your present circumstances. Essentially, you go somewhere else in your mind, so that painful stimuli cannot break through into your awareness. The ability to dissociate has allowed many people to endure unspeakable torment and torture.

Initially, when you are being verbally or physically abused, it requires intense concentration to keep your mind focused on something pleasant or neutral. Eventually, however, dissociation will impede your relationships when you no longer need to escape because the process becomes automatic. You dissociate whenever you experience uncomfortable emotions.

Your family members and friends may complain about how you seem to take mental holidays. They can be sitting right next to you, talking to you, looking into your eyes, but you are not there. They may need to raise their voices or touch you to bring you back. After they begin talking, you seem completely oblivious to what they were saying. Any suggestion that a conversation may be confrontive or uncomfortable triggers your mental departure.

You may have needed to dissociate when you were younger, but you don't have to anymore. You can learn constructive ways to deal with emotionally uncomfortable situations by following several of the suggestions presented in Part III.

Withdrawal

A preferred avoidance strategy of the Distant bonder is simply to ignore others, particularly in situations involving conflict or distress. If ignoring others is ineffective, Distant bonders typically withdraw from the situation. They leave the office, they go to the garage, they go take a nap, they run an errand. They just disappear. They just get up and leave, often with no indication of where they are going or when they will return. Other people often do not recognize these actions as control strategies, because there is no active attempt to subjugate someone else. However, these strategies do control interactions by effectively ending them.

When withdrawal does not work, some Distant bonders then may escalate to aggressive behavior. If you persist in trying to resolve a problem or in seeking emotional support, Distant bonders may respond with an intense display of anger that effectively causes *you* to withdraw. Their angry response is then reinforced. They do not need to use it very often, because most people are very uncomfortable with angry personal attacks or aggressive actions, such as someone punching a hole in the wall or breaking things. One or two of these episodes can teach you not to impede their withdrawal strategies. Some families live in constant fear of when Distant bonders will explode, even if they have done so only a few times.

Distant bonders prefer to use avoidance strategies that require no emotional displays on their part. Even their anger is designed to force others to let them withdraw. If a Distant bonder explodes occasionally, that usually reflects a loss of control and not a change in the underlying *Restrained* schema. If they explode with some frequency, then they also have an *Unrestrained* schema, and they flip back and forth between their *Restrained* and *Unrestrained* schemas.

A *Restrained* self schema does not mean that Distant bonders do not have feelings. The *Restrained* self schema views emotions as painful or a nuisance, something to be suppressed and ignored. Overt display of emotions, especially negative emotions, is to be studiously avoided. One should always be in control. So overt displays of anger by the Distant bonder typically are infrequent, but they can occur as just described. Because Distant bonders experience annoyance and resentment just as everyone else does at times, they try to dismiss those feelings. When they cannot, they might engage in what psychologists refer to as *passive-aggressive* behavior.

Passive-Aggressive Behavior

Instead of responding directly to someone's hurtful actions, a passive-aggressive response is indirect. For example, Brad is annoyed that a co-worker has been getting to work earlier and parking in a space that Brad had been accustomed to using. One morning Brad notices that the co-worker has left his car windows down and it is about to rain. As it begins to pour, Brad says nothing when he takes his seat at his desk next to his co-worker, but he feels pleasure thinking about the co-worker's possible reactions to his drenched car seats later in the day.

Sarcasm and sometimes joking and teasing are other forms of passive-aggressive behavior. Rather than directly confronting someone, people sometimes use jokes or teasing that have a hurtful edge for the listener. Engaging in passive-aggressive behavior is a way to get even with people without being honest about your feelings. If you confront Distant bonders about this behavior, they dismiss it by saying you are being too sensitive or you are misreading their intentions. They deny being aware of the effects of their actions or lack of actions. Passive-aggressive behavior is a common avoidance strategy of Distant bonders which frustrates others and increases the antipathy others feel toward them.

Other Avoidance Techniques

When their avoidance strategies don't work and their feelings slip into their awareness, Distant bonders may rely on more potent avoidance techniques: alcohol, drugs, sex, gambling, eating disorders. All provide a temporary escape from the discomfort that emotions can produce if they are brought into one's awareness. Distant bonders often select avoidance strategies that provide pleasure, emotional release, and involve few or no interpersonal interactions, at least face to face. Overeating is a common way to obtain pleasure and comfort with no social demands. Sex on the Internet is another impersonal strategy, as is an obsession with pornography and masturbation. When these strategies become a primary means of escape, some individuals may become obsessed with them. They fantasize about how and when they will engage in these activities. They often seem preoccupied, because, in fact, they are. Their spouses often describe feeling alone in their partners' presence. Such Distant bonders can have secret lives no one else knows about, not even people with whom they are living. These Distant bonders may feel justified in their pursuits, because, after all, other people never can fulfill their needs the way they can themselves. Yet they often feel ashamed of their activities, sometimes going to great lengths to conceal them. Any shame they feel becomes one more emotion to avoid and one more reason to engage in their avoidance strategies. It becomes an endless cycle.

If you are a Distant bonder, somehow you have to discover that feelings are your friends. Your emotions are a primary means of communication with yourself. Anxiety conveys the presence of a threat. Anger indicates possible mistreatment. Sadness is a response to a loss or a disappointment. Fear suggests risk or danger. Depression signals a painful loss. Laughter signifies pleasure or happiness. Your emotions are your body's way of telling you to pay attention: "Do more of this. Do less of that. Get out of here! Fix this situation. Don't let this happen. Get help!" Emotional awareness is essential for effective personal and interpersonal functioning. Avoiding awareness of your feelings means that you have shut down part of your brain. That is exactly what drugs and alcohol do. They anesthetize your brain, dimming or aborting your emotional awareness. Your other avoidance strategies try to do the same thing. Do you want to continue to shut down your awareness in order to survive? How much longer are you willing to be absent in your life?

An Absence of Empathy

Emotional suppression makes it difficult for the Distant bonder to experience empathy. For example, Rick seemed angry with his wife Julie all the time, ever since she was diagnosed with rheumatoid arthritis. He was angry that she had had to reduce her work hours to part-time, and that she was so tired when she came home from work, he had to do the household and child care tasks that she had always done. Rick had other things he wanted to do and now he had no time to do them. His life had changed drastically since Julie's diagnosis.

After Julie had begged him to come with her to her last medical appointment, her doctor told Rick that Julie had to cut back on chores and conserve her energy and that she would need his assistance. Rick had nodded his head in agreement, but now he was resenting how her illness was affecting him. He had complained to the doctor about how depressed Julie had become, how she never seemed interested in sex, and how she cried over everything. The doctor informed him that was due to the pain his wife was suffering and the side effects of the medications she had to take to control the pain. These symptoms were inevitable until they had the disease under better control. The doctor also told Rick that Julie would need him to be understanding and supportive. When Julie heard that, she felt even more hopeless. Rick had never been understanding and supportive. She understood that even a disease that was beginning to cause crippling changes and unbearable pain in her body could not trigger emotions in Rick that didn't exist.

Empathy means understanding how someone else feels. If you don't understand how you feel, you are not going to be able to decipher how someone else feels. The absence of the ability to empathize also makes it impossible for Distant bonders to know how they make others feel. Rick was completely oblivious to how his resentment was exacerbating Julie's depression. He was not upset about Julie's illness per se. Rick thought, "She will just have to learn to cope with that." He was upset that her illness was impinging on his freedom. He also didn't want to hear her talk about her symptoms or her fear of the future. Rick wanted his life to be the way it was before she became ill and he was angry with her because it was not. It was Julie's responsibility to fix this, not his.

This empathy deficit of Distant bonders has a profoundly negative impact on relationships. Most people seek emotional understanding and compassion in their close relationships. Someone without empathy will have a hard time offering either. Distant bonders are often quite surprised to discover how discontented or angry other people are with them. This is not necessarily denial. They truly are unaware. They are so focused on their own needs that they are oblivious to the impact that they have on others.

Loneliness

All of the strategies of the Distant bonder carry one major risk: loneliness. Distant bonders express a preference to be left alone. Other people are often glad to accommodate that preference. Distant bonders usually do not come across as particularly likable. They are self-centered, insensitive, indifferent, and uncooperative. Other people feel rejected and demeaned by them. Although Distant bonders report being happiest alone, many are aware of being disliked. While some dismiss their unpopularity as unimportant, others do feel a sense of sadness at this rejection. Over time, they may experience loneliness and a sense of frustration at not knowing how to be more likable.

For example, after Doug's third divorce, he was less resilient. He didn't pop back onto the singles circuit. When he went out, he felt empty and bored. Everyone seemed like a stranger. Nobody knew him, and no one cared about him even a little. In therapy, Doug confided:

> I now realize how lonely I have always been. I am afraid I will grow old alone. I think I always have told myself that I enjoy being alone, because I was running away from intimacy. I have avoided family outings, my kids' activities, developing friendships with other couples, and colleagues who have tried to develop closer friendships with me. I was afraid that they would expect commitments from me that I would not be able to keep or not want to. But I also was afraid that they would all let me down in the end, so I never invested in any of them.

If Distant bonding is your style, loneliness can actually be your best friend. Loneliness can be the painful stimulant that triggers a change in your behavior. Distant bonders who have no complaints about their lives are less likely to change. Why would they? Because other people keep complaining about them? No, they can either end those relationships or simply find more effective avoidance strategies. But if you are feeling lonely in your Distant Bonding Style, then some of your feelings are slipping through the grates of your control strategies. This is finally an opportunity for you to discover what your emotions are and to begin to act on them. You can learn how to be more likable and how to discriminate among people who will make your efforts at change worthwhile.

Modifying the Distant Bonding Style

Everyone with the Distant style has the hyperpositive self schemas of *Entitled*, *Intimacy Avoidant*, *Stubbornly Independent*, and *Restrained*. As with the Easy and Anxious styles, the strength of the schemas in the style can vary. In Sonja's case, her *Entitled* schema was predominant. While anyone with the Distant style has an *Entitled* schema, every Distant bonder does not necessarily have such a powerful *Entitled* schema as Sonja's. Some people with the *Restrained* schema are reluctant to verbally interact with anyone about anything. Others with the *Restrained* schema may be quite verbally skilled and even charming in social situations, but they avoid revealing personal information, particularly of a negative nature. Some Distant bonders can be socially charming if necessary, but there has to be an incentive, as there was for Sonja. For other Distant bonders, no incentive is great enough to extract social interactions beyond the bare minimum.

The same kinds of variability occur with the *Intimacy Avoidant* and the *Stubbornly Independent* schemas. The intensity of your hyperpositive schemas will not be exactly the same as that of another Distant bonder even though you have the same set of schemas. Pay attention to which of the schemas are most intense in your Distant style. This awareness will help you to personalize the strategies to change these schemas in the chapters ahead.

What if you are married to a Distant bonder? Can such spouses change? The question is not whether they *can* change, but rather whether they *want* to change. You may be quite miserable in the relationship, feeling unloved and unappreciated. However, if the Distant bonder is quite content, then how likely is change? The only change such spouses might welcome would be for you to decrease your complaints, and they can engineer that simply by being around you less or ignoring you more. I have had clients, however, who came in alone to work on their relationships with Distant bonders even though their Distant partners refused. In some cases, after the clients had made some changes to improve the relationship, their Distant partners were willing to come with them when they realized that therapy is about change, not blame.

Sometimes the clients seeking therapy changed so much that they no longer wanted to remain in the relationship with the Distant bonders. Other clients who understood that their Distant partners were not going to change tried to find ways to survive emotionally when, for various reasons, they felt they could not leave the marriage. If you are in a relationship with a Distant bonder who shows no desire to change, you will need to decide what direction to take. If you stay and your partner doesn't change, you will need to seek meaningful emotional connections elsewhere, or you will drown in your own loneliness. Predicting who will change is a very risky business, but it's a sure bet that the less people want to change, the less likely it is that they will.

Helping the Youthful Distant Bonder

As you saw with Doug and Pamela, their Distant Bonding Styles were already apparent in childhood and adolescence. If you have a son or daughter who is displaying this style, you can help that child change interaction styles that isolate or make social interactions difficult for him or her. However, you need to do this gently and not overreact. Many well-adjusted people are quite socially reserved and prefer solitary activities. The concern here is with the child or adolescent who shows signs of loneliness, isolation, social discomfort, or alienation from others. You also may find some of these suggestions helpful in your own interactions with adult Distant bonders. Even if these suggestions produce no changes in the Distant bonder, they are likely to make you feel more satisfied.

- *Entitled* schemas alienate others, so don't overindulge your children. If you are fortunate enough to be able to give them whatever they want, don't. If they want several things, let them choose one. If the things they want are not gifts for special events, i.e., birthday presents, have them earn all or part of the cost by doing chores. An excess of abundance usually corresponds with an absence of appreciation.

- On special occasions when your children receive several gifts, have them go through their things later and select an equal number of similar items, whether toys, clothes, or games, to give away. Be sure they don't pick broken toys or ruined clothing. Emphasize how much someone else will enjoy the item. Let them give the items to the charitable organization themselves. Model this behavior yourself with your own things. Discuss how fortunate you are to have so much and how if the circumstances were reversed, how grateful you would be for the generosity of others.

- Don't speak disparagingly of other people or different ethnic groups. Don't brag about your superiority, whether it is financial, educational, or whatever you think it might be. Your children will learn those attitudes and unwittingly offend their peers.

- Although you may have worked very hard to achieve whatever you have, you also have had good fortune whether in terms of health, timing, emotional support, contacts, or whatever. Acknowledge that. Show gratitude for whatever you have. Model modesty.

- Your children can learn empathy by engaging in spontaneous discussions with you about how others might feel in regard to tragic events such as natural disasters or deaths. Newspaper articles or television broadcasts will certainly supply the raw material for such discussions.

- When your children tell you something that happened to someone that they think was funny, but you realize was probably hurtful, gently discuss how the other person might have felt. Ask how they might feel in that same situation. Don't do this in a shaming way, but rather in a more speculative manner.

- Don't allow your children to think that they have to be the best to have your love and approval. Emphasize doing their best, not being the best.

- Praise your children's accomplishments, but also praise the accomplishments of other kids.

- Don't make winning the most important thing in the world. Don't rationalize why you or they lost. Congratulate their team's opponents and acknowledge that they played better. During a game, don't curse your children or team if they are losing. Don't call your kids or other players names. Don't blame others when you don't play well. If you want your children to be good sports, then model good sportsmanship.

- If you want your children to be more expressive, then model how to express feelings constructively. Verbalize what you are feeling and use a variety of words to describe your emotions. Acknowledge when you feel hurt, disappointed, rejected, or angry. Don't act as if those emotions are shameful. However, also show restraint in expressing your emotions. If emotional expression or control is not easy for you, the suggestions in Part III on changing the *Unrestrained* and *Restrained* schemas should be helpful for you and your children.

- Don't push your children to talk about their feelings. If you spend time with them and listen to them and remember what they tell you, gradually they will tell you more. Don't dispute what they say they feel even if you think they are describing the wrong emotion. If you model the difference at other times, they will catch on.

- Listen to your children. Let them know that they can talk to you about anything and you will not get mad, even if it is about you. Be available to them. Don't have them on some rigid schedule of access to you. If they can only talk to you when it is convenient for you, they will end up not talking to you at all.

- Respect your children's confidences. Don't share what they tell you with their siblings or anyone else. Betraying their confidences conveys that people cannot be trusted with their secrets. They will share less and less with you.

- Tell your children that bullying and teasing are not okay and that you want to know if people are mistreating them. If your children complain about being bullied or teased, find out the circumstances. However, don't overreact. Gather all the information before deciding on a course of action. Talk to your children about what they can do, what you can do, and what others can do. If your child is old enough, decide together on an action that will protect him or her. Don't take a course of action that could make your child vulnerable to retaliation.

- Model the schema of *Interdependence*. Ask for help yourself on projects when assistance would be helpful, even if it is not critical. Model cooperation, such as fixing dinner together or cleaning the garage together. Make working together fun. Take breaks together and have a special snack the kids like. These cooperative activities are the best times for conversations.

- If your children become frustrated doing something, offer to help, but don't insist, don't take over the project, and don't act as if they are stupid for not being able to figure it out on their own. Ask them what they have done so far on the project and where they ran into problems. Discuss possible strategies before anyone does anything. Let them try first if possible. Domineering parents or siblings can push children to become excessively independent or dependent.

- Avoid unnecessary criticism and include lots of praise and affection.

- Try to accept that some children are less cuddly than others. Respect that by not being intrusive about giving them physical affection when they are busy doing something. Discriminate between your needs for affection and their needs. Do touch and pat them frequently, and hug them when they seem to want that. If you find verbal or physical affection difficult, the schema change suggestions in chapter 11 will be helpful, because you need to increase your expressions of affection. Children need to feel loved. Affectionate words and loving hugs convey that.

- Don't model substance abuse. Don't model any addictive or obsessive behavior, such as staying on the Internet well into the night most evenings. Don't isolate yourself from your children for long periods of time.

- Eat dinner together as a family as many nights as you can—with the television off. Start a routine of discussing each person's day, talking about plans for the week and weekend, and events that could be of interest to your kids. Don't make meals a time for lectures or scoldings.

- Have your children participate in at least one social activity, whether sports, band, scouting, or whatever, on a regular basis. You can pick several possibilities and let them choose among them. Encourage your children to bring their friends home to visit and make their friends feel welcome.

- Don't allow your children unlimited access to television, video games, the Internet, or any other solitary activity that requires no social interactions. Check in with them to see what they are watching. You have the right and responsibility to monitor what comes into your home. You are the parent.

- If you are concerned that your child has no friends, spends all the time alone, and seems unhappy, talk to a teacher, school counselor, or a child psychologist. Describe your concerns and ask if they think if would be advisable to have your child see a therapist. Depressed kids often look like Distant bonders.

Assessing Distancing Strategies

Your Strategies: Here is a checklist for you to assess which of the Distant bonding strategies and characteristics you may have. Even if you think the Distant Bonding Style is not one of your styles, you may use some of that style's strategies, as these sometimes cut across different styles. Read through the checklist, and for each item that is descriptive of you, write one or two examples of that in your notebook. This information will help you identify the ways in which you create distance in your relationships.

I experience physical problems from my efforts at self-control.

I engage in activities requiring only superficial social interactions, such as sports or classes.

I don't encourage personal disclosure by others.

I dissociate or mentally feel as if I am somewhere else or almost out of my body watching.

I ignore others.

I withdraw from uncomfortable situations.

I become angry when others will not leave me alone.

I engage in obsessive or addictive activities.

I feel ashamed of activities I use to emotionally escape.

I keep some of my activities hidden from other people.

I have been told that others don't know me.

I have been surprised when others have told me they were upset with me.

I have trouble understanding how others feel or think.

I have felt intensely lonely at times.

Their Strategies: Next, review the material you have written about the people on your list, when you developed person schemas for each of them. Based on what you know, write the names of the people beside each item that you think describes that person. This will help you understand why you may feel distant when you are with that person.

He/she experiences physical problems from efforts at self-control

He/she engages in activities requiring only superficial social interactions, such as sports or classes.

He/she doesn't encourage personal disclosure by others.

He/she dissociates or seems preoccupied or altogether somewhere else at times.

He/she ignores others.

He/she withdraws from uncomfortable situations.

He/she becomes angry when others will not leave them alone.

He/she engages in obsessive or addictive activities.

He/she feels ashamed of activities used to emotionally escape.

He/she keeps some activities hidden from other people.

He/she has been told that others don't know them.

He/she has been surprised when told that others were upset with them.

He/she has trouble understanding how others feel or think.

He/she has felt intensely lonely at times.

PART III

Interactions, Changes, and Choices

9

Collisions: Schema Wars

When we wish to correct ... and to show another that he
errs, we must notice from what side he views the matter, for
on that side it is usually true.

—Pascal, *Pensees*

In this chapter you will put together all the information you have been assembling on yourself and the other people in your life. You will figure out your bonding styles, their bonding styles, and how those styles enhance or strain your relationships. As mentioned earlier, many people have styles that don't match the Easy, Anxious, and Distant Bonding styles. Here you will sketch out your own exact bonding styles for each of your relationships. You will be able to see if you switch schemas or entire bonding styles in your different relationships. You will be able to decide whether you have any unbalanced schemas that you want to modify. You also will be able to determine if other people have bonding styles that are especially problematic for you.

To help you understand your relationships, you first need to understand why interpersonal collisions are inevitable in anyone's life. Conflicts occur in almost all relationships. When you understand the sources of those conflicts, you can learn to avoid some and minimize the impact of others. Bonding schemas and styles can contribute to what seems like schema warfare. Bonding styles can strain relationships, because some styles are less compatible with each other. Flipping between styles and between schemas can produce chaos and tension within relationships by creating unpredictability. Developing new schemas can throw old relationships out of balance. These potential sources of schema conflict are discussed in detail, so you can understand the schema collisions in your life as you analyze your relationships.

Variations in Styles

In Part II you became familiar with the three common styles of bonding. You may have found that although one or more of the styles described you and your relationships to some extent, none was a perfect fit. That is not an unusual reaction. People can have characteristic bonding styles that don't match the Easy, Anxious, and Distant Bonding Styles; they also can switch between styles in different relationships and within the same relationships over very short periods of time (Bartholomew and Horowitz 1991; Baldwin and Fehr 1995; Baldwin, Keelan, Fehr, et al. 1996). Now you will see how there are many different possible styles and how you may have more than one. You will use this information later in the chapter to identify your individual bonding styles and which styles you use in your relationships with different people.

A bonding style consists of one schema from each of the four bonding continua of *Worthiness*, *Intimacy*, *Expressiveness*, and *Interdependency*. The Easy style consists of the four balanced schemas on these continua (*Worthy*, *Intimacy Comfortable*, *Expressive*, and *Interdependent*), the Anxious style consists of the four negative schemas (*Unworthy*, *Intimacy Driven*, *Unrestrained*, and *Dependent*), and the Distant style is comprised of the four hyperpositive schemas (*Entitled*, *Intimacy Avoidant*, *Restrained*, and *Stubbornly Independent*). However, you can have any combination of balanced, negative, and hyperpositive schemas and you may have more than one combination. For example, you could have a bonding style of the negative schemas of *Unworthy*, *Intimacy Driven*, and *Dependent* and a hyperpositive schema of *Restrained*. With this combination you would find the Anxious style quite descriptive of you, but you would seldom express your thoughts and feelings. This would mean that you would be more submissive, less controlling, and much less volatile than are most people who have the Anxious style.

You might identify with much of the Distant style but instead of all hyperpositive schemas, you might have a negative *Unworthy* schema instead of the hyperpositive *Entitled* schema. This would mean that you still keep people at a distance, but your motive is that you think they will reject you if they get to know you, so you are reluctant to be emotionally close. However, you do not come across to others as condescending and self-centered as do those with the

Distant style, because you do not have the *Entitled* schema. Rather than being seen as arrogant, you are more likely to be perceived as shy.

In these examples only one schema has been changed in the Anxious and Distant styles, respectively. Yet changing just one schema in a bonding style can have a significant impact in the way you perceive yourself and others perceive you.

Another possible bonding style might consist of the negative *Unworthy* and *Intimacy Driven* schemas, the hyperpositive *Restrained* schema, and the balanced *Interdependent* schema. With this style you would put your needs behind the needs of others (*Unworthy*), and you would want frequent reassurance that others care about you (*Intimacy Driven*), but you would be reluctant to let them know if they hurt your feelings or disappointed you (*Restrained*). You also would be comfortable asking for and offering help (*Interdependent*). This style would produce communication problems and very likely occasional passive-aggressive behavior because of your inability to directly express your feelings. So, you can see that the schemas in the bonding areas may group together in combinations other than the Easy, Anxious, and Distant styles.

Switching Schemas and Styles

Because people typically have more than one bonding style, switching from one style to another is a common phenomenon. For example, Kent has two different styles. He has the Easy Bonding Style with the four balanced schemas. He also has a second style that consists of the negative *Unworthy* schema and the hyperpositive *Intimacy Avoidant*, *Restrained*, and *Stubbornly Independent* schemas. His second style is activated when he is with strangers or people who are critical or judgmental. He anticipates that they will see that he is inadequate in some way and look down on him. So he keeps them at a distance, reveals little of his thoughts or feelings, and avoids asking them for help. However, when he is with people whom he views as warm and accepting, his Easy Bonding Style is triggered. Kent has different role and person schemas for these two categories of people, so his different role and person schemas trigger different bonding styles in him. His interactions are quite different with these two different sets of people.

However, Kent sometimes switches styles within the same relationship. When he first met Marilyn at work, his role schema for strangers activated his second style that kept her at a distance. Over time he observed her with various people in different situations and realized that she was friendly, thoughtful, and accepting of others. Gradually he developed a person schema of Marilyn as warm, accepting, and fun. This new person schema then activated his Easy Bonding Schema, which allowed him to be more open and expressive with her. After discovering that they both liked basketball, Kent and Marilyn attended several games together.

One evening after a game, Kent tried to kiss Marilyn, but she pulled back. Startled, he asked her what was wrong. She expressed surprise at his sexual attraction for her, and explained that she viewed their relationship as platonic. Furthermore, she said that she wanted to keep it that way since they worked together. Kent was stunned. Kent had thought that Marilyn's feelings for him were similar to his for her. He felt embarrassed and rejected. Then he apologized and agreed they could just be friends.

After that Kent's person schema of Marilyn changed, and their relationship changed. Now, Kent's person schema of Marilyn saw her as deceptive and superior, so his revised person schema of Marilyn triggered his second bonding style. He no longer joked with her or invited her to accompany him to any ballgames. He expressed no personal thoughts or feelings to her. He no longer asked for her help with any of his projects, and he did not offer to help her with any of hers. Kent illustrates how you can flip between styles with the same person. People do not just switch between styles randomly. Different triggers activate different styles. When Kent's person schema of Marilyn changed, that activated a different bonding style. Kent's person schemas of Marilyn are the triggers for his different bonding styles.

You may think that Kent's revision of his Marilyn schema is unfair, because her desire to not have romantic entanglements with her co-workers is prudent. Maybe his revision is "unfair," but his revision was strongly influenced by his *Unworthy* schema, which tends to interpret any rejection as somehow confirming that he is less worthy in the eyes of others. He didn't know that Marilyn had suffered greatly in her last job when her relationship with a co-worker ended at the man's request. Seeing him several times a day had been extremely distressing for her and made it difficult to get on with her life. Finally, she quit her job to stop seeing him. After that experience, she made a decision to never again become romantically involved with a co-worker. If Kent had worked elsewhere, she would have been interested in dating him, but she did not mention that, not wanting to encourage his feelings. Without this information, Kent personalized Marilyn's reaction and concluded that Marilyn thought she was too good for him, a notion that fit well with his *Unworthy* schema. When Kent flipped between bonding styles, he switched to different schemas on all four of the bonding continua. But people also can have different styles that differ on one, two, or three continua.

When Schemas Collide

Schemas can produce interpersonal collisions in any number of ways. Some bonding styles are simply less appealing to other bonding styles. Sometimes people create tension by unpredictably flipping back and forth between styles in the same relationship, as Kent did. Sometimes people develop new schemas, which can create new bonding styles no longer in sync with the bonding style of their partners. Incompatible schemas create other venues for collisions. Unfortunately, when relationships are in distress, schemas are often the culprits.

Bad Fits

Some bonding styles simply are bad fits with other bonding styles. Now that you understand the Easy, Anxious, and Distant Bonding Styles, which do you think would be more attractive to each other? Does the old saying, "Opposites attract," apply here? Apparently not. The idea that opposites attract seems to be limited to magnets. When a group of people were asked which of three hypothetical dating partners they found most attractive, the respondents all selected potential partners who were similar to their own characteristic bonding style. Easy bonders selected a partner described with the Easy style, the Anxious picked an Anxious partner, and the Distant chose a Distant partner (Frazier, Byer, Fischer, et al. 1996).

These findings are not surprising if you think about the schemas that constitute the different bonding styles. How happy would an Anxious bonder with the *Intimacy Driven* and *Unrestrained* schemas be with a Distant bonder with the *Intimacy Avoidant* and *Restrained* schemas? The Anxious bonder would be pushing for greater emotional closeness and personal self-disclosure, while the Distant bonder would always be moving in the opposite direction, feeling emotionally suffocated and psychologically probed.

Similarly, although an Anxious bonder would receive more closeness and openness from an Easy bonder, the Easy bonder would still be less inclined to offer the same degree of closeness that an Anxious bonder could find with another Anxious bonder who had the same intense need for emotional intimacy. Likewise, a Distant bonder with the *Intimacy Avoidant*, *Restrained*, and *Stubbornly Independent* schemas would be more comfortable with another Distant bonder rather than an Anxious or Easy bonder, both of whom would be less satisfied with the degree of detachment a Distant bonder would prefer. An Easy bonder's balanced schemas would be most compatible with another Easy bonder, who doesn't seem extreme on any continuum in either direction.

If people hypothetically prefer others with the same style, do Easy bonders end up with Easy bonders, Anxious with Anxious, and Distant with Distant? Not necessarily. Many factors play a role in what draws two people together in romantic and platonic relationships. Familiarity, location, availability, fate, temporary vulnerability, sexual attraction, shared interests, and an array of other influences all contribute to the connections people make with other people. Relationship choices are much less rational than most people might like to think. The bottom line is anyone can fall in love with the wrong person; wrong in the sense of how much turmoil is going to be experienced in the relationship. Easy bonders can fall in love with Anxious or Distant bonders, but the ride will not be a smooth one.

There is one bonding style combination that is a *very* bad fit: the Anxious bonder and the Distant bonder. Under stress, the Anxious bonder pushes for closeness while the Distant bonder seeks to escape. Each wants the exact opposite of what the other desires. This is a potentially volatile combination. Couples in which one person worries about being abandoned and the other is afraid of intimacy are at risk for abusive behavior as a result of violent behavior by the partner fearing abandonment (Roberts and Noller 1998). This pattern is true no matter whether it is the man or the woman who fears abandonment.

Other studies also have found links between the fear of abandonment and partner abuse (Dutton and Browning 1988; Dutton, Saunders, Starzomski, et al. 1994). In Camille and Alex's situation (see chapter 7), Alex's Easy bonding style prevented Camille's Anxious bonder's aggressive behavior from escalating into an abusive situation. But Camille still had to seek counseling to develop constructive ways to deal with her fear of abandonment. If you are in an Anxious bonder–Distant bonder relationship and your interactions even approach abusive language or behavior, consider counseling. Your relationship can be helped.

Always hesitate to rush into commitments based on any initial intense emotional attraction you may feel for another person. If this is truly a relationship made in Friendship or Partner Paradise, it will last. And never confuse lust for good judgment. They have little in common, if they are not altogether incompatible. You are unlikely to show much good judgment about a relationship when you are so obsessed with someone that you walk into doors or back over fire hydrants thinking about that person. The women who were drawn to the Anxious Bonder Matt (see chapter 7) initially were immensely attracted to him, but with time as their familiarity with him increased their attraction diminished. Furthermore, those who did not rush into commitments with him found it much easier to extricate themselves than those who readily acquiesced to his suggestions for greater intimacy.

Even though Anxious bonders may prefer Anxious bonders and Distant bonders may desire Distant bonders, that does not mean they will experience smooth sailing. With two Anxious bonders, both will be subject to emotional distress, jealousy, and insecurity. With two Distant bonders, there will be little communication, many misunderstandings, a lack of connections, and an absence of deep emotional investment in each other. Many people who had previous predominantly Anxious or Distant styles were more easily able to move toward an Easy style with the support and love of someone with more balanced schemas. You can still work to balance your schemas if you are in a relationship with an Anxious or Distant bonder, but you may experience more resistance from them. Now, let's see how relationships are strained by other schema phenomena.

Flippers

People who flip between schemas or styles within the same relationship can be very confusing to the other person in the relationship. Kimberly is a twenty-seven-year-old teacher, who married her college sweetheart, Kevin, right after graduation. Kimberly wanted children immediately, but Kevin wanted to wait until he was more established in his career. Kimberly reluctantly agreed to obtain a high school teaching position until that time. From the beginnings of their relationship Kevin had been jealous and possessive, but Kimberly found his jealousy appealing, interpreting it as a sign of how much he loved her, and feeling that she was the center of his attention at these times. After their intense courtship, she often felt neglected by him, because he was consumed with doing well in college and then by his career.

When Kimberly went out with her girlfriends while Kevin studied or worked, he would become jealous if later she told him about any men with whom they had interacted. Initially, he discouraged her from spending time with her friends. Over time he became increasingly controlling. He wanted to know where she was at all times, who else was present, what she wore, how much she had had to drink, what time she got home, and so forth. Typically, these interrogations escalated angrily, with Kevin calling her various epithets and storming off. Later, he would express great remorse with promises to change his ways.

As Kevin increased his efforts to control Kimberly, she admitted that she engaged in more activities and behaviors that upset him, in an effort to resist his control. She also acknowledged that her actions were effective in getting his full attention, while compliance with his requests netted her nothing. Kimberly also admitted that she was accustomed to getting her way and resented it when Kevin wouldn't go out with her. Furthermore, she revealed that she felt great resentment because of his wish to delay having children.

An analysis of Kevin and Kimberly's bonding styles will help explain their problematic interactions. Kevin has primarily one bonding style with Kimberly: the negative schemas of *Unworthy, Intimacy Driven*, and *Unrestrained* and the balanced schema of *Interdependent*. He also has a person schema of Kimberly as being socially superior to him, as she comes from a wealthy background and is very attractive. Kevin needs a lot of reassurance in his relationship with Kimberly because of his fear that ultimately she will realize that he does not deserve her (*Unworthy, Intimacy Driven*). Because Kevin is so easily threatened, his jealousy is quickly aroused by any indication that she is interested in anyone else or if anyone else expresses interest in her whether she reciprocates or not (*Unworthy, Intimacy Driven*). When Kevin becomes jealous, he interrogates Kimberly and becomes verbally abusive (*Unrestrained*).

Kimberly has two bonding styles with Kevin and switches back and forth between them. One style consists of the negative schemas of *Intimacy Driven* and *Dependent*, the hyperpositive *Entitled* schema, and the balanced *Expressive* schema. Her other style consists of the hyperpositive schemas of the Distant Bonding Style: *Entitled, Intimacy Avoidant, Restrained*, and *Stubbornly Independent*.

In both styles Kimberly expects to be the center of Kevin's attention and to have her way. When Kevin focuses his attention on her, Kimberly's first style is active. On those occasions she feels she deserves all of the attention he gives her (*Entitled*). She wants him to tell her repeatedly how devoted he is to her and how he could never imagine leaving her for any other woman (*Intimacy Driven*). She seeks his advice on any decisions she has to make (*Dependent*), and she expresses her own feelings and thoughts openly (*Expressive*).

However, when Kevin does not give Kimberly the attention she demands or does not agree with her, she flips to her Distant Bonding Style. She maintains her *Entitled* schema of feeling superior to Kevin, but she flips on the other three bonding continua. She acts cold and indifferent to Kevin, goes out with her single friends, and drinks and flirts with other men (*Intimacy Avoidant*). Kimberly doesn't ask for Kevin's advice on anything (*Stubbornly Independent*), nor does she tell him that she feels neglected by him (*Restrained*).

The person schema of Kevin that activates Kimberly's Distant style is a Kevin who seems less devoted to her because he does not pay as much attention to her as she craves and has always received from her family. Her other bonding style is activated by her person schema of Kevin as being awestruck by her and always wanting to please her. So Kevin's different behaviors activate Kimberly's different person schemas of Kevin, which in turn activate her different bonding styles with him. Clearly, this is not a relationship made in bonding heaven.

Kimberly's ability to switch styles is anathema to Kevin's insecurity about himself and their relationship. If neither party modifies their bonding styles, their interactions could escalate to Kevin becoming physically abusive. However, this relationship is salvageable, as you will see in chapter 12.

Changers

Although many people do flip between styles within the same relationship, other people develop new schemas that create new bonding styles. Relationship problems can ensue when one member develops a new style that no longer is compatible with the other person's.

When Gwen and Rudy met and during the first several years of their marriage, they both had bonding styles consisting of a negative *Unworthy* schema and the hyperpositive schemas of *Intimacy Avoidant*, *Restrained*, and *Stubbornly Independent*. During their childhoods, Gwen had been verbally, physically, and sexually abused by her stepfather, and Rudy had been verbally and physically abused by his father. Neither of their mothers had ever intervened on their behalf. Schemas of a poor self-image (*Unworthy*), a fear of closeness with others (*Intimacy Avoidant*), a reluctance to express personal thoughts or feelings (*Restrained*), and a need to not be obligated to anyone (*Stubbornly Independent*) are understandable outcomes from such experiences. Gwen and Rudy also had role schemas of other people as basically uncaring and untrustworthy.

The couple met a few years after high school when they worked the same night shift at a shoe factory. Because they had breaks at the same time they got to know each other gradually. They discovered a shared enthusiasm for horses and began to go riding on their days off. They felt comfortable together, because neither pressed for too much closeness nor probed too much about the other's personal history. In spite of that, they both felt closer to each other than they ever had to anyone else previously. They both felt safe in the relationship and married. Their marriage seemed to work for them, but it was not without problems.

Their *Restrained* schemas meant that differences of opinions were never discussed, and compromises were never reached. One of them would just give in, and both felt resentment when they were the one to capitulate. Their *Stubbornly Independent* schemas frustrated each other, because the unwillingness of each to ask for help meant that some tasks were never finished and much time was often wasted. As time passed, there was an increase in unspoken hostility and distance between them, with each feeling more alone and alienated.

Although this particular style is not one of the three common styles described earlier, I have encountered this combination of *Unworthy, Intimacy Avoidant, Restrained,* and *Stubbornly Independent* repeatedly in my practice with many couples who shared this set of bonding schemas and histories of abuse. I also have observed this bonding style in many individuals who do not have histories of childhood abuse, but certainly have had experiences that contributed to an *Unworthy* schema and a distrust of others. This variability underscores the point that similar schemas can be developed through entirely different experiences.

People with this style (*Unworthy, Intimacy Avoidant, Restrained,* and *Stubbornly Independent)* truly desire emotional closeness even though they fear that they are too unworthy to deserve it. Often this particular schema combination spurs people into therapy, because this style leads to intense loneliness and sadness, which is exactly what happened to Gwen. When she recognized the increasing emptiness and tension in her life, Gwen sought counseling.

A therapist helped her address the sources of her unbalanced schemas and helped her to see how those schemas had protected her in her relationships with her parents by keeping them at a distance. When she was a child she had needed to isolate herself emotionally from her stepfather's abuse and her mother's neglect. The schemas had enabled her to do that.

However, as an adult, those same schemas now trapped her in a bonding style that prevented her from forming emotional ties and from feeling understood and loved. Over time Gwen worked through her feelings of having been betrayed by her parents and she came to understand that her *Unworthy* schema resulted from inappropriate and inexcusable behavior by them. As she gained a greater sense of self-worth and learned how to express herself more openly to others, her schemas began to shift. Gradually, she began to develop the balanced schemas of *Worthy, Intimacy Comfortable, Expressive,* and *Interdependent.* She liked the closeness that began to develop with her therapist and with a few of her friends. But she was no longer comfortable with how disconnected she felt from her husband.

However Rudy's schemas were not changing, and he sensed Gwen's increasing frustration with him as she tried to create better communication and more closeness between the two of them. Both

Gwen and Rudy began to wonder if their relationship could survive the changes Gwen was undergoing. At that point, Rudy asked to enter therapy with Gwen. He was willing to try to change, because even though he rarely expressed it, he deeply loved her.

This style of *Unworthy, Intimacy Avoidant, Restrained,* and *Stubbornly Independent* differs from the Distant Bonding Style only on the *Worthiness* continua, with the Distant bonder having an *Entitled* schema instead of an *Unworthy* schema. However, that single schema difference makes an enormous difference in one's openness to change and receptiveness to therapy. People with the *Entitled* schema have a hard time acknowledging their flaws and tend to expect others to change to accommodate them. Although often fearful of condemnation, people with the *Unworthy* schema are more willing to look at themselves and explore ways to change when faced with the alternative of losing one of the few loving relationships they might have.

The problems in Rudy and Gwen's relationship became more apparent after Gwen began to develop new schemas during therapy. However, new schemas can develop without either intent or awareness. For example, many people with *Unworthy* schemas develop *Entitled* schemas after achieving impressive professional or financial success. Then, the partner they chose when they were young and struggling and had *Unworthy* schemas no longer matches what they think they now deserve. They might insist their partners undergo cosmetic surgery to become more compatible with their new *Entitled* schemas or they might just dump their partners and acquire "trophy" wives or husbands.

In any case, when one person in a relationship changes a schema, the relationship can be thrown into a crisis, but this is certainly not inevitable. You may come to experience greater joy in a relationship as the other person develops a new *Worthy* schema to replace an old *Unworthy* one. An increased sense of worth can make that person more confident, more willing to try new things, and less threatened by any successes you have. So schema change in one person can produce either positive or negative outcomes for the other person and for the relationship, but some kind of impact is almost inevitable.

Incompatible Schemas

Schema wars can ignite when people develop new schemas and when they flip between schemas in the same relationships. But sometimes schema conflict is generated simply because people have fundamentally incompatible schemas. Although everyone develops schemas, the *content* of schemas is greatly influenced by one's culture.

This is especially true of the bonding schemas. Cultures teach quite specific expectations about appropriate interpersonal and personal behavior. Schemas that are viewed as appropriate in one society may be viewed as inappropriate in another. The *Expressiveness* continuum best illustrates that.

While the *Expressive* self schema is viewed as appropriate in the United States by most people, some cultures value the *Restrained* self schema as far more appropriate. In those cultures, expressing personal thoughts and emotions is unacceptable. Different cultures also vary greatly in role schemas deemed appropriate. For example, role schemas for husbands and wives have great discrepancies among cultures. What is considered appropriate behavior for wives in the United States differs substantially from what is appropriate for wives in Saudi Arabia or India.

Cultural differences in role schemas can create tension between cultures, but they are especially problematic between people from different cultures who marry. Neither may be aware at the outset of the marriage how different their various role schemas are nor how discrepant their expectations of each other will be.

Even within the same country there are various ethnic groups and different religions that encourage different role schemas. However, individuals from the same ethnic and religious backgrounds also may have incompatible schemas. Remember Megan and Michael from chapter 1 who discovered that they had very different role schemas of marriages. Megan's *marriage* role schema expected husbands and wives to readily exchange thoughts, whether they were positive or negative, and not to hold back emotional intensity. Michael's *marriage* role schema expected husbands and wives to refrain from criticism or arguments and to never show anger or disgust. Although Michael and Megan came from the same Boston Irish-American neighborhood and had attended the same Catholic church, their parents had modeled very different styles of interaction. Those parental styles were the driving force behind the marriage schemas that Michael and Megan developed.

Role schemas also can produce conflict when they appear to be in conflict with reality. In chapter 2, you may remember that Frieda was frustrated and disappointed with her husband George because Frieda's role schema of a husband was one who eagerly pitched in with child care and who was understanding when the wife was not interested in sex. However, Frieda's role schema of a husband was the exact opposite of her person schema of George, depicting George as seldom helping with child care and being obsessed with sex. Now, in truth, George was not obsessed with sex, but he was much more interested in sex than Frieda's role schema of husbands predicted he would be. The discrepancy between Frieda's role schema of husbands and her person schema of George made it seem to Frieda as if George were obsessed with sex. The expectations that your role schemas produce can be quite incompatible with the real people who fill those roles in your life, and this discrepancy can be the source of much friction.

You Are Not an Island

Contrary to what songwriters Simon and Garfunkel passionately asserted, they are not islands and neither are you. In any relationship you are part of a dynamic social system. A *dynamic social system* refers to two or more people who have reciprocal connections with each other. *Reciprocal connections* mean that the two (or more) people connected in some way have an effect on each other. In other words, in a dynamic social system, change by one party has an impact on the other person (or people) in the system. Then the impacted person's reactions have a subsequent effect on the original party. In any dynamic system, change in one part will be felt by other parts.

A dyad is the simplest dynamic social system because a dyad involves only two people. In a dyad, any changes one person makes will have some kind of impact on the other person, whether it is a spouse, a child, or a colleague. Most people are part of several dynamic systems.

You are connected to the people with whom you live, the people at your workplace, and the people in any of the other regular activities in which you participate, such as religious or social groups. You are a part of these systems, whether you like it or not. If you change, you could have an effect on the other people in your system. In turn, other affected people could react, generating new impacts on you. Interpersonal systems are never static. People are always reacting and adjusting to other people in their various systems.

Manuel and Linda and Their Children

Consider how the people in the following dynamic social system—a family—affected each other. Manuel and Linda have two children, Connie, fourteen, and Diego, eleven. Three years ago, Diego was diagnosed with moderately severe asthma. Diego had had recurrent colds in past winters, but that year his symptoms worsened with no times of respite in between asthma attacks. One evening Diego's breathing was so labored that Linda had to take him to the hospital for emergency treatment. After that, Diego began a regimen of daily breathing treatments and scheduled inhalations from his asthma inhaler, which Linda monitored conscientiously. For the first year he still had to make occasional trips to the emergency room for additional treatments. The last two years Diego has not required emergency treatment even when he has had flare-ups.

Originally, everyone in this family had the balanced schemas of the Easy Bonding Style. The kids showed some typical sibling rivalry but both felt secure with their parents and they were good playmates at times. The parents enjoyed both of their children and did not show any favoritism. After Diego's diagnosis of asthma, there seemed to be a shift in the family system. Diego now received special treatment. Because Diego's physical activities had to be restricted, Linda and Manuel purchased some special video games for him. Connie had to let Diego use the computer whenever he wanted to play, as she was able to do other things. Family activities and vacations were scheduled around Diego's asthma, depending on the allergy seasons in different places. Linda spent more time with Diego, checking on his medications and listening to his lungs. She would get upset with Connie for arguing with Diego, as Diego's wheezing could worsen when he became angry and yelled. Linda cleaned Diego's room, because his room needed to be dust-free. But she insisted that Connie clean her own room and help with other housecleaning chores.

Linda noticed that Connie was opting out of family activities and spending more of her time alone in her room or with her boyfriend. When Linda took Diego to the doctor, Connie complained about how Diego exaggerated his symptoms, which angered Linda and led to reprimands for Connie. When Connie spoke to Linda, Linda allowed Diego to interrupt because she wasn't sure whether he was going to tell her he was having trouble breathing. Finally, Linda noticed that Diego's asthma had precipitated a shift in all of the family interactions. She realized that she had become much more focused on her son and more impatient with her daughter. She recognized that Diego had begun to develop an *Entitled* self schema and Connie an *Unworthy* one.

Linda decided that she had to change the imbalances that had developed in her parental behavior. She sat down with Diego and told him that he was old enough to monitor his own use of the inhalers. She showed him how to read his peak flow meter, the tube that he blew into that registered his lungs' air volume. He was instructed to use the inhaler when his volume fell below a certain level. If that did not work, then he was to tell Linda. Linda stopped allowing him to interrupt her conversations with Connie. She started visiting Connie's room in the evenings to chat with her daughter. When Connie would come to her to talk, Linda would stop whatever she was doing and pay attention. If Connie said she didn't want to participate in a family activity, Linda would express disappointment, encourage her to join them, and show pleasure when Connie would. Linda also increased her physical affection for Connie, going into her room each evening to kiss her good night.

Initially, Diego increased his interruptions, but each time he broke into a conversation, Linda firmly asked him to wait. After a couple of weeks, the interruptions decreased noticeably. She observed that Diego did not use his inhaler as often as he should have, but she could tell that he was not in any serious trouble breathing. So she ignored those instances and praised him when she saw him use his peak flow meter and inhaler. She added household chores that Diego could do without experiencing breathing difficulties each Saturday when the family cleaned house. She restricted the use that both kids had to video games, so that their access was the same. Only when Diego was restricted from going outside was he allowed to have greater access to the computer. Linda made these changes without great fanfare, simply stating the new rules when the situations would arise.

With Linda's changes Connie began to blossom. She seemed happier. She began to ask to go on family outings. She came home from school and looked for her mother to tell her about her day. Connie stopped complaining about Diego's asthma and seemed more interested than critical when Diego needed to see the doctor. Although Diego had been resistant to the changes at first, he seldom interrupted after Linda no longer accepted that behavior. He began to use his inhalers more appropriately. He developed other activities to replace the void created by his limited access to the video games. He became less dependent on Linda and his entitled attitude began to subside.

The relationship between Linda and her husband also improved. When Linda was favoring Diego over Connie, Manuel had complained that Linda was playing favorites because of Diego's asthma. Linda knew she was giving more attention to Diego, but she felt justified and was hurt by Manuel's lack of understanding.

Over the last few years, the family had seemed split between Linda and Diego versus Manuel and Connie. Manuel had stopped punishing Connie when she did something wrong, never held her accountable for her schoolwork, and also complained about Linda's obsession with Diego's asthma. After Linda implemented her changes with her children, the tension between her husband and herself also decreased.

This example illustrates the reciprocal reactions that occur in a dynamic social system. Linda changed her parenting behavior out of her concern for Diego's asthma, which necessitated an increase in her attention. Manuel, Connie, and Diego all adjusted their behavior in reaction to the changes Linda made and the circumstances surrounding Diego. Their reactions then had an impact on Linda and each other. There are no bad guys in this example. Linda did the best she could, but eventually she noticed that Connie was being ignored while Diego was being too accommodated. Linda implemented a thoughtful plan to rebalance the family system. The *Entitled* and *Unworthy* self schemas that Diego and Connie, respectively, were beginning to develop, soon were reintegrated into their original *Worthy* self schemas. You can see how changes in Linda produced changes throughout the family system; and then how changes in the other family members had subsequent effects on Linda, which, in turn, affected them. The importance of reciprocal effects will be addressed carefully when you develop your schema change plan. You will need to consider how others might react to any changes you make *before* implementing your change strategies.

Relationship Analyses

Throughout this book you have been developing your person schemas of the important people in your life in a separate notebook. At this point, you should have a fairly complete picture of your person schemas of other people. Now, you will be able to use that information to better understand your relationships with those people and the bonding styles you have with each of them. You can do that by following the directions presented below to complete the "Relationship Chart" that follows in the next part of this chapter.

Instructions for Working with the Relationship Chart

First, examine the Sample Relationship Chart on page 197 to see how to fill out the chart. After the example, there are five blank Relationship Charts for you to complete. Select five people from the list of names you made in chapter 1. Try to include your parents or parental figures and at least one romantic partner. Also try to include two problematic relationships. On each chart write the name of the other person and circle whether this was a constructive or problematic relationship, or both. In the second column, "Relationship," indicate what the nature of the relationship is, i.e., sibling, boyfriend, supervisor, and so forth.

You can duplicate these charts to analyze relationships you have with other people you listed in chapter 1. The more relationships you analyze, the more clearly you will see which schemas in yourself and in others are problematic.

"My Style"

For each person you named in the chart, under "My Style I" write in the bonding schemas that you think best describes *you* in that relationship. Select one from each of the bonding self schema continua. Do that for each relationship listed. Don't hurry through this part. Carefully think about the entire relationship before you decide. The bonding schema descriptions are listed in Appendix A for your convenience. Pick the schemas that best fit you for each relationship.

You may find that you have or had *more than one* type of style or set of schemas during a relationship. For example, you may have one style with that person when you are happy and a different style when you are unhappy. If so, under "My Style II," write down your second set of bonding schemas, and if you have a third style, put that under "My Style III." Sometimes a style will vary only on one schema. It doesn't matter which style you list under I, II, or III. The numbers are there just to designate different styles.

"Their Style"

Your bonding style *alone* does not determine the quality of a relationship. People in relationships with you also have bonding styles. Their styles may or may not be similar to yours. Review the information that you wrote for each person when you did the previous exercises to complete your person schemas of them. Review the list of bonding schemas again. Then for each person you named, under "Their Style I" write the bonding schemas that best describes them in their relationship with you. You may feel that the other person has or had more than one bonding style with you during the relationship. If so, also list the schemas of the other styles each person has in the relationship with you. Again, their styles can vary on one, two, three, or four continua.

"Relationship Description"

For each relationship you listed, briefly describe how it is or was for you and the other person under "Description of yourself in the relationship" and "Description of other person in the relationship." Describe how you are or were in the relationship, and how the other person is or was. Your descriptions can include behavior, thoughts, and feelings. Here are some examples of descriptors for a variety of relationships:

- *Most comfortable I have ever felt in a relationship*
- *Always felt accepted even when we disagreed*

- *Wonderful at first, then over time turbulent, with lots of anger expressed by both of us*

- *Like a roller coaster—the good times were great, but the bad times were terrible*

- *I never felt I understood the other person*

- *I always felt there was a distance between us and I didn't know how to bridge it*

- *Other person seemed less invested in the relationship than I was*

- *I felt very loved, almost adored, at first, but later I felt constantly monitored and judged*

- *I never could convince the other person of my commitment to the relationship*

- *The other person was terribly jealous of me*

- *I often felt I was walking on egg shells*

- *Sometimes the person would be warm and loving and then other times cold and aloof*

- *I never felt I could please the other person*

- *I always felt the other person was picking at me*

- *At times I would get jealous and sulk*

Now, in the blank Relationship Chart describe each of the relationships you listed, describing yourself and the other person.

"Relationship Impact"

Next to "Impact of relationship on yourself" and "Impact of relationship on other person" describe the impact of each relationship you listed. What effect has the relationship had on you? Does it make you feel good or bad about yourself or both? Does it influence the way you treat other people or how you handle your responsibilities, in either a positive or negative way? Does the relationship make you better, worse, or no different as a person? If the relationship has changed you, describe how you have changed. Likewise, what impact does the relationship seem to have on the other person? Describe how you think the relationship has affected the other party.

After you complete the Relationship Chart, you will find at the end of this chapter on page 203 a series of questions to guide you in analyzing the information in your chart.

Sample Relationship Chart

Example: Kevin, who was described under "Flippers" earlier in this chapter, illustrates how to complete this chart. He describes his relationship with his wife, Kimberly.

[Kevin's chart]
Name of other person: Kimberly   **Relationship:** My wife

[Next Kevin lists the schemas that describe his different bonding schemas with Kimberly.]

Continuum	My Style I	My Style II	My Style III
Worthiness	*Unworthy*		
Intimacy	*Intimacy Driven*		
Expressiveness	*Unrestrained*		
Interdependency	*Interdependent*		

[Below Kevin lists the bonding schemas that Kimberly has with Kevin.]

Continuum	Their Style I	Their Style II	Their Style III
Worthiness	*Entitled*	*Entitled*	
Intimacy	*Intimacy Driven*	*Intimacy Avoidant*	
Expressiveness	*Expressive*	*Restrained*	
Interdependent	*Dependent*	*Stubbornly Independent*	

Description of yourself in the relationship: I try to buy her what she wants, because I know she is used to having expensive things. I get jealous quickly and often. I lose my temper, say mean things, call her names, even break things sometimes. Later I am ashamed and apologize.

Description of other person in the relationship: She switches from being loving and attentive to being cold and uncaring. When she is cold, she flirts with other men and taunts me about it. She gets angry when she doesn't get her way. She always has to be right. She never admits to being wrong. She never apologizes.

Impact of relationship on you: Emotionally exhausting. I have a jealous streak, but it has never been like this before. I hate being so out of control. I hate how changeable she is. It's like she has two different personalities, and I never know who is going to show up.

Impact of relationship on other person: Sometimes she almost seems to enjoy our fights, as if she gets off on the intensity of the interactions.

Relationship Chart

Relationship: Constructive, Problematic, Both

Name _____ Relationship _____

Continuum	My Style I	My Style II	My Style III
Worthiness	_____	_____	_____
Intimacy	_____	_____	_____
Expressiveness	_____	_____	_____
Interdependent	_____	_____	_____

Continuum	Their Style I	Their Style II	Their Style III
Worthiness	_____	_____	_____
Intimacy	_____	_____	_____
Expressiveness	_____	_____	_____
Interdependent	_____	_____	_____

Description of yourself in the relationship: _____

_____

Description of other person in the relationship: _____

_____

Impact of relationship on you:_____

_____

Impact of relationship on other person: _____

_____

_____

Relationship: Constructive, Problematic, Both

Name _____ Relationship _____

Continuum	My Style I	My Style II	My Style III
Worthiness	_____	_____	_____
Intimacy	_____	_____	_____
Expressiveness	_____	_____	_____
Interdependent	_____	_____	_____

Continuum	Their Style I	Their Style II	Their Style III
Worthiness	_____	_____	_____
Intimacy	_____	_____	_____
Expressiveness	_____	_____	_____
Interdependent	_____	_____	_____

Description of yourself in the relationship: _____

_____

Description of other person in the relationship: _____

_____

Impact of relationship on you:_____

_____

Impact of relationship on other person: _____

_____

_____

_____

_____

Relationship: Constructive, Problematic, Both

Name _____ Relationship _____

Continuum	My Style I	My Style II	My Style III
Worthiness	_____	_____	_____
Intimacy	_____	_____	_____
Expressiveness	_____	_____	_____
Interdependent	_____	_____	_____

Continuum	Their Style I	Their Style II	Their Style III
Worthiness	_____	_____	_____
Intimacy	_____	_____	_____
Expressiveness	_____	_____	_____
Interdependent	_____	_____	_____

Description of yourself in the relationship: _____

_____

Description of other person in the relationship: _____

_____

Impact of relationship on you:_____

_____

Impact of relationship on other person: _____

_____

_____

_____

_____

Relationship: Constructive, Problematic, Both

Name _____ Relationship _____

Continuum	My Style I	My Style II	My Style III
Worthiness	_____	_____	_____
Intimacy	_____	_____	_____
Expressiveness	_____	_____	_____
Interdependent	_____	_____	_____

Continuum	Their Style I	Their Style II	Their Style III
Worthiness	_____	_____	_____
Intimacy	_____	_____	_____
Expressiveness	_____	_____	_____
Interdependent	_____	_____	_____

Description of yourself in the relationship: _____

_____

Description of other person in the relationship: _____

_____

Impact of relationship on you:_____

_____

Impact of relationship on other person: _____

_____

_____

_____

Relationship: Constructive, Problematic, Both

Name _____ Relationship _____

Continuum	My Style I	My Style II	My Style III
Worthiness	_____	_____	_____
Intimacy	_____	_____	_____
Expressiveness	_____	_____	_____
Interdependent	_____	_____	_____

Continuum	Their Style I	Their Style II	Their Style III
Worthiness	_____	_____	_____
Intimacy	_____	_____	_____
Expressiveness	_____	_____	_____
Interdependent	_____	_____	_____

Description of yourself in the relationship: _____

_____

Description of other person in the relationship: _____

_____

Impact of relationship on you:_____

_____

Impact of relationship on other person: _____

_____

_____

_____

_____

Analyzing Your Relationships

After you have completed the Relationship Chart on the six people from your list, read what you have written. The purpose of this analysis is to observe any patterns or trends in both your constructive and problematic relationships. As you consider the questions listed here, jot down in your notebook any thoughts or observations you may have.

First, focus on yourself.

- How do your *styles* differ in your constructive and problematic relationships?

- How do your unbalanced self schemas create problems for you in your relationships?

- How does your *behavior* differ in your constructive and problematic relationships?

- How are your *feelings* different between the two kinds of relationships you described?

- How did your self schemas change in any of the relationships?

- What unbalanced schemas seem to be problematic for you in these relationships?

- How would your relationships be easier if you had more balanced self schemas?

- What characteristics in other people tend to evoke your balanced self schemas?

- What is it about other people that seems to trigger your unbalanced schemas?

- Do you have role or person schemas that cause you to react to other people differently?

- Are these role or person schemas balanced, negative, or hyperpositive?

- How could you balance any unbalanced role or person schemas that you have?

Next, focus on the other people in your relationships. Compare the bonding styles of the other people in the relationships that are and are not problematic for you.

- How are the people with whom you have constructive relationships similar to each other?

- What do the people with whom you have problematic relationships have in common?

- What is it about these two different groups of people that allows you to have constructive relationships with one group and troublesome relationships with the other?

- Does there seem to be a difference in the bonding styles or self schemas of the people in your problematic and constructive relationships?

- Do other people have self schemas or bonding styles that seem to trigger different schemas or bonding styles in you?

- How do their unbalanced self schemas affect other people?

- Or are they different with other people?

You have now identified which bonding styles you have in different relationships. You have also identified the bonding styles of the other people in your relationships. By systematically analyzing these relationships, you are now able to identify problematic schemas that you and other people have.

Knowing how to identify how your schemas contribute to relationship distress is essential for you to develop an effective schema change plan later. Your analysis also should help you identify whether certain self schemas in other people make it easier or harder for you to have positive relationships with them. Identifying the unbalanced self schemas of other people will make their behavior and emotions more understandable to you. Later you will see how this awareness can help you change the impact their schemas have on you.

The next two chapters will focus on how schemas are changed. In chapter 10 you will see how schemas can be changed unintentionally by various events. These disruptive events are called "schema busters," because they can challenge your schemas, and they have far-reaching effects on everyone within your different social systems. Chapter 11 will teach you how to intentionally modify your schema system. You will learn how to develop a personal schema change plan to become the person you want to be.

10

Schema Busters: Infidelity, Divorce, and Death

*Life is not a static thing. The only people who do not change
their minds are . . . in cemeteries.*

—Sen. Everett M. Dirksen, press conference,
Washington, D.C., January 1, 1965

New schemas do not develop readily, but people develop them
throughout their lives. Typically, your self schemas have existed
much longer than most of your person or role schemas, so developing new self schemas can be more difficult than developing or modifying person and role schemas. Nonetheless, you can develop new
schemas, regardless of whether they are self, person, or role schemas.

In the last chapter, Linda and her family demonstrated how significant events in people's lives can affect their schemas as well as the
schemas of other people in their social systems. Certain events, such
as infidelity, divorce, death, and health problems can be viewed as
schema busters because they are especially likely to precipitate the
development of new schemas and to affect bonding styles. However,
any major change in your life can challenge your current schemas to
incorporate those changes. When your existing schemas can't incorporate extremely discrepant information, the development of new
schemas becomes an option. The birth of a child or the inability to
have children, a disfiguring surgery or an accident, and job changes
either for better or worse are significant events that can be potential
schema busters. These events can lead to new schemas that may be
balanced or unbalanced, as you will see. This chapter analyzes a variety of potential schema busters, so that you can determine their
impact on your life.

All significant events have the potential to cause schema
changes, and many common events precipitate changes within our

social systems. These changes often reverberate unpredictably for different people in the system. For example, having balanced schemas is no guarantee that you will not develop unbalanced schemas, as you saw in chapter 9 with Linda's children, Connie and Diego. Connie and Diego had *Worthy* self schemas, but they began to develop the unbalanced schemas of *Unworthy* and *Entitled*, respectively, as a result of differential treatment by their mother. Changes in your social systems can cause new schemas to develop, weak schemas to become stronger, and strong schemas to become weaker. Some events have such a major impact on social systems that their potential to modify schemas is huge. Let's take a look at these schema busters.

Infidelity

One classic schema buster can be the discovery of a partner's infidelity. Of course, the impact of such a realization depends on the quality of the relationship and the implications of the affair, but affairs rarely have little impact. If you have always trusted your partners' loyalty and integrity, never doubted their love, and unhesitatingly confided in them over the years, the discovery will be devastating. Not only will you be reeling from their betrayal, but also from confusion and shock. In an era when infidelity can mean the transmission of deadly diseases, the potential consequences of infidelity to your life can be terrifying. Besides feeling savaged by the adulterer, you question your own judgment and wisdom: "How could I have been so blind? What was wrong with me that I didn't see what was happening?" You may vacillate between wanting to deny the reality of the situation, wanting to annihilate your partner and the other person, and wanting to destroy yourself.

Infidelity is an extremely potent schema buster. People with the balanced schemas of the Easy Bonding Style who have been blindsided by a partner's affair may change in either direction on their schema continua. Some people may move toward the hyperpositive *Intimacy Avoidant* schema, keeping a distance from any prospective partner and promising themselves that they will never put themselves in such a vulnerable position again. Those people also may develop new role schemas with a cynical view of all possible mates as deceitful. Others may move toward a negative *Intimacy Driven* schema, rushing into another relationship to reaffirm their own sense of desirability. Their still shaken sense of themselves propels them to seek premature commitments in relationships, relationships that may reveal themselves to be glaringly ill-advised with the passage of time.

Del

Del was stunned when he accidentally came across correspondence between his wife, Shirley, and another man on her church committee. When he confronted Shirley with the letters, she confessed to a two-year affair. During the next several days her recent patterns of pervasive lying were laid bare, with her numerous business and church-related trips revealed as having been sexual rendezvous while Del stayed home to care for the children. Shirley showed little remorse, blaming Del for working too much and not showing enough interest in her sexually. There were neither apologies nor assurances that the affair would end. Shirley moved into an apartment and arranged temporary visitation with the kids. Del filed for divorce.

Del had an Easy Bonding Style with Shirley, whom he had married eight years earlier. Their relationship had been exciting and fun in the beginning, but with the children came more responsibilities and less time for getaways. Del had viewed that as a natural evolution of a marriage and he had treasured the family life that he had missed as a child. In reviewing their relationship, he recalled that after their second child was born, Shirley had seemed less content—until a couple of years ago, at which time he now knew she had begun her affair. He had never doubted Shirley's word or even considered that she might be unfaithful. Suddenly he had no wife, his children would be regularly absent from his home, and his future was in turmoil because both incomes were necessary to maintain their lifestyle.

Del began to develop the schemas of the Anxious Bonding Style. He became increasingly emotionally dependent on his children, seeking reassurance that they would never leave him (*Intimacy Driven*). He interrogated the kids about their visits with their mother and alternated between angry outbursts about her sinful actions and uncontrollable sobbing, blaming himself for losing her (*Unrestrained*). He began to treat the kids, who were only five and seven, as confidants and engaged them in major decision making (*Dependent*).

He quit attending church, because he felt humiliated that the entire congregation knew about his wife's affair; he was angry with himself for not earning more money; and in his mind he blamed himself for not keeping Shirley happy (*Unworthy*). These are not atypical reactions after a revelation of infidelity or during adjustment to the dramatic changes that often result. Whether Del will develop permanent negative schemas depends on a variety of factors, but without constructive intervention, he is on the road to developing an Anxious Bonding Style that will be painful for him and his children.

Dean

An affair does not inevitably mean the end of a relationship or only negative outcomes. Frequently it can be the impetus to examine a meaningful relationship and to discover what has gone awry and fix it. Unbalanced schemas that contributed to the affair can be identified and balanced schemas can be cultivated.

Dean had *Unworthy, Intimacy Avoidant, Restrained*, and *Stubbornly Independent* self schemas. He didn't feel good about himself, was uncomfortable about emotional intimacy, had a difficult time expressing his thoughts, and was compulsively independent, always needing to appear to be in control. The relationship between Dean and Mary, his company's new receptionist, started as a friendship, chatting at work, then taking coffee breaks together, and finally escalating to a few sexual encounters at her apartment near their office. The sex wasn't any better than it had been with Shelby, his wife, but the younger woman's attention made him feel better about himself and the excitement of the affair energized him and helped him to ignore the added stress he was feeling at work and in money matters.

Shelby always had been Dean's only source of emotional support, but she had had less time for him since the birth of their children a few years earlier. Soon after Dean's affair with Mary began, Shelby sensed something was wrong and with little effort she uncovered the truth. She was distraught. Dean expressed genuine shame and remorse. Both loved each other and wanted the marriage to last.

In counseling, they addressed the issue of how Dean's unbalanced schemas had increased his vulnerability to the affair. He had been feeling increasingly incompetent in his responsibilities, which he viewed as further evidence of his inadequacy (*Unworthy*). He was unable to talk about his feelings and the shame he felt at not being able to handle his stress (*Restrained*), but he didn't want to ask for help from anyone (*Stubbornly Independent*). He kept Shelby at enough of a distance that she couldn't see how overwhelmed he was feeling (*Intimacy Avoidant*). The decrease in sexual activity between them had eliminated Dean's primary way of obtaining emotional intimacy with his wife (*Intimacy Avoidant*). Counseling addressed how his unbalanced schemas had prevented him from doing something about his issues in a constructive way with Shelby, who was devoted to him.

Dean worked on changing his behaviors and attitudes to try to develop balanced schemas that would benefit both of them. In addition, Dean and Shelby both made other changes to reestablish the primacy of their relationship, which over time became far closer than it had ever been in the past.

Personal Growth and Crises

Psychologists have long viewed crises as opportunities either for destruction or growth. A crisis always has an impact on you, positive, negative, or both. Someone with an *Unworthy* schema who has long suspected infidelity may finally leave a relationship that only reinforced a sense of inadequacy. Discovering that life is much better not living with someone who denigrates you can be liberating. Gradually, you may develop a *Worthy* schema, as a result of exposure to supportive and nonjudgmental friends and by realizing how self-serving your partner's behavior was.

If you and your partner remain together, you may develop an *Entitled* schema. If you were the one who was betrayed, you may view your needs as paramount now, if not forever. Your partner, who may feel overwhelming guilt, may buy into this arrangement initially, but over time, enormous resentment with unpredictable outcomes will ensue. Or your *Worthy* schema can be so assaulted by the discovery that you begin to doubt your desirability and blame yourself for what has happened, especially if your partner encourages that interpretation, until gradually you develop an *Unworthy* schema.

Wendy

Few people walk away unscathed by an affair, not even the third party. If you are the third party, your sense of integrity and worth can be so damaged that the development of an *Unworthy* schema seems inevitable. Consider Wendy's experience.

When she was twenty years old, while living at home, Wendy finished a draftsman program at a local junior college. She quickly found a good-paying job with advancement opportunities at an architectural firm. Her job was to assist Phil, one of the firm partners who eagerly guided her development. As they became an efficient team, Wendy enthusiastically worked long hours overtime with her boss on various projects. With Phil's support, she received several increases in pay, so she was able to afford her own apartment. Once she was living alone, however, her relationship with Phil changed.

In the evenings after they finished their work, Phil took her to romantic dinners, and confided how unhappy he was in his marriage, and how trapped he felt because of his children. Wendy idolized Phil; he was handsome, successful, kind, and respected in the firm. She was awestruck and flattered that he was interested in her. Soon enough the relationship became sexual. Phil assured her that he was going to ask his wife for a divorce, but the time was never quite right.

When Phil's wife discovered the affair, she insisted that Phil fire Wendy. Phil told Wendy he had refused to fire her, but that she would have to leave voluntarily. He said, "The architectural community is a small family. I'll give you a good reference." He warned her that if she didn't go quietly, her career would be ruined. He made additional remarks, emphasizing that no one would believe he had initiated the affair. Women were always coming on to him. His wife was a former beauty queen. They were prominent in society. Wendy was not in their league.

Wendy was filled with anguish, shame, and terror. She had always viewed herself as a moral person. She had loved Phil, believed his tales of marital woe, felt sorry for him, and believed he needed her. She had begun to imagine their life together. Now she had nothing, not even her sense of integrity. Wendy entered her relationship with Phil with balanced schemas of *Worthy*, *Intimacy Comfortable*, and *Expressive*, and a negative schema of *Dependent*. Her *Worthy* and *Intimacy Comfortable* schemas had been brutally challenged, and the seeds of the *Unworthy* and *Intimacy Avoidant* schemas had been sown.

Emotional versus Sexual Needs

Affairs are usually about emotional needs, not sexual ones, as Dean's story illustrates. Even emotional affairs that are devoid of sex create emotional damage to partners. Discovering that your partner is more emotionally invested in someone other than you is crushing, with or without sexual infidelity. The presence of both is even worse. Affairs are never benign, but the impact of an affair on all the parties depends on a variety of factors, such as the degree of emotional attachment, the level of financial and physical dependency, the existence of other supportive relationships, and the changes and amount of disruption that ensue from ending a relationship, to name only a few factors. The type and strength of your schemas will determine how you withstand such an event and whether balanced schemas rebound, unbalanced schemas become more entrenched, or new schemas emerge, balanced or unbalanced.

In Del and Shirley's case, Del's characteristic Easy Bonding Style was pushed aside by a new Anxious Bonding Style. Shirley's deceit had been so meticulous and extensive that Del was completely devastated by the discovery. Her two-year affair with another church member he knew made Del feel publicly humiliated. Her absence of remorse left him angry and bereft. Shirley's simultaneous sexual involvement with him and another man nauseated him. The upheaval in finances and child care arrangements overwhelmed him. In Del's case, the extent of deceit and the results of the discovery were so pervasive and incomprehensible that none of his bonding schemas were able to integrate the experience. Consequently, new schemas emerged—new schemas that were the negative schemas of the Anxious Bonding Style.

Del's Easy Bonding Style was not eliminated, but after this experience it became much less frequently activated. Some people still triggered his Easy style as they always had, but with anyone with whom he had a real or potentially close relationship, his new Anxious Bonding Style was evoked. Del illustrates how people can develop different styles even as adults, and that you don't erase a previous style by developing a new style. You simply change how often the previous style is active.

If you have multiple bonding styles, you have learned, whether consciously or not, to automatically discriminate between people, so that certain person schemas you have will trigger one style and other person schemas you have will trigger another style. This process is identical to what happens when children develop different bonding styles, which are triggered by different people.

In Shelby and Dean's case, Shelby also had an Easy Bonding Style prior to her discovery. Her balanced schemas also were challenged to integrate an event that was extremely discrepant from her schema expectations. However, Dean's remorse, his acceptance of responsibility for his actions, and his willingness to change made it easier for Shelby to integrate the experience into her balanced schemas eventually. Shelby also may have had stronger balanced schemas than did Del at the outset.

Shelby and Del both illustrate how various factors influence the extent of how disruptive infidelity will be to schemas. Although the focus here has been on sexual affairs, *any* act of betrayal in a trusted relationship can produce schema change if the impact is sufficiently severe. Betrayal between parents and children, siblings, friends, and colleagues are all potential schema busters. Chapter 13 will revisit betrayal, in an effort to help you resolve any acts of betrayal you have experienced or committed.

Divorce

Divorce is another major schema buster. Few people go through a divorce without experiencing some impact on their schemas, whether temporary or permanent. Although one out of two marriages currently ends in divorce, many people who experience divorce still feel stigmatized by the experience and view themselves as failures and somehow defective. Even people who leave brutally abusive spouses often feel guilty, because they failed to change their partner, they didn't leave earlier, or they made such a poor marital choice. If you did not want a relationship to end, divorce causes you to question your worth, desirability, and judgment and almost everything else about yourself. As with infidelity, divorce can cause schema change from either unbalanced to balanced schemas or balanced to unbalanced schemas.

Del illustrated how schema change can occur in the betrayed partner, but children are just as susceptible to schema change caused by infidelity and divorce. Del's seven-year-old daughter, Paige, became her father's caretaker, worrying about him, trying to comfort him when he was distraught, and dreading his anger, fearful that he might leave her, too, if she couldn't keep him happy. Paige's Easy Bonding schemas began to weaken as she developed the negative *Unworthy* schema and the hyperpositive schemas of *Intimacy Driven*, *Restrained*, and *Stubbornly Independent*. Paige blamed herself that her mother left, because she hadn't been a better daughter (*Unworthy*). She constantly sought reassurance from her father that he was not going to leave her and her younger brother, Peter, as her mother had (*Intimacy Driven*). She stopped expressing her own feelings, never showed her frustration or anger, and constantly appeased her little brother, so that her father would not become upset with them (*Restrained*). Paige tried to become self-sufficient and take care of all her father's and brother's needs, so that she and Peter would not be a burden to her father (*Stubbornly Independent*).

The needs of both Paige and Peter were neglected while their parents focused on their own needs and feelings during the divorce. Five-year-old Peter also showed schema changes, but not in the same manner as Paige. Peter developed two new styles in addition to his Easy style, one that became characteristic with Paige and another style that became characteristic with his parents. With Paige, Peter developed a new hyperpositive schema of *Entitled* and new negative schemas of *Intimacy Driven*, *Unrestrained*, and *Dependent*. The causes of Peter's new schemas are obvious. Peter now always got his way with Paige, because Paige never wanted Peter to upset their father (*Entitled*). His sister became so effective at meeting Peter's daily needs that he became increasingly dependent upon her (*Dependent*). Because Paige took such good care of him and was the only person in his family who had not emotionally abandoned him, Peter became increasingly fearful of losing her (*Intimacy Driven*). Peter also learned that his sister was extremely responsive to any emotional displays by him, so these increased (*Unrestrained*). Unfortunately, Paige often slipped into appeasing Peter's expressions of anger or frustration by bribing him, which reinforced both his *Unrestrained* and *Entitled* schemas.

With his parents, Peter developed a different style although it also included the *Entitled* and *Restrained* schemas that were present in his new style with his sister. When he was with his parents, he developed a Distant Bonding Style. Peter's mother slipped into a pattern of indulgence with him, because it made dealing with him easier and allowed her to avoid discussing her actions and choices (*Entitled*).

His father lost sight of Peter's pain and confusion about his mother's departure. His mother was so involved with her own needs that Peter was an afterthought at best. Neither parent addressed the bewilderment and grief Peter experienced at the emotional loss of both parents. Emotionally, Peter just withdrew from them, and neither responded (*Intimacy Avoidant*). His expressions of sadness, anger, and grief were ignored by his parents, and he was being encouraged by his sister not to do or say anything that would upset either parent (*Restrained*). Because both parents were now so unreliable, Peter stopped expecting much from either, and eventually no longer wanted any help or interference from either of them (*Stubbornly Independent*). So now, Peter has three bonding styles, as shown in the columns here:

Continuum	Style I	Style II	Style III
Worthiness	*Worthy*	*Entitled*	*Entitled*
Intimacy	*Intimacy Comfortable*	*Intimacy Driven*	*Intimacy Avoidant*
Expressiveness	*Expressive*	*Unrestrained*	*Restrained*
Interdependent	*Interdependent*	*Dependent*	*Stubbornly Independent*

Peter's Style I, the Easy style, had been characteristic of him in the past, but it later became quite infrequent. Eventually, his sister activated his Style II, and his parents triggered Style III, the Distant Bonding Style. In the past, his sister and parents had triggered his first style of Easy bonding. The radical changes in his family system resulted in Peter changing his person schemas of Paige and his parents, so they now triggered one of his two new styles.

After his parents broke up, Peter saw his sister, Paige, as the only person who cared about him and consistently tried to meet his needs, but sometimes she got quite disgusted with him, which worried him about whether she might abandon him, too. Peter saw both of his parents as no longer reliable or as loving as they had been in the past. In addition to Peter changing his person schemas, Paige and her father Del both changed their person schemas of Shirley in negative directions. Paige also began to see her father as emotionally unpredictable, dependent on her to assume the role his wife had left, and also as someone who might leave her, too. Paige's person schema of her brother Peter changed, as Peter changed. Paige loved her brother, but she began to see him as manipulative, clinging, and demanding.

Not only can a divorce affect your person schemas about yourself and specific other people, it also can cause changes in your role schemas. Both Paige and Peter developed new role schemas of mothers as untrustworthy and self-centered; fathers as dependent and emotionally unpredictable; marriages as resulting in painful endings. Peter's role schema of sisters as strong, reliant, dependable, and loving was strengthened, but now it evolved to seeing sisters as almost omnipotent. Paige began to develop a role schema of brothers as still lovable but also as burdensome, emotionally demanding, and manipulative. Her emerging role schema of men viewed them as self-centered, manipulative, and needy. You can imagine what kind of impact these new role schemas could have in their future relationships as well as in their current ones.

The Development of New Schemas

Psychologists don't know how long it takes to develop new schemas, but there seems to be a period of initial instability. If more evidence continues to support the new schemas, those schemas become more developed, stronger, and more likely to survive. For example, if Del had sought counseling quickly after Shirley moved out, he might have been able to work through his grief and distress by understanding how this situation came to be and he might have learned how to better manage his loss. This realization then might have allowed him to incorporate the entire event into his Easy Bonding schemas.

If that had happened, his role schemas also might not have taken a major negative shift, although his person schema of Shirley certainly would still have been changed. Hence, his Anxious Bonding Style schemas would have diminished in the absence of further evidence to support them. His Easy Bonding Style would have become more prominent again. He would have stopped being overly reliant on his daughter and become more supportive of both of his children, reverting to his previous way of interacting with them. These changes would then have allowed Paige and Peter to shift back into their former interaction patterns, and their Easy Bonding Styles would have become characteristic of their interactions with each other and their father once again. Their interactions with their mother would still have shifted, but how much they shifted would depend on her behavior. If her behavior remained quite discrepant from how she previously was with them, Paige and Peter may have still demonstrated schema changes, but the new schemas would have been primarily limited to their interactions with their mother.

There are three major points to understand from this discussion of Del and his children.

- First, developing new schemas is not an instantaneous process. Some amount of time is required for newly developed schemas to become stabilized.

- Second, some amount of evidence is required to support the new schemas, but if there is sufficient contradictory evidence during their development, the schemas are unlikely to survive because they won't fit that person's reality. In other words, if new schemas don't help you make sense of your world, they will disappear.

- Third, even if new schemas are developed, how frequently they are activated will depend on how many situations trigger them. If Del had sought counseling in time to keep his children from developing new negative schemas, both Paige and Peter might have developed new schemas to form a different bonding style in their interactions with their mother. Those styles might have been limited to interactions only with their mother and not necessarily generalized to other adult females. In other words, the children's new schemas for their mother would not necessarily be generalized to include their aunts or schoolteachers. Only certain women who reminded the children of their mother might trigger those same styles.

Dating

Dating after a divorce can be another major influence on schema development. The behavior of the people whom the divorcees date certainly can influence their schemas, as well as influencing the schemas of their children. The new person would form a new social system with the divorced partner and his or her children, and thus everyone's behavior will have an effect on everyone else within that system.

When Del started dating Joan, a woman with no children, Paige and Peter had different reactions. Paige was eager to welcome another mother, but she was also apprehensive about being abandoned again. She was overly accommodating to Joan, not wanting to alienate her in any way. Paige's new bonding style of *Unworthy*, *Intimacy Driven*, *Restrained*, and *Stubbornly Independent* were activated, because Joan was another potential mother and Paige wanted her to stay with her family and take care of them. On the other hand, Peter kept Joan at bay. Joan triggered his new Distant Bonding Style, just as his own mother did. He had learned he couldn't trust mothers and was not about to be pulled back into that kind of relationship. Why invest in another mother who also might abandon him?

Fortunately, Joan had an Easy Bonding Style and she understood what had happened to both children. She helped Del and Paige shift the adult responsibilities of the family back to Del. She didn't take Peter's distance personally and reached out to him without being intrusive. Gradually, both children got to know Joan and discovered that they could trust her not to leave even when they misbehaved. Over time, both kids shifted to Easy Bonding Styles with her. Had Joan had an Anxious or Distant style, the problems already developing would have been exacerbated.

For example, an Anxious style would have made it hard for Joan to restrain herself from pushing too hard to develop closeness too quickly. She would have been more inclined to take Peter's distance personally, and would have reacted with hurt feelings or possibly pushed even harder. If Joan had had a Distant style, she would have been likely to withdraw from Paige's efforts at immediate closeness, and she would have been comfortable with Peter's distance, and unlikely to reach out to him. So, you can see how dating relationships after a divorce can influence the schema formation and bonding styles of everyone involved.

Health Problems

An illness in any family member affects all family members. Illnesses typically require adjustments in other family members to varying degrees. Some people accommodate those adjustments more easily than others. In chapter 8, Rick illustrated the unbalanced hyperpositive schemas of the Distant Bonding Style. His wife, Julie, made their relationship work by meeting all of his needs and seldom requiring help with child care or household tasks even though she also worked full-time. However, when her rheumatoid arthritis prevented her from continuing those tasks, their relationship became strained because Rick was asked to assume some of Julie's responsibilities, which was inconsistent with his *Entitled* schema. Furthermore, Julie always had been healthy and had never viewed herself as needing a lot of emotional support. But Rick's apparent indifference to her pain and obvious anger about her newly diagnosed illness made his *Intimacy Avoidant* schema become glaringly obvious and caused her to begin to reevaluate their relationship.

Not only can illnesses disrupt relationship balances, they also can produce changes in schemas. As you saw in chapter 9 with Diego's diagnosis of asthma, illness can produce significant changes in schemas in the person with the illness and in others within that person's social systems. In Diego's case, his preferential treatment began to develop a hyperpositive *Entitled* schema in him and a negative *Unworthy* schema in his sister.

Chronic illnesses may cause unbalanced schemas that are either negative or hyperpositive. Those with serious acute or chronic illnesses may develop *Unworthy* schemas, because they begin to view themselves as somehow defective and perhaps as a burden to others. This is particularly so if their illness produces significant strain on a family's finances or necessitates major changes in the way the family functions.

Seriously ill people also can develop negative *Dependent* schemas, if their survival depends on the increasing care and support of others. In contrast, some people who are seriously ill may develop or strengthen their hyperpositive *Stubbornly Independent* schemas in an effort to avoid burdening others. In spite of compromising their well-being, they may struggle mightily to remain independent and not to have to request assistance or be dependent on anyone for anything.

Unbalanced schemas on the *Intimacy* continuum also can be affected. The demands of an illness can make people fearful that others will abandon them now that they require so much care, or are not who they were at the beginning of the relationship. This can result in the germination or enhancement of the negative *Intimacy Driven* schemas. Such people may fear, and not necessarily unrealistically, that they will be abandoned and they begin to seek frequent reassurance that other people will not leave them. In contrast, other seriously ill people may develop hyperpositive *Intimacy Avoidant* schemas, assuming that others will view them negatively if they have a physical impairment. They may begin to keep others at a distance in an effort to hide their physical problems.

The impact of illness on individuals and their families depends on the severity of the illness and the adjustments and accommodations necessitated by it. However, those with more balanced schemas can accommodate change more easily than those with the unbalanced schemas. Thus, sometimes even a minor illness or limited demands can strain a relationship when one person has strong unbalanced schemas, as demonstrated by Rick. In his case, the demands were significant, but one could safely predict that he would resent any demands.

Death

Clearly, death can have a major impact on the survivors' schemas. The circumstances of a death, its suddenness, and the role of that person in your life will influence the effect of a death on you. The death of a parent when you are a child likely will have a different impact than if you are a middle-aged adult. Your self schemas also can influence the impact of a death.

For example, Thelma and Harry had been married for fifty-three years when he had a fatal heart attack. Harry had had the Easy Bonding balanced schemas. Thelma had balanced schemas of *Worthy*, *Intimacy Comfortable*, and *Expressive* schemas and unbalanced schemas of *Dependent* and *Unworthy*.

Harry and Thelma had married the summer after Thelma's graduation from high school. They had assumed traditional roles agreeably, with Harry as the breadwinner, handling all financial and insurance matters, and the primary decision maker. Thelma had taken primary responsibility for raising their four children and for meals and house care. This certainly is not meant to imply that every woman in a traditional role has a *Dependent* schema, but Thelma had entered the relationship with one. The marital arrangement Harry and she developed prevented the schema from being particularly problematic. When the children grew up and left home, Harry and Thelma did almost all of their activities together, from grocery shopping to antique hunting. Both had viewed their marriage as a happy, fulfilling relationship.

When Harry died suddenly, Thelma was forced to confront her *Dependent* schema at the same time that she was struggling with her grief over the loss of her lifetime partner. Being dependent on Harry for many things had been comfortable for both of them, but now Thelma was thrust into responsibilities for which she had minimal or no experience. Her sense of being overwhelmed intensified her anguish over Harry's death. Her diabetes became unstable, she had difficulty sleeping, and she slipped into a clinical depression. As a child in an impoverished family, Thelma had had an *Unworthy* schema when she first met Harry. Over the years Harry's respect and admiration for her had been the primary catalyst in Thelma developing a strong *Worthy* schema. The loss of Harry's support and her shame of being so overwhelmed by new responsibilities reactivated her *Unworthy* schema, which further exacerbated her depression.

Thelma's history illustrates how people can have unbalanced schemas and still maintain satisfying relationships. However, the loss of a relationship can precipitate greater distress for those with unbalanced schemas because their problems then can become apparent. Furthermore, Harry had had no history of heart problems, so neither had addressed the need for Thelma to become more competent at his tasks. Both had assumed that Harry would outlive Thelma because of her diabetes.

As you can see in Thelma's case, unbalanced schemas make people more vulnerable to greater distress when they must deal with the death of a loved one. Unfortunately, even balanced schemas do not prevent schema shifts from occurring as a consequence of the death of someone close to you.

As a young child, Bobby had the balanced schemas of the Easy Bonding Style. But when he was nine, his dad died of cancer. For the previous eighteen months his father had gradually lost a great deal of weight and had become weaker and weaker, especially during the last few weeks. Bobby's parents told him that his dad's increasing feebleness was due to the chemotherapy that was going to cure him. So, Bobby was sure that his dad would recover in spite of how ill he was.

One afternoon his mother sent Bobby to the neighbors' house. When he was allowed to return home, his grandmother told him his dad was in heaven. Bobby thought she was kidding . . . until he saw his dad's body on the bed, his eyes wide open, his skin cold to the touch. His mother and older brother were sobbing. His two-year-old sister was playing with her toys on the floor in the living room, seemingly unaware.

For many nights Bobby cried himself to sleep. He missed his dad so much. His dad had wrestled with him in the evenings and played catch and rode bikes with him on the weekends. His dad had been funny and always made his mom laugh. After his dad died, his mom never laughed. She cried most of the time. His older brother seemed angry all the time. Bobby learned to stay out of his brother's way. His little sister, whom he loved, spent most of her time at his aunt's house.

About a month after his dad's death, the family had to move to an apartment in a poorer neighborhood. Bobby didn't know any of the kids at his new school and he spent most recesses standing alone by a tree. He began to hate school and usually didn't do his homework. Nobody noticed when he did. Bobby was in sixth grade, his first year of middle school. "Hate" does not even describe the way he felt about school now. He had no friends, but there were more kids who picked on him, teasing him for being fat, for wearing glasses, for dressing in clothes too big that had once been his brother's.

He started skipping school. He left home in the morning and then sneaked back after he knew his mom and brother were gone. He crawled in through the window to his room and spent all day there, watching television and eating. He drew pictures of what he would like to do to all the kids who teased him, to the teachers who scolded him for not turning in his homework, to his brother who was so mean to him. Maybe someday he could get even with them. For the time being, it was good enough just to be away from them.

The death of a loved one can precipitate the development of unbalanced schemas, especially in young people. However, the changes may really be signs of depression, not a permanent style change. Bobby had withdrawn into himself and no one tried to reach in after him and pull him back. He was angry, depressed, and alone. The person he loved the most in the world had died. His mother essentially disappeared into her own grief, only reappearing to yell at him about something. Inevitably, Bobby began to develop the schemas of *Unworthy, Intimacy Avoidant,* and *Restrained.*

One day the school contacted Bobby's mother and told her about the absences. When she confronted Bobby about it, she suddenly saw how miserable he was, and she remembered how he had always loved school before his father died. He had done his homework eagerly, and proudly showed his parents what he had learned every day. He had been happy and well liked by the other kids. He had always been a little chubby, but had been a high energy boy who engaged in lots of physical activities with his dad. Now she realized that he had become so heavy that almost any physical activity was difficult for him. He sat around in his room or on the couch and snacked almost continuously. The Bobby she had known had disappeared.

The next day Bobby's mom arranged for him to be seen at a mental health clinic. The counselor told her that Bobby was depressed. Bobby needed counseling to work through his grief and all the subsequent losses and changes attached to that. After several weeks of counseling, Bobby's mom began to see glimmers of the funny little boy Bobby had been. About six weeks later, the counselor began to see the family together. Over the next two months Bobby's depression disappeared. His whole family began to readjust to their loss and to change the destructive interactions among them that had begun to develop. Bobby was lucky to have a mom who was able to rescue him from this slide, even though she was still dealing with her own agony. By addressing all the changes that had taken place in the family's life, the family counseling prevented Bobby from developing a permanent change in his bonding schemas.

The powerful impact of a death can precipitate a variety of schema changes. The painful loss of a loved one can result in someone developing a hyperpositive *Intimacy Avoidant* schema to avoid ever experiencing such pain again. On the other hand, having experienced such a loss, some people become terrified of abandonment and require repeated reassurance that they will not be left again, thus developing a negative *Intimacy Driven* schema. If a person is treated with kid gloves and granted special privileges for a substantial time after a death, that person may develop a hyperpositive *Entitled* schema. If a death precipitates an array of negative losses in a person's life and a drop in status, as with Bobby, a negative *Unworthy* schema may evolve. Experiencing a death does not lead inevitably to the development of unbalanced schemas, but certainly the consequences of a death must be addressed to prevent that very thing.

Other Busters: Parenthood, Infertility, and Disfigurement

Any significant positive or negative event can produce schema changes. Remember Lindsay from chapter 1 who had such a negative role schema of mothers? Unexpectedly, Lindsay found herself unhappily pregnant. She did not want to become the kind of person her role schema of mothers described, but her husband was so pleased about the prospect of a baby that she could not even broach the subject of terminating the pregnancy. With great trepidation and sadness, Lindsay went through an uneventful pregnancy that produced a healthy baby girl. Although unsure of her maternal abilities, Lindsay was surprised at how much pleasure she derived from her new daughter so quickly. She found she enjoyed taking care of the baby's needs and felt a new contentment in being able to comfort and care for her.

Over the next few years Lindsay experienced several schema changes. She developed a new role schema of mothers as happy, nurturing, competent, and loving, a reflection of the type of mother she had become and of several mothers she had met in her daughter's play group. Lindsay developed a new role schema of children as lovable, responsive, entertaining, dependent, malleable, and vulnerable. Whereas she had always had an *Unworthy* self schema, she now developed a new *Worthy* self schema. Her newly discovered nurturing abilities made her more confident about her own worth.

In addition, Lindsay's experience with her own daughter made her realize how unrealistic her mother had been with her when she was a child. Her mother's criticisms and hurtful comments had made Lindsay feel undeserving and inferior. She realized that she had not been a bad child. She was not inferior. She simply had been a child, but her mother had been unable to grasp that. As Lindsay began to view her child self differently, and her adult self as a competent, nurturing mother, her *Worthy* schema grew stronger. Numerous positive schema changes resulted from the birth of her daughter, which initially she had viewed as an ominous event.

Another challenge to schemas can include the inability to have children. This circumstance can affect your self, person, and role schemas. If you have been identified as having a physical inability to reproduce, you may begin to develop an *Unworthy* schema because you may now view yourself as defective. If your partner has been identified with the problem, your person schema of your partner may change to someone who is impaired. And if the infertility problem is a result of contributing factors from both of you, you may see yourselves as a defective and inadequate couple.

Whether such an unhappy outcome happens depends on many factors, including how much your schemas base their worth on being able to reproduce. If your image of yourself is based primarily on being a parent, the loss of that possibility may shatter your sense of who you are. On the other hand, people who are unable to have children often invest in other caregiving activities, which satisfies their nurturing needs, produces much pleasure in the aid they provide to others, constructively connects them to other people, and reaffirms their self-worth.

Disfiguring accidents or surgeries, such as mastectomies or amputations, can impact schemas on the *Worthiness* continuum in a similar way to infertility, generating painful *Unworthy* schemas. But unwanted, dreadful events do not inevitably produce negative schema effects. Often they can produce positive schema changes. For example, the loss of a major basis of your self-worth, such as your appearance or your ability to reproduce, can force you to reconsider how you evaluate worth and might push you to expand your views of what makes someone worthwhile.

Whether events produce negative or positive schema changes depends on a variety of factors, including the person's current schemas, their personal vulnerabilities, their support systems, and other circumstances, such as financial stability, health, and so forth. The impact of any event also depends on what Chaos Theory recognizes as the presence of certain random influences in all of our lives, that which we usually call fate.

Although there are many predictable patterns in nature, yourself, and others, there are also a number of unpredictable events that may have a daily impact on your life. Sometimes random events, such as a stroke or a tornado, can be devastating by themselves, while others are distressing only when they occur simultaneously with other stressors. When several stressful events occur in close proximity, your resources may be stretched too thin to absorb them all, making you more vulnerable than you normally are. Some events are almost always potential schema busters, but the impact of other events may depend on timing.

Identifying Your Schema Busters

Go back to chapter 3 and review your bonding self schemas. What self schema changes have you made over the years? Schema strength refers to frequency, intensity, or both. A schema can be viewed as strong because it occurs frequently. A schema also can be considered strong if it occurs infrequently, but is very intense when it does manifest. For example, you may have the balanced *Intimacy Comfortable* schema with nearly everyone, but whenever you are around a former partner who betrayed you, you flip to the *Intimacy Avoidant* schema.

In the chart below indicate which of your self schemas have changed during your lifetime. In the space beside the schema name, put a "W" if a self schema has become weaker in intensity or in frequency. If a self schema is stronger in intensity or frequency, mark it with an "S." Put an "N" if you think the self schema is new and you don't remember it existing when you were younger.

Continuum	Negative	Balanced	Hyperpositive
Worthiness	__ Unworthy	__ Worthy	__ Entitled
Intimacy	__ Intimacy Driven	__ Intimacy Comfortable	__ Intimacy Avoidant
Expressiveness	__ Unrestrained	__ Expressive	__ Restrained
Interdependent	__ Dependent	__ Inter-dependent	__ Stubbornly Independent

Schemas don't just appear or disappear randomly. Changes in your life cause schema changes. In the chart below, list your schemas that have changed and describe what you think the factors were that contributed to those changes. Sometimes the causes are obvious, such as the schema busters described in this chapter. However, sometimes the causes are less apparent. For example, perhaps you have noticed that you developed a new *Expressive* schema some time ago and that your *Restrained* schema is now weaker, seldom being triggered.

In thinking about two such changes, you may remember that your *Expressive* schema seemed to emerge after you were promoted to your first management position and had completed a management training program on effective communication. Over the years you may have applied those techniques in your work and personal life, as well as having read numerous books on that subject. You may think that these factors greatly contributed to the development of that schema. Your response would look like the example below.

Schemas Changed: Likely Causes or Influences of Schema Changes

Expressive: Developed after began communication training and from reading books.
Girlfriend Lori (now wife) reinforced my efforts to communicate more.

Restrained: Weakened after learned how to express myself more clearly and directly.

You also can list person and role schemas that have changed. For example, Del would describe a new person schema of his ex-wife Shirley, as a result of her deceitfulness. Lindsay would describe a new role schema of mothers as loving, nurturing women as a result of her experiences with her baby. On the lines below, or in your notebook, list your schema changes and what you think contributed to those changes.

Schemas Changed: Likely Causes or Influences of Schema Changes

_____

_____

_____

_____

_____

_____

_____

Identifying Their Schema Busters

Try to do this same exercise for the people who you listed as important in your life in chapter 1. First, for schemas that you think have changed in them, indicate in the chart whether, to your knowledge, their schemas became weaker ("W"), stronger ("S"), or are new ("N"). Then, list those changed schemas and describe what you think were the contributing factors to those changes. Remember to also list any person or role schemas that you think have changed. Think about what schema busters or other more subtle influences could have been involved in their schema changes. With some of the people on your list you probably won't know this kind of information, but you most likely will for at least a few of them.

Name of Other Person: _____

Continuum	Negative	Balanced	Hyperpositive
Worthiness	__ Unworthy	__ Worthy	__ Entitled
Intimacy	__ Intimacy Driven	__ Intimacy Comfortable	__ Intimacy Avoidant
Expressiveness	__ Unrestrained	__ Expressive	__ Restrained
Interdependent	__ Dependent	__ Inter- dependent	__ Stubbornly Independent

Schemas Changed: Likely Causes or Influences of Their Schema Changes

_____

_____

_____

_____

_____

Name of Other Person: _____

Continuum	Negative	Balanced	Hyperpositive
Worthiness	__ Unworthy	__ Worthy	__ Entitled
Intimacy	__ Intimacy Driven	__ Intimacy Comfortable	__ Intimacy Avoidant
Expressiveness	__ Unrestrained	__ Expressive	__ Restrained
Interdependent	__ Dependent	__ Inter-dependent	__ Stubbornly Independent

Schemas Changed: Likely Causes or Influences of Their Schema Changes

_____

_____

_____

_____

_____

_____

_____

This exercise has several purposes. One is to make you aware of how schema change is possible. If schema change can occur unintentionally, certainly it can also take place intentionally. Your past schema changes of yourself and others provide evidence that you will be able to change your schemas.

Another purpose of the exercise is to make you aware of schema changes in yourself and others that have been harmful. This recognition can enhance your understanding of your relationship problems. With this awareness you have a choice: whether to modify your unbalanced schemas and reawaken other less active balanced schemas or to allow matters to remain as they are.

11

Becoming the Person You Want to Be

*All of my relationships would go smoothly if I always could
be the person my dogs think I am.*

Schema busters are events that often shift schemas unintentionally. In this chapter you will discover how to make intentional changes in your schema system. You will find various ways to inhibit your problematic unbalanced schemas and to develop new balanced schemas. After reading about the different strategies to change schemas, you can select which strategies seem most relevant for you. Your choices will depend on your particular problematic schemas. By the end of this chapter, you will be able to develop a personalized schema change plan to meet your goals.

Building Balanced Schemas

Based on your analysis of your relationships, you have identified which of your schemas are causing you problems. Before you select which schemas to modify first, read through the suggestions for changing schemas. Some schemas may seem easier for you to change than others, so you may want to start your changes with those. Remember, people often have both negative and hyperpositive schemas on the same continuum, and they can flip between them. In those cases, you will be trying to build a balanced schema in the middle. For example, if you switch between the negative *Unworthy* and hyperpositive *Entitled* schemas, you will be trying to replace each with the same balanced *Worthy* schema.

Building a Worthy Self Schema

A *Worthy* self schema will allow you to treat yourself with respect and compassion without demeaning or neglecting others. You will be able to value yourself as you are even if you are trying to change. You will be able to enjoy the success of others without feeling envious or inadequate.

Shifting from *Unworthy* to *Worthy*

Be fair to yourself. People with an *Unworthy* schema usually can identify some—if not many—other people whom they view as worthwhile. However, they seem to have two different sets of criteria for worth: one set for others and one set for themselves. If this is descriptive of you, then first you need to level the playing field by creating one model of worth that you can apply to everyone, including yourself.

What do parents tell their children when they send them off to their first day of preschool? "Be kind. Be nice. Play with everyone. Share. Tell the truth. And pick up after yourself." These instructions include important ideas about the qualities most people think constitute a worthwhile human being: kindness, compassion, acceptance, generosity, trustworthiness, and thoughtfulness.

The *Unworthy* schema often causes people to think that they must do something special to be worthwhile. However, being attractive, wealthy, talented, or famous are not prerequisites for being worthwhile. Those attributes may draw attention to you, but they don't make you any more worthwhile than anyone else. If a mega-rich movie star donates $100,000 of a multimillion dollar salary to a charity, is that a greater contribution than a mother on welfare who gives her second sweater to a neighbor who has none? Both are generous acts. The amount does not make one more worthwhile than the other. Anyone can be kind, compassionate, accepting, generous, trustworthy, and thoughtful. What else are you insisting of yourself to be deemed worthy? Do other people have to meet those same standards?

To develop a *Worthy* schema, you need to know how you are evaluating worth, so do this next exercise to find out how you do evaluate it. To determine the criteria in your model for worthiness, take out your separate notebook and on a fresh page, list the names of those whom you think are worthy people. For each person, describe the qualities you think make them worthwhile. Next, on a new page, write "Model" at the top and then list the qualities that all the people on your list share. This would be your model of your criteria for worthiness. Note that if you have extraordinary qualities listed, which you or most could *never* develop, such as the ability to win the Nobel prize, then those are not legitimate qualities of worthiness. Qualities of human worthiness must be possibilities for everyone and cannot require special talents or attributes.

Do what will help you respect yourself more. For each of your worthiness qualities, provide examples of how you have them or how you don't. If there are qualities on the list that you think you do not have, then figure out what you need to do to develop those qualities. For example, perhaps you think you are not trustworthy because you have often betrayed confidences. You can change this. If you think you can't keep a secret, then ask the person not to tell you the secret for that reason. If you think you can, then when you are tempted to break your promise, vividly picture how the other person would react if you were to reveal that confidential information. If you want to tell someone else, force yourself to call the person who trusted you with the secret to get permission before you do so. Each time, ask yourself how you would benefit from your betrayal, and conjure up an image of how ashamed you felt in the past when you repeated a confidence that you had been requested to keep secret. The point is that if you really believe you don't have a quality essential for feeling you are a worthy person, then develop it. Simply berating yourself won't change anything, except to strengthen your sense of unworthiness. Incidentally, *trying* to be a better person is a quality of worthiness that you could add to your model.

Stop doing things you disrespect. What is it about yourself that you think is so bad? Is there something you have done or something you are doing that makes you unworthy? If you are doing or not doing something that generates feelings of unworthiness, write down what those things are. What actions would you need to take to change this? With a serious problem, you may need professional guidance to help you make lasting changes. With milder issues, you can make changes on your own, but probably you can benefit from a support person. Find someone who you trust and respect to help you set realistic change goals and to support your efforts to change.

Maybe you think you are not a good enough parent. If that is the case, in your notebook make a list of what you (or anyone) needs to do to be an adequate (not great) parent. Put checkmarks by the constructive things you are doing, and remind yourself that these behaviors make you worthy. Figure out how you could do some of the things that you are not currently doing and start doing them. Simply taking some steps to change is an act of worthiness.

Shame often prevents people from seeing themselves as worthwhile. If you are engaging in activities of which you are ashamed, you will need to stop. If you need help to stop, then get it. If your shame is about an act from the past, then you will need to forgive yourself to free yourself from your *Unworthy* schema. If so, then you will want to read about forgiveness in chapter 13. If you feel ashamed of attributes or actions of your family, the section on forgiveness and acceptance in chapter 13 will be helpful for that, too.

Treat yourself and others better. People with *Unworthy* schemas often are mercilessly critical of themselves and frequently of others, as well. They feel so bad about themselves that acknowledging anything good about someone else makes them feel more worthless. People with an *Unworthy* schema usually treat themselves quite shabbily if not outright cruelly. They need to stop treating themselves and others so harshly. Stop using black-and-white thinking. People don't have to reach a particular threshold of goodness to be worthy. Trying to be a better person is an act of worthiness. Stop allowing yourself to say or think hateful things about yourself or others. Focus on your positives rather than dwelling on your shortcomings. Do the same with others. Do something nice for yourself every day, whether it is letting yourself sleep twenty minutes longer or watching a television show you enjoy. You have to stop being mean to yourself and become the best friend you always wanted. People with a *Worthy* schema are kind to themselves and others.

Be assertive. Unworthy people often tend either to be nonassertive or aggressive or vacillate between the two. Assertive behavior is hard for someone who has an *Unworthy* schema. How can you stand up for yourself if you feel so worthless that you deserve no respect? If you are nonassertive, you often allow other people to disrespect you until you reach a point where you explode aggressively, then feel ashamed, and retreat into nonassertiveness again. If you are aggressive, you are usually angry and anticipating disrespect or nastiness from others, not realizing that you are instigating most of it. If you want people to treat you with respect, you have to treat yourself and others with respect. Assertive behavior is respectful behavior that respects your rights and the rights of others. Learning to be assertive will help you shift to a *Worthy* schema. You will find the suggestions in this chapter and chapter 12 for changing the *Restrained* and *Unrestrained* schemas helpful. You also can benefit by reading Alberti and Emmon's *Your Perfect Right* (1995). This is an easily understood presentation of how to be assertive instead of aggressive or nonassertive. Assertive training programs might also be helpful.

Shifting from *Entitled* to *Worthy*

Develop empathy. Learn to see the world through the eyes of other people. You can do this by observing different people in various settings who seem less fortunate than you. Think about what their lives may be like. What is it like to be elderly and have to drive in congested traffic, not be able to hear, have to use a walker, or spend most of the time alone? Imagine what it is like to be a single parent and never have anyone with whom to share responsibilities, to have to ration your use of air-conditioning or heating oil because you can't afford to use them all the time, to not be able to afford medical care, or to know that your family will experience financial disaster with any unexpected expense. What is it like to be restricted to a wheelchair, never able to go anywhere without first figuring out routes that literally won't stop you in your tracks, and have to drive around parking lots looking for spaces to accommodate your wheelchair because some entitled person who was perfectly healthy parked in the only handicapped space in the lot? What is it like to be blind and never see the faces of the people you love or watch your children grow up? What is it like to not be able to speak English well and have other people treat you with disdain when you can't understand them?

How would your life change if you were paralyzed, blinded, brain damaged, or burned beyond recognition? How would these factors affect your freedom, your relationships, your job opportunities, or your recreational pursuits? The point of this exercise is to help you develop empathy by learning to see the world through the eyes of those less fortunate, and to gain compassion for those who have obstacles to overcome every day just meeting their routine needs. As you pay more attention to other people, avoid finding ways to blame them for their plight. When you are thinking critical thoughts about other people, stop and imagine what it must be like to be them. Try to make these kinds of observations whenever you go anywhere. This process will help you to pay more attention to others and to develop a less judgmental attitude.

Treat everyone with respect. Pay attention to the way you treat other people, especially anyone who you view as inferior. Think about how you treat store clerks, secretaries, or service people who come to your home. Do you look through them as if they are not even there? Do you treat them differently than you do people you deem equal or superior to you? Does your voice, attitude, or manner differ between those two groups? If so, work on treating people in the first group the same as you do people in the second. Don't allow yourself to use an arrogant, condescending tone with anyone. Don't act as if others are incompetent. Most people are doing the best they can. They don't need any grief from you. Maybe they aren't as smart or clever as you are, but that does not mean they are worth any less. You might be surprised to realize that when you treat store clerks rudely, observers think you are the jerk, not the store clerk. People tend to identify with the person being humiliated, not the person who is doing the humiliating. Changing the way you treat the *least* powerful people you know can be a major step toward developing a *Worthy* schema and developing the respect that you may mistakenly think you already have.

Elevate the needs of others. A *Worthy* schema views the needs of others as important as one's own. An *Entitled* schema views your needs as more important than those of other people and is a primary reason people with *Entitled* schemas are seen as selfish. If you want to develop a *Worthy* schema, you will need to pay as much attention to the needs of others as you have been paying to your own.

Now, on a fresh page in your notebook, list the people with whom you have regular contact. For every one of them, identify something that you could do that would please them. Preferably, these should be acts, not gifts. Smiling and saying hello to the receptionist, calling a relative to talk for a while, offering to run an errand for someone, or cleaning the kitchen after dinner are examples of the kind of acts that are responses to others' needs. Then, start systematically performing the acts on your list. Pay attention to how the recipient reacts. Your only goal is to produce some amount of pleasure in that person's day. You are not trying to generate a positive act in return or even a thank-you. If you tell your partner that you will clean up the kitchen after dinner if you do not have to do the laundry, that does not count. That is negotiating to get what you want in exchange for something. Negotiation is a good process to meet the needs of each other, but this exercise is to help you focus solely on meeting the needs of someone else with no expectation of anything in return. Your goal is to learn to experience the pleasure that comes from truly altruistic acts. Other ways to meet this goal are to become a volunteer or to make charitable donations anonymously.

Learn to concede graciously. If you have the *Entitled* schema, you usually expect to have your way. Review the last few days and think about how many times you got your way in your interactions. Did you go to dinner at the restaurant you wanted, to the movie you preferred, or did others change their schedules or preferences to accommodate you? Do you expect others to do things in your time frame? Do you get annoyed if anyone keeps you waiting? Do others usually have to wait for you? When you play a game, do you have to win?

Do you get angry at your teammates if they don't play as well as you expect? Do you always have to be right? If you have an *Entitled* schema, the answer to most of these questions is yes.

Try to imagine how it feels to live with someone who never lets you have your way without sulking, getting angry, or expecting a favor in return. Imagine how it feels to never win at anything or ever be right. How would it feel to always be second best? That wouldn't feel too good, would it? And it doesn't for the people who experience that with you either. Contrary to the impression you think you make, people are not awestruck by you. They often feel annoyed by your need to feel superior and may not enjoy being around you. To create a *Worthy* schema, start giving in on choices that are not important. That includes restaurants, movies, and what time you go to church. Don't turn games or discussions into exercises to demonstrate your superiority. Praise other people for their skill or effort. Acknowledge other people's ideas. Admit when you are wrong. Making other people feel good about themselves does not diminish you in their eyes. Indeed, it usually does the opposite.

Learn to discriminate between your desires and needs. Entitled people tend to view their desires as essential needs: season tickets for football, a motor boat, expensive clothes, luxury cars, fine jewelry, and so forth. You may have come to see such things as essential for your happiness, but these are luxuries, not needs. Neither your breathing nor your heart will be impaired if you have none of those things. They are not needs.

Write down all the things that are important to you. Then go back and identify which are needs and which are luxuries. Living in a $150,000 house is a luxury. Having a roach-free apartment in a safe neighborhood may be a need. Driving an expensive car is a luxury. Having a reliable car that doesn't break down frequently may be a need. After you have made your list, think about how often you become upset because of not getting your *needs* met? How often do you get upset by not getting the *luxuries* on your list? Is your reaction often out of proportion? How dramatically would your life change if you didn't have tickets to the symphony, had to give up your boat, shop at less expensive stores, couldn't eat at expensive restaurants, or didn't win at games? Would it change the way your friends treat you? If so, you may be surrounded by other entitled people who will disappear in a heartbeat if your fortunes change.

In the future when you are upset, ask yourself, "Why is it so awful if I can't have this? . . . if I lose this game? . . . if I am wrong? . . . if I have to eat something I don't relish? . . . if I see a movie someone else prefers? . . . if I have to wait for someone else? . . . if someone else has something I don't have? . . . if I have to change my plans?" The key word here is "awful." Not getting what you want is usually not awful. It may be boring, inconvenient, or disappointing, but seldom is it truly awful. Stop acting as if it is. That reaction makes you feel far worse than the situation does. Your elevated expectation that you must always get your way is what causes the reaction, not the actual situation. When you are upset because your sense of entitlement is not met, remind yourself of the people you have been observing who must get by on far less than you do. Would this be a big deal to them?

Building an Intimacy Comfortable Self Schema

An *Intimacy Comfortable* self schema will allow you to be comfortable being yourself with others. You will be able to give your love to others without wanting to possess them. When relationships end, you will be able to rebound eventually and have other meaningful close relationships.

Shifting from *Intimacy Driven* to *Intimacy Comfortable*

Recognize when you feel threatened. What emotional management strategies did you discover in chapter 7 under "Assessing Your Anxious Bonding Strategies" that applied to you? When you use those strategies, you will find the *Intimacy Driven* schema lurking nearby. With an *Intimacy Driven* schema, destructive and often controlling strategies are frequently triggered by the fear of being excluded or abandoned.

When you feel threatened, remind yourself of the ways in which the other person has been trustworthy. Visualize positive images of that person. Don't let your mind dwell on upsetting, imaginary images. If the other person's plans change, remind yourself that there probably is a reasonable explanation. Practice giving others the benefit of the doubt. Don't readily attribute negative motives or deceitful actions to them. Instead of looking for signs of abandonment or rejection, start a list of what different people do to show that they care about you. Add to this list on a daily basis. Use that information to create positive images to replace your negative ones. Then focus on those positive and realistic images whenever you feel threatened by abandonment or betrayal.

Don't demand that others care only about you. Remind yourself that everybody can care about more than one person. If someone shows affection or concern for someone else, that does not mean there has to be a simultaneous decrease in that person's feelings for you. For example, if your children love your ex-partner, that does not make them less able to love you. Whether they love you or not depends on you. The *Intimacy Driven* schema readily fosters jealousy. When you are feeling threatened in a relationship, use the arousal management techniques you will find in chapter 12, under "Managing Emotions," to control jealousy, anxiety, and anger. Recognize how you try to control the attitudes and behavior of others when you feel threatened. Routinely ask yourself, "How would I feel if someone did to me what I am doing?" Identify the power struggles you create. Whenever you can, drop your end of the rope. Ask yourself whether you have a right to ask others to make the changes you want just to decrease your insecurity. Give people as much freedom as you can, or you will drive them away by your effort to control them.

Don't idealize others. No one is perfect, nor do they need to be to have satisfying relationships. When you meet new people, stop yourself from idealizing them. Don't create hyperpositive person schemas. Remind yourself that everyone has shortcomings just as you do. The *Intimacy Driven* schema tends to encourage overvaluation of others and undervaluation of yourself. When you idealize someone, you make yourself feel more vulnerable in that relationship. You also create unrealistic expectations of that person. When people who have been idealized by you reveal their human frailties, you are so disappointed that you tend to flip them to the other extreme, creating a negative, unbalanced person schema. Review your person schema lists that you have been developing on the people in your life. Are there any on your list whom you have seen that way—first at the hyperpositive end and then at the negative end? Work very hard on creating balanced person schemas of the people you know. Try to balance the unbalanced ones, whether they are hyperpositive or negative person schemas. People are rarely extremes, so look for some realistic information that you can add to the unbalanced schemas to balance them.

Accept differences. Stop viewing differences as rejections. Remind yourself that you are more focused on yourself than others are, because you are so fearful that you will be rejected if your flaws are seen. Remember, too, you may be the one who rejects others as soon as they do anything you interpret as disapproval. Can others have different opinions, interests, likes, or dislikes without your viewing that as a sign of rejection? Reverse the circumstances. For example, when you disagree with someone, does that mean you don't like that person, or is that just your honest opinion? Accept that people who care about you will not be identical to you. If someone wants time alone, do you view that as rejection? People vary in how much personal time they need. When you are doing certain things, do you want to be left alone sometimes? When you get upset about any perceived differences, reverse the situation, and ask yourself if you would apply the same interpretation to yourself. Work on being more tolerant of differences.

Accept criticism constructively. Do you become upset when anyone criticizes you? Do people have to accept you exactly as you are? Do others often have to retract their criticism or apologize before you are nice to them again? All of us do things that irritate each other. If you are unable to hear the complaints of others, how can you respond constructively? By not being able to listen to others' complaints, you force them into not asking for changes that might improve your relationship, which only puts the relationship at greater risk. If someone asks you to please not talk with your mouth full of food, that doesn't mean you are unlovable. It just means that person wants you to eat with your mouth closed. When you ask others to change something, are you implying that they are bad people? Good relationships require ongoing constructive feedback. When you get upset with feedback, you close the door to opportunities to improve your relationships. You also increase the chance of being blindsided by others' intense resentment when they no longer can keep silent.

Expand your emotional support system. How could you receive more emotional support beyond your current network? Don't make a partner or your parents your only social support system. You need a bigger network, because only one or two people won't always be available to you. Don't make your children your source of emotional support. That is not fair to them. Have adult confidants. Although you need a support network of at least a few people, you also need to become your own primary support person.

Your *Intimacy Driven* schema came into being when you felt extremely vulnerable to abandonment, which occurs typically during childhood. Remind yourself that you are no longer the helpless child you were when you were so vulnerable and had little if any power over your life. You now have many more options than you did then, plus more mature reasoning abilities. If you can calm yourself down, you can tap into those abilities. There are exercises in chapter 12 that will teach you how to calm and nurture yourself in times of stress. You are much more powerful than your *Intimacy Driven* schema allows you to think.

Shifting from *Intimacy Avoidant* to *Intimacy Comfortable*

Invest in other people. If *Intimacy Avoidant* has been a long-standing strong schema, follow the suggestions later in this chapter for changing the *Restrained* schema at the same time that you work on the *Intimacy Avoidant* schema. You can work on changing *Restrained* and *Intimacy Avoidant* schemas simultaneously, because your changes in either often support both new balanced schemas of *Expressive* and *Intimacy Comfortable*.

If you have family and friends, you can increase your investment in them by spending more time with them, asking them about themselves, listening closely, remembering what they say, and subsequently inquiring about those issues. Invite them to do more with you. In addition, you need to identify a few people that you might like to know better. If possible, pick people that have an Easy Bonding Style, because they will make it easier for you to interact with them and they won't be overly intrusive. The easiest step would be to find someone like this at work. Make a point of going by once or twice a day, saying hello and engaging in some small talk about the business, their work, or something in the news. Remember what they tell you, so you can follow up on that at a later conversation, especially anything personal. Over time your conversations will evolve into more personal interactions.

Share yourself. In addition to paying more attention to others, you need to be more open about yourself. In your interactions, include some relevant comment regarding your life or your own opinions, such as, "It sure is difficult to have a family member be ill in another state. That happened to me when my dad had bypass surgery back East. I couldn't get much time off, and I worried all the time," or "Losing a dream is tough. I always have been disappointed that I wasn't able to finish my degree." This gives the other person permission to inquire further about what you have said.

To increase emotional intimacy you need to remember what others tell you, inquire about that on subsequent interactions, and begin to share more of yourself with them. In other words, you need to let other people know that you care about them and value them enough to share part of yourself. If you observe Easy bonders, they do that. They are open about themselves and they show a genuine interest in others.

Be committed. You can learn to invest more in others and to share more of yourself, but you must make a commitment to change, or you will be inclined to slip backward. Try to apply these changes with various people, even with those who interact with you briefly but regularly, such as the dry-cleaning operator or the grocery clerk. You will be surprised at how responsive people are when you ask how they are doing, actually are interested in their replies, and remember their names. You can meet additional people through special interest groups or by engaging in a volunteer activity where you will interact with many of the same people on a regular basis. Over time, you will discover that you have similar interests to some of these people, which will allow you to suggest doing something together. Volunteer activities where you are personally engaged in helping someone else are especially valuable ways to discover how your personal investment matters. Be selective in what you decide to do. Once you have decided, make a commitment to do this for six months, because for some time you will be struggling against your old *Intimacy Avoidant* schema's push to withdraw.

Stop your avoidance behavior. At the end of chapter 8 you identified ways that you create distance between yourself and others. Now that you are aware of what you do, you can begin to change. Pay attention to what triggers your distancing reactions. Conflicts, requests for greater intimacy, and stressors are common triggers. Once you have a list of triggers, you need to identify other ways of responding. People who rely on avoidance strategies often do not have alternative coping strategies. The suggestions in this chapter and chapters 12 and 13 will be helpful. You may want to seek therapy to learn new ways of responding, especially if you have relied on addictive avoidance strategies. One helpful step is to tell your family that you are trying to stop your avoidance behavior, so that they can be supportive of your efforts. The key is to hang in there. Don't allow yourself to act on your initial response to withdraw or to push others away. Just remaining present is a step forward for you. Use the arousal management procedures described in chapter 12 to help reduce your tension as you change coping strategies and remain engaged with other people.

Building an Expressive *Self Schema*

An *Expressive* self schema will allow you to express your thoughts and feelings honestly and constructively to others. You will be able to accept your feelings as a natural part of who you are and not feel overwhelmed by them.

Shifting from *Unrestrained* to *Expressive*

Moving from an *Unrestrained* to an *Expressive* schema is so important that all of chapter 12 is devoted to how to do this. So, if this is the work you think you need to do, see chapter 12.

Shifting from *Restrained* to *Expressive*

I have no musical ability, or at least none that has been uncovered to date. If you asked me to sing in front of you, I would be reluctant, uncomfortable, and if forced to do so, embarrassed if not humiliated. People with a *Restrained* self schema feel the same way when asked to express their emotions and discuss their feelings. Their hesitancy is not just stubbornness. For a variety of reasons, they have learned that expressing their feelings was not in their best interests. Perhaps you say, "Trust me. I want to hear about your feelings." That is no more reassuring to them than if you told me that you would not laugh if only I would sing. How do you know how you will react to me? You have never heard me sing. These are the same thoughts that occur to people with the *Restrained* self schema. Moreover, they often don't even know how to begin. They have been ignoring their feelings for years, if not for decades. How can they even recognize what they are feeling? If you understand this, then you can appreciate the need to go slow and start simply with someone who wants to move from a *Restrained* to an *Expressive* self schema. Because those with the *Restrained* schema often have no idea how to change, a lot of specific suggestions are offered here.

Expressing your thoughts and feelings does not mean that you have to go around emoting like a Shakespearean actor. It just requires simple, straightforward statements about what you think, what you like or dislike, and how you are feeling. These simple statements will make others feel more connected to you. You also will notice that most people will respond the way you would hope they would to these statements. Even if they don't, at least you will know that they are aware of where you stand or how you feel. Start trying to use some of the statements listed below. The more you do this, the easier it will become.

I like it when you . . . [describe specific behaviors].

I don't like it when you leave the toothpaste in the sink, your towels on the floor, the gas tank on empty, etc. [describe behavior].

That hurts my feelings when you do . . . say that . . . , when you make fun of me about . . . , when you criticize my brother about . . . [describe behavior].

It makes me feel good when you do . . . , say . . . [describe behavior].

Please stop doing [be specific] . . . . I don't like that.

I was disappointed when . . . .

I think you look nice.

I like how you smell.

I feel sad when . . .

I feel happy when . . .

I was proud of you when . . .

I am worried about . . .

I wish you wouldn't do . . . It makes me nervous.

I feel irritable about . . .

I am not mad at you. I just am thinking about a project at work.

I need your help.

I am not in a bad mood. I just had a hectic day and need a little time to unwind.

I appreciate what you did for me when . . .

I am sorry for when I did . . . , or when I said . . .

I am sorry I hurt your feelings. I didn't mean to. I will try to change [describe behavior to be changed].

I am ashamed of the way I acted when I . . . I hope you can forgive me.

I don't want to do that.

I don't like that very much.

I am sorry you didn't get the position.

I hope you are feeling better.

I am sad about what happened to you.

Simple statements of what you are going to do also increase the connections other people feel toward you. When you just walk off or go to your room, the other person often cannot tell if you are upset, angry, or tired. He or she doesn't know if you are going away for a few minutes or for the rest of the day. You can use the following statements with family members or roommates. This is not to suggest that you have to be accountable to someone. Rather the purpose here is to increase the depth of your connections to these people. These statements suggest that you see them as people who matter to you, not as pieces of furniture.

I feel tired. I am going to go lie down.

I don't feel well. I am going to take an aspirin and go to bed.

I'll be back in a few minutes.

I'm going to go work on my project in my office.

I'm going to run over to the drugstore. Do you need anything?

I don't want to talk about this right now, but I will after dinner.

In addition to increasing your verbal output, you also need to pay attention to your facial expressions. Many people with the *Restrained* self schema have learned to keep their face expressionless. Facial expressions are critical to human interactions. People are better able to respond to your needs if you give them more cues. If you are older, you can get an idea of what your typical facial expression is by the lines on your face. If you have no lines on your face, guess who is not giving away any cues? Look at yourself in the mirror and read the above listed statements meaningfully—that is, read them with some feeling. Does your facial expression remain the same, no matter what you are saying? If so, practice smiling when you say the positive phrases. Practice smiling in general. Start saying hi to people, look in their eyes, and smile. You will be surprised at how many people will smile back at you. If they don't, that doesn't matter. This is your exercise, not theirs.

If you think your facial expression looks kind of mean, try to soften it, no matter what you are saying. When you are giving people negative feedback or asking for them to make a change, a mean or angry expression conveys that you do not like them and that may precipitate a hostile or fearful reaction. You can smile when you ask for changes or give negative feedback, indicating that you are not angry, although you would like them to do something different. You can even start by saying, "I am not mad at you, but I would like . . ." Mean, angry expressions drive people away. If this is your typical expression, you may be having that effect a lot more often than you intend.

People with a *Restrained* schema need to increase their awareness of their own feelings. Here is a simple exercise to help you do that. Think of the last few times when you have felt either upset or happy. In your notebook, write a description of the situation, who was there, and what happened. Try to remember your thoughts and actions in the situation and describe them. At the end of the paragraph, list the feelings that you had in the situation *and* the feelings that you had writing about the situation. Repeat this exercise on a daily basis. No one has the same feelings all the time. Even with a *Restrained* schema you have fluctuations in your feelings although your fluctuations may be more subtle, because you have been holding them in check for so long. The purpose of doing this exercise regularly is to make you more aware of your feelings, to help you identify what they are by naming them, and to know what they feel like when you are feeling them. Then, as you become more adept at recognizing your feelings when they are happening, this will allow you to recognize them in the moment. There will be many times you will benefit from expressing your feelings in the moment with another person with some of the statements you have just learned.

Building an Interdependent *Self Schema*

An *Interdependent* self schema will allow you to ask for help when you need it and to offer assistance to others when that is appropriate. You will be able to see that some degree of dependence on others is acceptable and not a sign of personal inadequacy. You will feel confident in your ability to handle most life tasks on your own.

Shifting from *Dependent* to *Interdependent*

Dependent is often associated with the *Intimacy Driven* schema. As long as you are convinced that you cannot handle life on your own, you will be terrified of the prospect of abandonment, regardless of how improbable it might be. As you become more interdependent, you will feel less anxiety in your relationships. Even if *Dependent* is your only unbalanced schema, you will feel a decrease in tension as you change, because being dependent means you view yourself as vulnerable. From birth to adulthood you became less dependent, so throughout your life you have already become more self-sufficient, yet somehow your *Dependent* schema has remained unmodified. First, let's look at how you have changed in the past. What are some ways in which you became less dependent from childhood to adolescence, and then from adolescence to early adulthood, and, if you are past thirty, from early adulthood to your current age? Also note what helped you make each of those changes from dependency toward adult independence. Do that in your notebook.

Identify how you are dependent now. Describe the various ways you currently are dependent in your notebook. Leave space for each example, preferably one page for each example.

Develop specific plans to become less dependent. For each way in which you are dependent, describe what you would need to do to become less dependent. For this item, you might want to ask others for suggestions on how you could change, but think of what you can do to change now, and ask for suggestions later. Then select one item that you want to change and describe in detail a more specific plan to make this transition from dependency.

Here is an example. *I depend on my partner to handle all of the finances. I want to become more financially competent and to assume some of the responsibility. Steps I can take to do this: Every Saturday morning we will go through the bills together, and I will enter the amounts in our expense journal. Then we will discuss how to decide which bill is paid, from which checking account, and how much. Then I will write the checks. I also will balance my checkbook at the end of each day before I go to bed if I wrote any checks. After we do this together for two months, I will handle the bills on my own, but we will discuss together our payment strategies for any bill that is not routine. After I am able to do this, the next thing I will do is learn about our investments and insurance plans and develop a systematic way of keeping track of that information for myself.*

Take specific, graduated steps to change. In the example above the person identified specific and gradual steps to increase financial competency. Being interdependent means that you still can rely on other people for some things, but that you try to assume responsibility for what you can. For whichever item you select, develop a plan with specific steps that are graduated over time. Pick the *easiest* item on your list. This is not an exercise in heroics. The goal is to increase your sense of confidence and to increase an *Interdependent* self schema within yourself. Use this same procedure as you work through your list, but work only on one or, at most, two items at a time. Also pay attention to other ways that you are dependent, small or large, and add those to your list as you notice them. *Your goal is not to eliminate any dependency, but rather to decrease it by increasing your independence.* Once you have developed the confidence and/or competence to do something new, it is a *necessity* to do that something new on your own. Whether someone else helps you with that task in the future may be an *option*, but for now, you must try to do it by yourself. The lack of options is what increases your anxiety and makes you feel helpless with a *Dependent* schema.

Shifting from *Stubbornly Independent* to *Interdependent*

You must recognize what your stubbornly independent behavior has cost you in the past. If you have a *Stubbornly Independent* schema, first you need to list examples of when you needed help and didn't get it. Think of situations that you messed up because you wouldn't ask for help. Think of examples of when you or others were hurt or inconvenienced by your stubbornness. Write those examples in your notebook. Again, be sure to leave some space between each example. Now, think of how you could have handled those situations if you had had an *Interdependent* schema. Write those alternatives after each example.

Identify current situations where you could use assistance. Next, in your notebook list current situations where you might be able to use some help even if it isn't absolutely necessary. Include both trivial and major tasks. Leave space between each task.

Start asking for help. Under each task, list the names of people whom you might ask for help. Think of how you would ask each person, for example, "If you have a few minutes now [or a few hours on Saturday], could you help me with a project [describe what it is]?" Next, select one of your items and ask for help with it. Afterwards, express your thanks and offer to return the favor sometime when that person needs help. Don't keep score and feel obligated until you can return the favor. This is not a formal contract. Most people feel pleased to be able to help other people, at least occasionally. In fact, sometimes people become offended when someone does not ask them to help when that person is obviously struggling doing something alone. They often assume the other person thinks that they are incompetent to help. If your son offers to help fix dinner, with a *Stubbornly Independent* schema you would be likely to say no or give him only menial tasks. Eventually, he will get the picture. Remember, your behavior has an impact on others. Eventually they will not want to help you.

Implementing Schema Changes

After you identify which schemas you want to modify and select the changes you are going to make, consider what effect those changes will have on the people around you. As discussed earlier, most people are part of several social systems. If you change, you will very likely have an effect on other people in your systems. Their reactions, in turn, could affect you.

To illustrate, if you have the *Restrained* schema and begin to make changes to develop the *Expressive* self schema, other people can be affected by those changes. If in the past, you have not expressed your wishes to co-workers, nor set limits on what you would or would not do, your co-workers may be taken aback when you begin expressing yourself. Your co-workers may resist your new behavior, if they have been comfortable having you do tasks that they disliked. In this situation, by anticipating their reactions, you can anticipate that they may challenge you. You can prepare to be persistent. You don't need to become angry or accuse them of taking advantage of you for years. You may have trained them to do so by your own acquiescence or by not expressing your feelings. You just need to be aware that you will have to be persistent about making changes that others may not like. If this is an important change for you, then don't give up. Stick to your plan.

If you do anticipate that there will be resistance to a change you want to make, you may find it helpful to discuss your plans with the people who will be affected by your changes *before* you implement them. Describe what you plan to do and explain that your changes are *for* you, not *against* them. Tell them your goal is to change *yourself*, not *them*, and that you don't want them to think that you are angry or upset with them because you are changing. You also can discuss how your changes might affect them and how they feel about that. As a result of such a discussion, you might decide to modify some of your changes or you might decide that your change plan is appropriate unmodified. Whichever, a discussion like this can help avoid misinterpretations of your motives.

If you are in an abusive relationship, being aware of the impact your changes could have on the other parties in your systems is critical. In that kind of situation, as stressed earlier, although you need to get out of the situation, you need to do it under the guidance of an expert in domestic violence. Even if you are not in such a situation, you still need to carefully think about how other people will react to your changes. You may be surprised to discover that some people may be ecstatic about the changes you want to institute. Perhaps together you could identify ways that they could support your changes. Whatever the case may be, assess the impact of your intended changes on other people *before* you implement them.

Schema Change Plans

In developing a schema change plan, there are certain steps to follow that will help you focus your efforts and consider the impact on other people. Let's look at the schema change plans of some of the people described in this book. Doug, described in chapter 8, had a Distant Bonding Style. Having gone through three divorces and having virtually no relationship with his children, Doug wanted to change his bonding style by first working on his schemas on the *Intimacy* continuum. His plan follows:

Doug's Plan to Change His *Intimacy* Schemas

Steps to strengthen Doug's balanced *Intimacy Comfortable* schema:

1. I will take responsibility for developing a relationship with my son and daughter. I will apologize to them for not being more involved in their lives and tell them that I want to change our relationship and become close to them if they are willing to give me another chance. I will do this by writing them a letter and then I will follow up with a call a few days later and ask if they will give me another chance. I will begin calling weekly. I will make a few notes during the conversa-

tions, so that I can remember what they tell me and follow up on what they said in my next call. I know they may act distant for a while, because I have never followed through before and they will be skeptical, but I won't use that as an excuse to stop trying. I will block off times on my schedule to have them come and visit me every three months. I can afford to do that. When they come, I will take off work and spend the time with them interacting, not just sending them out to do things on their own.

2. I will focus on developing platonic relationships with two of the women who have been in relationships with me for years and whom I think really like me as a person. I will tell them what I am doing: that I am trying to learn how to be comfortable in caring relationships that don't involve sex.

3. I will initiate efforts to develop friendships with some of the men at my office who have invited me to do things with them over the years. I will initiate some activity out of the office with one of them at least once a week and ask them to have lunch with me at least twice a week.

Steps for weakening Doug's hyperpositive *Intimacy Avoidant* schema:

1. I will not have sex with anyone I meet or know until I decide that I really want that person to care about me and me to care about her.

2. I will engage in only one sexual relationship at a time.

3. I will not walk away or withdraw when people want to talk to me about their feelings or inquire about mine.

4. I will stop avoiding areas of conflict. I will talk things out with other people.

Obstacles: My son and daughter might be reluctant at first. We will need to talk about their feelings. I will listen to how hurt they have felt. I will have to prove to them that I am committed to changing.

Support: Over time, I think my kids will be supportive of these changes. I think my two women friends will like the idea of us developing closer friendships.

Support People: my two women friends.

Kevin was described in chapter 9 as having intense problems with jealousy in his relationship with Kimberly. In addition to working on his *Unrestrained* and *Expressive* schemas on the *Expressiveness* continuum by following the suggestions you will find in chapter 12, he also wanted to work on his *Intimacy* schemas.

Kevin's Plan to Change His *Intimacy* Schemas

Steps for strengthening Kevin's balanced *Intimacy Comfortable* schema:

1. I will try to expand my emotional support system so that Kimberly is not my only support person. I have a good friend from college who wants to play tennis with me, but I am always working. I will make a regular time with him to do this weekly. I also will be more open with him about some of the things I worry about at work, because he has always been trustworthy. One of the older guys at work has been supportive of me and I like him. I could initiate more contact, like going to lunch with him, to get to know him better.

2. I also will get involved in a service organization. The Kiwanis organization has asked me to come to their meetings. I need to do something besides just work. This would give me a chance to meet some new friends and for Kimberly and me to meet some new couples.

3. I will make a list of the things Kimberly does to show me that she loves me. I will visualize those images when I am feeling threatened by her other social activities.

4. I will make more time for social activities with Kimberly, because she has told me that she feels unimportant to me when all I do is work. I also will meet her for dinner in the evenings even if I have to go back to work after that.

5. I will be honest with Kimberly about how I sometimes feel in a bind, because I want to work hard to earn money to buy her nice things, but then she gets angry that I don't have time to do things with her. I will ask her if we can set up a budget for us that we both agree to, so she won't see it as imposed by me.

Steps for weakening Kevin's hyperpositive *Intimacy Driven* schema:

1. I will make a list of the things I do to control Kimberly. I will try to be aware of when I do these and remind myself that I am probably feeling threatened and try to figure out why, so I can address the actual issue.

2. I also will remind myself that Kimberly intentionally tries to make me feel jealous when she is not getting enough attention. In those situations, I will calmly talk to her about how that hurts my feelings and how we need to try to compromise to meet both of our goals. For example, if I have to work on the weekends, I will take Friday and Saturday nights off to do something with her.

3. I will stop criticizing her friends and the way she dresses, because I always liked it before we were married. I will remind myself that I am afraid that other men will be attracted to her and seduce her, but I know that Kimberly is not easily seduced and that she has never been unfaithful in any of her relationships. Even though she is a flirt, she values fidelity. I also will remind myself that the reason I feel so easily threatened is because of my *Unworthy* schema, and that I am going to work on changing that too, after I have made headway with *Intimacy Comfortable* and the *Expressive* schemas.

Obstacles: Kimberly may not be too crazy about the budget, but if we figure it out together, that might help.

Support: Kimberly wants me to work less and for us to have more friends and to spend more time together. She would love for me to be less controlling and would support any efforts I made in that direction.

Support Person: My tennis friend.

Observe how specific the steps for schema changes are in both Doug's and Kevin's plans. Vague steps are almost impossible to implement, because you are unsure of what to do. Develop specific, small steps. Do only one or two at a time. Don't move on to another step until you feel the previous step has become almost automatic for you. In making schema changes, it also can be helpful to tell some of the people involved what you are trying to do. In Doug's case, he plans to tell his two women friends. In Kevin's case, he is going to tell Kimberly what his strategies are. Both know those people will support their efforts. Having a support person can be critical to prevent you from becoming overly discouraged when you run into obstacles. When trying to change your schemas, obstacles are inevitable. They just mean that you have to revise your plan a little. Identify at least one person who can serve as your support person, and talk with that person at least once a week about how things are going, even if everything is going well.

Your Schema Change Plan

For each continuum, circle the schemas you want to strengthen and the ones you want to weaken:

Continuum

Worthiness	Unworthy	Worthy	Entitled
Intimacy	Intimacy Driven	Intimacy Comfortable	Intimacy Avoidant
Expressiveness	Unrestrained	Expressive	Restrained
Interdependent	Dependent	Interdependent	Stubbornly Independent

1. Select one continuum where you have circled schemas. Below write the name of each schema that you want to change for that continuum. You might list only a negative or hyperpositive schema for a continuum because you have only one of them. List both if you have both. Always list the balanced schema, because you need to strengthen that one at the same time you are weakening either of the unbalanced schemas. Then, review the material in this chapter on building schemas for those schemas you wish to change and list the actions you plan to take for each schema.

Continuum:

Balanced Schema:

Steps to strengthen this schema:

_____

_____

_____

Negative Schema:

Steps to weaken this schema:

_____

_____

_____

Hyperpositive Schema:

Steps to weaken this schema:

_____

_____

_____

2. If I make these changes in these schemas, what obstacles might I face?

3. What support can I get for making these changes?

4. Who can I use for my support person?

   Repeat Steps 1-3 for additional schema changes you want to make on the other continua, but focus only on one continuum at a time.

Continuum:

Balanced Schema:

Steps to strengthen this schema:

_____

_____

_____

Negative Schema:

Steps to weaken this schema:

_____

_____

_____

Hyperpositive Schema:

Steps to weaken this schema:

_____

_____

_____

2. If I make these changes in these schemas, what obstacles might I face?

3. What support can I get for making these changes?

4. Who can I use for my support person?

12

Keeping Your Cool

All emotions are pure which gather you and lift you up; that emotion is impure which seizes only one side of your being and so distorts you.

—Rainer Maria Rilke, *Letters to a Young Poet*

Everyone has emotions, but people vary widely in how they deal with their emotions. The self schemas of the *Expressiveness* continuum reflect these differences. People with the hyperpositive *Restrained* schema are less aware of their feelings and less able to discriminate among different feelings than those with a negative *Unrestrained* schema or those with a balanced *Expressive* schema. For those with the hyperpositive *Restrained* schema, their lack of understanding of their own feelings makes it difficult for them to recognize emotions in other people and to respond appropriately.

Individuals with the negative *Unrestrained* schema have the opposite problem. They are excessively sensitive to their emotions and to the emotions of others. However, they have a difficult time modulating their emotions. While their emotions are appropriate to the situation as they see it, those emotions are often out of proportion. People with the balanced *Expressive* schema are able to identify and understand their emotions and regulate and use them effectively. They also are able to identify emotions in others and to react appropriately. These skills are viewed as emotional competencies.

The *Restrained* group has a deficit in emotional awareness. The *Unrestrained* group has a deficit in emotional management. The *Restrained* group also has an emotional management problem once they learn to be aware of emotions, because they have relied only on suppression for managing their emotions. Although you are hard-wired at birth to feel emotions, emotional competencies are learned. Children develop emotional competencies by learning to distinguish among their feelings, manage them effectively, and recognize and respond constructively to the emotions of others. However, children whose role models are emotionally incompetent are less likely to learn emotional management skills. The result of not learning these skills is the development of either the *Restrained* or *Unrestrained* unbalanced schemas. A family that models expressing anger with physical aggression may produce a child who imitates that aggression or the opposite, the suppression of feelings. Without appropriate models and guidance, children are less likely to develop the balanced *Expressive* schema. Information on how to shift from the *Restrained* to the *Expressive* schema is provided in chapter 11. Now you will learn how to move from *Unrestrained* to *Expressive*, but first you need to understand the role that interpretation plays in emotions.

Emotions

Emotions are a combination of interpretations and biochemical changes. An emotion is not just a physiological activity. At some level of awareness there is an appraisal or an interpretation of an event or experience. For example, after waiting thirty minutes for someone to meet you, you begin to feel angry. Your anger is not a random emotion. You have interpreted the lateness to mean something along these lines: "She is always late. She never thinks about anyone but herself. She doesn't care if this will make me late getting back to work. I have asked her to call if she is going to be delayed, but she never does."

Your anger is the result of what you tell yourself about the situation. The same experience could produce anxiety: "She is never late. She would call if she were going to be more than fifteen or twenty minutes late. I shouldn't have asked her to drive over here to meet me in this weather. Something must have happened to her." How you interpret any experience depends on your knowledge, which includes your relevant schemas. In the first case, lateness is characteristic of the person schema you have of this woman, while in the second example it is not. This influences the way you interpret the event. The interpretation influences the subsequent physiological reaction. Together, the interpretation and physiological reaction create an emotion.

Are all interpretations conscious? No, interpretations can take place without your conscious awareness. Suppose late one evening the hair stands up on the back of your neck and your pulse begins to race, and you suddenly feel afraid. Yet you cannot identify any particular stimulus; it's not something of which you are consciously aware. But some stimulus associated with danger in your knowledge system, perhaps a sound or a draft of air, has activated your brain at a preconscious level of your awareness. Your brain interprets the stimulus and acts on the interpretation by stimulating a physiological reaction, which you now notice consciously.

Similarly, anger, anxiety, and jealousy are not random emotions. A stimulus activates your brain, then your brain interprets that stimulus and produces an appropriate physiological response, resulting in the emotion that you *feel*. Although you might be very aware of your *feelings*, often you are unaware of the *interpretations* that produce a particular emotion. So, *an emotion consists of an interpretation followed by a biochemical reaction that you feel.*

To better manage your emotions, you need to be aware of the kind of interpretations that produce anger, anxiety, and jealousy. Anger is usually the result of interpretations that you or someone you care about has been demeaned, treated unfairly, or prevented from obtaining an expected goal. Anxiety is associated with interpretations that something bad is going to happen and you will not be able to handle it. Jealousy occurs with interpretations that someone you care about views another person as more desirable, more competent, or more positive in some way than you—and the belief that this perception will weaken or change the other person's attachment or feelings toward you. Whenever you experience one of these emotions, try to bring to your awareness the interpretations underlying the emotion and then evaluate the evidence supporting those interpretations. You will learn how to do that in the next section.

Managing Your Emotions

Until you gain better control of your emotional reactions, you will find it difficult to modify other unbalanced self schemas. Your unharnessed emotional reactions will keep you in a state of turmoil and impede your plans to change other schemas. To modify your *Unrestrained* schema, first you need to dispel the myth that you can't change your emotional reactivity. Of course you can. Even if you have an inherently more reactive nervous system, you still can modify your reactivity. You may never be as laid back as Mr. Rogers, but you can move in his direction.

If you have a problem with intense reactions of anxiety, anger, or jealousy, you have to learn how to contain those feelings and express them in a more constructive fashion. Unchanged, they will continue to harm you and the people in your life. The procedures that are described next will work for you. *This is a guarantee.* But they will work only *if* you apply them repeatedly and consistently. *You can't give up.* You can do this and you must if you want to stop alienating the people you love.

Some people excuse their emotional reactions by saying, "My mother says I always have been emotional" or "Hotheads run in my family." Both of those statements may be true, but neither would preclude you from being able to change. *You cannot come up with any legitimate reasons that you cannot change.* You can change. Not to change intense negative emotional reactions is unfair to the people in your life. The harm of excessive anger or jealousy may be obvious, but even overwhelming anxiety is stressful for others. For example, intense anxiety in parents is very hard on children, who either withdraw into themselves or try to become their parents' caregivers. Gaining control of your emotions is *your* responsibility. The people around you are not obligated to tolerate or excuse your emotional excesses. *You* need to change, not them.

Gaining Emotional Control

The goal is *not to eliminate* these emotions. Anxiety, anger, and jealousy are not abnormal emotions. You are not a bad person for having these emotions. All humans feel such feelings at times. Anxiety, anger, and jealousy are messages to alert you that something needs your attention. There may be legitimate reasons for those emotions, or they may result from erroneous interpretations of events. In either event, you need to pay attention to these feelings and figure out what is happening and what actions to take. These emotions become problematic only when they become too intense. When they are too intense, they disrupt your thinking, impair your judgment, and can result in actions you will later regret. The goal is to shrink the intensity of the feelings, so that you can thoughtfully analyze a situation and then implement effective problem-solving strategies. You can apply these procedures to yourself or use them with a partner, friend, or child who has a problem with emotional overreactivity.

Manage Your Impulses

Don't react impulsively. When you are feeling panicky or on the verge of losing control, the first thing you must do is calm yourself. Problem-solving skills become impaired when a person is experiencing intense emotions, whether anxiety, anger, depression, or whatever. This means that the first step is *not* to try to solve the problem at that moment. Whatever actions you might take in a moment of panic, fury, or despair are unlikely to be the actions you would select if you were calmly considering alternatives. The first step is to calm yourself down to a point where your breathing is normal, your pulse is no longer racing, and you are not sobbing uncontrollably. Here are the steps you must follow to do that.

Calm Your Thoughts

Calmly talk to yourself. Talk to yourself, out loud or in your head, in the way that you would talk to a distraught child. Think about what other people have said to you in similar situations that was effective or what you said to other people when they needed to calm down. Say those same things. Or say things like, "I have time to think about this. I can work this out. First I need to just calm down. Then I can figure something out. I don't need to do anything until after I've calmed down."

What keeps your emotional intensity at an extreme level are the repeated tales of terror you tell yourself. You keep envisioning worst-case interpretations of events, no matter how unrealistic those images might be. People who repeatedly experience intense emotions lack the ability to self-soothe. They may nurture and comfort others extremely well, but they fail to apply those skills to themselves. You can calm yourself down by changing what you say to yourself and by changing how you breathe, which you will read about below.

Calm Your Breathing

An essential part of calming yourself is to regain control of your breathing. When you are distressed, your breathing becomes more rapid and shallow. This causes an imbalance in your oxygen and carbon dioxide, which contributes to the physiological symptoms you experience. By changing your breathing pattern, you will readjust the imbalance and experience some relief in your symptoms quickly. Changing your breathing pattern is *very easy* to do, but you must do the following exercise for at least *five minutes*, not just a few seconds.

Breathing exercise. You can do this exercise either sitting or lying down. Place one hand on your abdomen and one hand on your chest. Slowly inhale and then slowly exhale, counting in your head "one thousand one, one thousand two, one thousand three, " and so forth until you have finished inhaling or exhaling each time. Eventually your inhalations and exhalations should have the same count. In other words, if an inhalation takes you up to "one thousand four," so should the exhalation. Gradually pace your inhalations and exhalations to achieve this balance, but don't force it. You may require several practice sessions to achieve this balance. Practice doing this breathing procedure at least four times a day, so that when you are upset you will be able to do it effectively.

If you breathe through your nose, this exercise is a little easier. If you can't breathe through your nose, it will still work, but be sure when you inhale not to take large gulps of air and then exhale rapidly and forcefully. Rather, breathe in slowly and smoothly. When you exhale, slowly blow the air out through pursed lips. By the end of five minutes, you should be able to increase your count by one or two and equalize your counts for inhaling and exhaling. You also should notice that the hand on your chest is moving less and the hand on your abdomen is moving more. These changes mean that you no longer are breathing shallowly from your chest but more deeply from your abdomen.

While you are doing this breathing exercise, you need to do whatever helps you stay focused on it. Usually that means either closing your eyes or focusing them on a particular object, such as your watch, and then continuing the exercise for five minutes. If your mind wanders, and it usually will if you are quite distraught, bring it back to the counting. You can't pay attention to your counting and simultaneously think about anything else. If you are thinking about something else, you are not counting. Just keep bringing your mind back to the counting whenever it drifts away. Don't get upset with yourself if your mind keeps drifting away from the counting. Just keep coming back to it. As the minutes pass, you will find it easier to stay focused on your breathing. Be sure to do this exercise for at least five minutes.

People who have developed a chronic shallow breathing pattern may need some extra help. If you have trouble stilling your chest as you breathe, try the following techniques that have been used successfully by people who have panic disorders (Craske 1996).

Lie face down on the floor, with your arms stretched out and your head turned to one side, resting your cheek on a tissue or cloth on the floor. This position makes it easier to keep your chest still and to breathe more normally. Lie in that position, inhaling and exhaling several times, counting slowly in your head. After four to five minutes, turn over on your back. Place a book on your abdomen and continue breathing and counting for a few more minutes or for as long as you like. Focus on the book slowly rising with each inhalation and falling with each exhalation. Use these positions if you have trouble changing your shallow breathing while in a sitting position. Once you have learned how to breathe less shallowly lying down, you can apply this technique while you are sitting or standing to relax yourself.

Use Healthy Distractions

Find engaging distractions. If you are still agitated even after you have regulated your breathing, do something to distract yourself or something that will make you feel better immediately. Distractions that can help you continue to calm down are activities that engage your attention but do not require much mental effort. For example, read a magazine, watch a television show, or clean out a desk drawer. Do anything that will engage your attention for a little while.

Many people who have pets find that petting them is very soothing. Stroking a pet or even watching fish in an aquarium produces physiological changes that are very calming. If you have a pet, find it. Don't just grab it, because some pets don't like that and will struggle to get away, which will only upset you further. Just sit down beside it and pet it. Pay attention to how pleasant that feels and to your pet's responses. Or go to your fish tank and watch your fish for a while.

Exercise is another way to calm down. In fact, it is one of the most effective ways to reduce emotional intensity. You can get that effect from even mild exercise. Go for a brisk walk, or if you have exercise equipment, use it for a little while or for as long as you want.

Music has soothed people's nerves for centuries. Lie on a bed or sit back in a chair and listen to music that calms you, not music that revs you up or makes you feel sad. "Somebody-done-me-wrong" songs are definitely not helpful. Or do whatever else you can think of that will engage your attention for a while. Whatever you do, do this until you are feeling calmer. Make a list of activities that you can use for this purpose in the future, so you can begin to do them quickly when you need them. *Don't use alcohol or drugs to distract or calm yourself.*

Analyze the Problem

After you have calmed down, think about the situation that upset you. If you want to wait until later to do this, that is fine. But you need to do this at some point. Distraction is not the solution to the problem. The distracting activity is only to calm yourself down until you can think more clearly about the problem. Then follow these steps.

List the Facts

Thanks to television reruns, for about twenty years *Dragnet's* fictional Los Angeles police detective, Joe Friday, has said repeatedly,

"The facts, ma'am, just the facts." Obviously Joe was a closet psychologist ahead of his time. He knew that premature interpretations lead to false accusations. You need to follow his advice. List the facts regarding what happened. No interpretations. No conclusions. Just the facts. Facts also can include events that did not happen. For example, "Jack did not show up for lunch" or "Mary did not call back last night" are facts. What doesn't happen can be as important as what does happen, as Sherlock Holmes noted in *Silver Blaze* when he discovered the critical clue was what hadn't happened: the dog had not barked, which revealed that the dog knew the culprit.

To illustrate how to list facts, Camille wrote this, "I saw Alex laughing with that redhead. I know he finds her more attractive than he does me. He's going to dump me if she'll go out with him." Of course, this example includes more than just the facts. So, let's break it down:

Fact: *I saw Alex laughing with that redhead.*

Interpretation: *I know he finds her more attractive than me.*

Interpretation: *He's going to dump me if she'll go out with him.*

To do this step properly, Camille should have written only one sentence: *I saw Alex laughing with that redhead.* That was the only fact that she listed. When you make your list of facts, be sure to ask yourself after each statement, "Is this a fact or an interpretation?" If it is not a fact, scratch it out or erase it.

Link Interpretations and Emotions

Describe your interpretation of the facts and the emotions associated with each interpretation. After you have listed all the facts, list your interpretations of those facts. Then, for each interpretation, list the emotion associated with that interpretation. This will help you in identifying all of your interpretations more completely. Remember, you may have more than one emotion involved in a situation. Identify all of the emotions you feel and add any additional interpretations or assumptions. Remember, too, that one emotion can be attached to more than one interpretation, and one interpretation can be attached to more than one emotion.

Camille described her emotions as jealousy, anxiety, and anger. Her jealousy was based on her interpretation that because Alex seemed to enjoy being with another woman, he would find Camille less desirable in comparison. Camille believed that Alex was going to leave her for this other woman, which triggered her anxiety. Her anger stemmed from her interpretation that she could not stop this chain of events, she would lose this important relationship, and she would be unable to handle things on her own. After she wrote this out, she realized that being unable to handle things on her own also made her feel anxious, so she added anxiety to her list. To figure out your interpretations, just ask yourself what the facts mean to you. Ask, "Why am I upset by what I saw or heard?" or "Why do these facts make me feel this particular emotion?"

Identify Schema Sources

Identify your schemas associated with your interpretations and emotions. In Camille's example, her negative *Unworthy* and *Intimacy Driven* schemas are connected to her interpretations. Her interpretation of what she observed is that the redheaded woman is more attractive than she is *(Unworthy),* Alex will dump her if the redhead wants to go out with him *(Intimacy Driven),* and Camille will not be able to handle things on her own *(Dependent).* These interpretations may seem like several big leaps, but *people with unbalanced schemas make big leaps.* That's a primary problem with unbalanced schemas. *They generate extreme conclusions and expectations, which produce intense emotions.*

With the Anxious Bonding Style, people like Camille are easily convinced that others will leave them because they are less worthy than other people. They are insecure, easily threatened, and tend to anticipate the worst. So their *Unworthy, Intimacy Driven,* and *Dependent* schemas conjure up dreadful scenarios, and then their *Unrestrained* schema acts on them, allowing their emotions to surge. Think about this: If Camille really believed that Alex was about to leave her for this stranger, wouldn't she be distraught?

Identify the Evidence

List the evidence supporting and challenging your interpretations. Since your interpretations produce your emotions, your emotions will subside if your interpretations turn out to be invalid or questionable. Analyzing your interpretations is critical in emotional management.

List the evidence that supports your interpretations. The evidence that supports Alex leaving is that he insisted Camille get therapy or he is going to leave. He also said he can't tolerate her angry accusations anymore. He had a redheaded girlfriend in the past who broke up with him.

List the evidence that challenges your interpretations. What evidence challenged the interpretation that Alex would leave Camille for another woman? Alex has never been unfaithful to Camille. He hardly even knew this woman. He is friendly with everyone, men and women. He has many female friends, and Camille knows that he has no romantic involvement with any of them although several are very attractive, and one is a redhead. Alex said he doesn't want to leave, but he can't stay if Camille doesn't stop her angry tirades at him. He was obviously relieved when Camille told him that she had started counseling. He volunteered to participate in her counseling whenever she wants. He frequently expresses love and affection to her. He does not have a history of bailing out of relationships when they become problematic. He tries to work things out.

Evaluate your two lists of evidence for and against your interpretations. Which seems more substantial? After Camille did this analysis, she concluded that the evidence challenging her interpretation was much stronger than the evidence supporting it. In some instances, this analysis allows you to see your interpretation does not fit the evidence and you can stop there. However, at other times you will still have doubts. If so, then you need to continue with the following steps.

Identify Alternative Explanations

If your analysis of the evidence for your interpretations still seems valid to you, next ask yourself, "What alternative explanations might exist for what I observed or was told?" *You must identify at least one benign interpretation.* To do this step, Camille wrote, "Alex is polite to everyone. Maybe he was just being polite. Or maybe he does like her, but that doesn't mean he wants to go out with her." If you cannot think of an innocent interpretation, ask someone else for suggestions. This means just presenting that person with the facts—without including your negative spin on them. Those who have unbalanced schemas often have difficulty thinking of benign interpretations. You may need to have one or two friends who can serve as consultants as you develop this skill.

Identifying benign interpretations does not mean that your negative interpretation is wrong. Your interpretation may be right. For example, your partner may be cheating on you. But if you typically overreact and misinterpret ambiguous information, you will have less credibility with others and even with yourself. Your partner will be able to cite all the other times you made false accusations, which will undermine your confidence in your own analysis of the current events. The purpose of these procedures is to help you make reasoned analyses and implement rational decisions. You may choose to end a relationship or take other actions, but they need to be actions that are thoughtfully considered and maintain your self-respect.

Gather More Information

Seek clarification or additional information. At this point, you should have lists of the facts, of both negative and neutral interpretations, and of the evidence consistent and inconsistent with your primary upsetting interpretations. How can you find out which interpretations are accurate? By gathering more information. Start by asking questions. Asking questions means asking questions, not initiating a military bombing offensive. Don't assume maliciousness on the part of the other party. Don't blame. Don't attack. Assume innocence. Ask questions in a calm, nonaccusatory manner. If you put people on the defense, they react defensively even if they're innocent. "Why were you flirting with that redhead?" is not a helpful question. "What were you and the woman with the red hair talking about?" or simply, "Who was the woman with the red hair?" asked in a calm, curious voice that does not imply ulterior motives on Alex's part would be a good opening for Camille.

Go into the situation with the expectation that there is a benign explanation for the facts. When people respond to your questions, *listen* to them. Don't interrupt. Let them finish what they are saying. Then, ask additional questions if you need further clarification. Don't approach this as a legal interrogation. Don't seek additional information with a closed mind, eagerly looking for any hint that your worst-case interpretation is correct. If you do that, you are likely to overlook important information.

Keep a Record

Record your steps. Do this entire procedure, starting with the listing of facts, in a notebook or a computer, so that you can reread what you have written as often as you need to refocus yourself. Initially, don't do these steps in your head. Once you are familiar with the different steps in the entire process, you can do them in your head, but not at the beginning while you are learning how to react differently.

Worst-Case Preparation

If gathering additional information agitates you, you may be anticipating discovering information that confirms your worst expectations. If so, then it might be helpful to consider the worst possible situation before you seek more information. You need a plan to deal with your most dreaded outcome. If you can deal with the worst case, you can deal with anything.

List Your Worst-Case Scenario

Identify worst-case scenarios. What would be the worst case possible? Camille's worst-case scenario is that Alex will leave her.

Identify Your Fears

What would happen if the worst case occurred? Ask yourself what would happen or how your life would change if the worst case actually happened. Identify all the possible outcomes that you think could happen in the worst case. Camille thought that if Alex left her, she would be alone, no one would care about her, no one would think she was special, no one would be there if she needed help, and she would miss the emotional and sexual intimacy that she had with Alex.

Develop a Worst-Case Plan

Figure out how you could manage the worst case. Address each of the possible worst-case outcomes separately. For each possible outcome, figure out how to buffer the effects you fear. These ideas should be realistic, not Pollyannaish suggestions. Camille wrote the following for each of her feared consequences.

I will be all alone: I have other close friends I could see more often; my mother and I are close; my friend Norma is always asking me to do things but I never have time now, so I could do more with her.

I will have no one who cares about me: my friends do care about me but whenever I have a boyfriend they complain that I just drop them; I could re-invest in those relationships; my mom and dad care about me.

No one will think I am special: Norma thinks I am special; we have been friends for years even though recently I have neglected her; my parents think I am special; I have never had much trouble finding boyfriends, so it is likely that I will meet someone new who will think I am special—although probably not another "Alex."

I will have no one to help me if I need help: Norma and my parents have helped me at times in the past; I really can handle a lot of things on my own now; I was taking care of myself before I met Alex; I am in good shape financially.

I will miss the emotional and sexual intimacy I have with Alex: I will miss this, but I could make it a little less painful by increasing my intimacy with my friends; I will eventually get over the pain, because I did in past relationships; this would be harder, because I love Alex more than I have loved anyone in the past, but I think the pain would eventually subside.

Estimate Worst-Case Probability

Estimate how likely the worst-case scenario is. Ask yourself how probable your feared worst case is. In estimating the probability, consider whether similar circumstances in the past have produced this outcome. If under similar circumstances different outcomes occurred, why would you think this outcome is more likely now? Camille thought that Alex might be more inclined to leave her now, because she had been so hard to live with for the past several weeks. Yet she had agreed to see a counselor, as Alex had requested, and he had been pleased about that. Camille felt that, realistically, the likelihood of Alex leaving right now was low.

Recognize Your Survival History

Remember your resilience. What if the worst case-scenario is likely to take place? People do leave people. And some worst-case scenarios are much worse than Camille's. What if your partner is going to leave you and you need the medical insurance for a chronic illness, because you cannot work and cannot afford any alternative insurance? In such a case, it is even more important that you follow these procedures, because you need to think calmly and clearly about your options. Becoming intensely emotional and making threats toward others or yourself will not help, but will only further distress you and antagonize other people.

Think about the times when you have gotten riled up and been emotionally out of control for hours or days, but in the end you did what you were dreading during your emotional tirade. Ask yourself, "Will being distraught change the outcome, or will it only delay the inevitable and probably exhaust me?" Lots of truly rotten things happen to people during their lives, but the reality is that they somehow survive those events. However, some people seem to survive better than others, because they seem to know when to shift from resistance to acceptance. The harder you resist an inevitable change, the more difficult coping with it will be. You can't reverse misfortune or accidents. You can't force someone to love you. You can't prevent death. You can't undo many things in life. The longer you try to fight what you can't control, the worse you make it for yourself.

Often people refuse to accept the obvious out of fear that they will not be able to handle what is happening. They resist as long as they can, and who can blame them? How do people survive devastating experiences, such as the death of a child, a rape, disfigurement, or any other horrific experience? They do it with the aid of the resilience they never knew they had. Most people think they could never endure such tribulations—until they have no choice. People often underestimate their resilience. Think about some of the most difficult situations in your past. Did you think you couldn't survive them? Yet, here you are, reading this book–you did survive them. You are a survivor. Remind yourself of this in the future when you doubt yourself.

Big No-No's

Certain actions and words are *always* inflammatory. They serve to antagonize or hurt. They seek to wound, not repair. They move you further from reconciliation and mutual understanding. They destroy your self-respect and the respect of other people for you. Don't do these anymore.

- Swearing, cursing, name-calling
- Being sarcastic, ridiculing, mocking, displaying contempt
- Kicking, throwing things, breaking anything, hitting the wall, or pounding the table. Don't engage in any physical act of aggression, whether directed at another living being or an inanimate object. Speeding is an aggressive act. If you are upset, do not drive anything with a motor.
- Trying to get the kids to side with you
- Trying to get the kids to be nasty to their other parent
- Making your children afraid of the other parent
- Threatening other people
- Threatening yourself

Stopping the use of these tactics may not be easy, but you must stop them. Ultimately they destroy your relationships. You always have a choice of whether to do any of these hurtful actions or to refrain from doing them. If you give yourself permission to do them, you'll do them, but sooner or later shame and regret will follow.

Aren't these actions sometimes justified? What about when another person hurts you deeply? Ask yourself this, "Will any of these actions undo that hurt?" Could these actions contribute to an escalation of hostility between you and the other person until someone gets completely out of control? Would you want your children to learn these behaviors as ways to resolve differences? Would you be proud to have others know of your behavior? Sometimes you are hurt and angry enough to want to do something to retaliate, but retaliation is always a destructive process with an unpredictable outcome.

Anger Management Strategies

Let's revisit Kevin and Kimberly. Kimberly would go out without Kevin, flirt with other men, tell him about it later, and sometimes even say that she had exchanged telephone numbers with them. These were facts. Kevin experienced jealousy, anger, hurt, and anxiety about these facts. What are Kevin's interpretations of these facts and what are the schemas that caused his jealousy, anger, hurt, and anxious feelings?

Emotions	Interpretations	Kevin's Schemas
Anger	*Kim is trying to hurt me intentionally.*	Kevin's Person Schema of Kim
Jealousy	*Kim is interested in other men.*	Kevin's Person Schema of Kim
Hurt	*Kim thinks I am inadequate.*	Kevin's Person Schema of Kim and Kevin's *Unworthy* schema
Anxiety	*Kim is going to leave me.*	Kevin's Person Schema of Kim and Kevin's *Intimacy Driven* schema

In these situations, Kevin responded with destructive actions. He was verbally abusive, broke things, and threatened to hurt Kimberly and the other men. Even though Kimberly's behavior is understandably upsetting to him, Kevin is responsible for maintaining self-control. *No matter how angry someone else makes you feel, you are responsible for controlling your behavior.* Before you react with any destructive behaviors, ask yourself what you want your actions to accomplish. When you are extremely upset, use the procedures described earlier to regain control of your emotions.

If your anger is still easily ignited, then go through the following steps, as Kevin did.

What is the goal of my destructive behavior?

I want Kimberly to apologize. I want her to tell me that she will stop being flirtatious, stop encouraging other men to come on to her, acknowledge to others that she is committed to me, and tell me that she loves me more than she does anyone else.

Do I ever get any of those responses when I engage in these attacks? If yes, how so? If not, what happens?

No, Kimberly just reacts angrily, and the interchange between us escalates viciously. Then we don't speak for days until I can't stand it any longer. Finally, I apologize and promise not to act like that again. But of course I do the next time she does that stuff.

What could be or have been the consequences of my aggressive behavior?

Kimberly could get mad enough at me to have me arrested for domestic violence. That would give me an arrest record and hurt me professionally as well as personally. I also could hurt her, someone else, or myself when I get so out of control. I would lose everything I have worked for. My family would be grief-stricken and ashamed of me.

How could I achieve my goals constructively?

I could sit down with her sometime when we are not upset with each other and explain how her actions make me feel. I would describe my interpretations of her behavior and ask her if I am interpreting her actions accurately. I would ask her if I am doing anything to encourage that behavior that I dislike. Then, I would ask how we both could change to improve this situation.

The problem in Kevin's situation is not his emotions. The problem is his behavior in reaction to those emotions. This is a good illustration of the difference between appropriate and inappropriate jealousy. Having your committed partner go out, engage in flirtatious behavior, and exchange phone numbers probably would create jealousy in most people. But with the *Unrestrained* schema, your reactions are usually excessive and distract the focus from the real issues. Your destructive reactions become the focus of attention rather than the original event. Someone with an *Expressive* schema would be more able to discuss the situation constructively and not risk the potential consequences of out-of-control actions.

This is not to say that jealousy is not a problem in itself for some people. Camille frequently experienced jealousy in her relationship with Alex and she had been jealous in previous relationships also. When you experience negative emotions such as anger, jealousy, or anxiety frequently and in many different situations, unbalanced schemas are the culprit and must be examined. If you have seldom experienced jealousy in any relationships but a particular one, then you need to look at the schemas of the other person as closely as you look at your own. People with either an *Entitled* or *Intimacy Driven* schema often try to instigate jealousy in others intentionally to get their attention or to be reassured of how much they care. Kimberly had both—the *Entitled* and *Intimacy Driven* schemas. To improve this situation, both Kevin and Kimberly need to change their schemas and their behavior. However, whether Kimberly changes or not, Kevin still needs to stop his destructive behavior.

Eliminate Ruminating

You have to stop ruminating. Ruminating refers to reviewing upsetting images over and over without trying to truly problem-solve the situation. Ruminating about upsetting events maintains high levels of emotional intensity. Even if you follow the procedures described in this chapter, you may be prone to dwell on upsetting events. Stopping this is essential to learning to manage your emotions. When upsetting images come into mind, you need to try to change the focus of your attention. Rumination is only partly involuntary.

You have to decide you are not going to dwell on these images and that you are only going to think about them when you are actively engaged in problem solving. At any other times, force yourself to think about something else. You will be surprised at how much of your ruminating you can stop by this simple active effort to focus on other things. You also can describe in writing what is upsetting you. Writing out your feelings can give you insights into what your interpretations and fears might be if they are still unclear. Writing is useful for all negative emotions, but it is especially helpful for anger. Just write out your feelings uncensored, and then destroy what you have written. Do not give anyone something you have written in anger. Do this several days in a row until your ruminations become minimal and the intensity of your emotions subsides.

Build Balanced Schemas

Balance your negative person schemas. When people are very upset with someone, they often are dwelling on extremely negative schemas of that person. By depicting someone as particularly odious, you fuel intense negative emotions. Actively try to balance those negative schemas. Frequently, the other person is someone for whom you have had strong positive feelings in the past. Force yourself to recall what you liked or admired about that person. Try to recall specific positive memories of that person. Then make a list of both their positive and negative qualities. When your extreme negative person schema comes up again, force yourself to review this person's good qualities. Then follow the procedures described above to stop ruminating. More suggestions to stop ruminations can be found in chapter 13.

Know Your Limits

Remove yourself from potentially anger-provoking situations. While you are learning the procedures to manage your emotions more effectively, you need to remove yourself from any situation that you think will make maintaining control more difficult. If out of control behavior has been descriptive of you for a long time, you may have a difficult time implementing these procedures to the extent that you want. In that case, a counselor may be able to assist you in your efforts. Being willing to seek help is evidence of having at least a little of the *Worthy* schema, because it demonstrates that you think you are worth helping.

Long-Term Emotional Management

If emotional overreactivity is descriptive of you, follow the procedures described in this chapter to regain control of your intense emotional reactions. However, you also need to take steps to lower your overall level of tension. People who are emotionally overreactive and have a high level of tension are readily thrust into intense reactions, because they already are so close to their threshold to react. There are a number of things you can do to reduce your overall level of tension. These are not short-term interventions. These are long-term strategies to make your life less stressful and you less vulnerable to overreacting. Think of these as lifestyle changes.

Emotional Analysis

First, analyze your emotional intensity. Has it gotten worse lately or in the last several months? Was there a noticeable increase at some time in the past? Has there been an increase in other stressors in your life? What factors could be contributing to this increase in tension? Review the last year and write down the changes that have taken place in your life. Circle the ones that you think are most significant. What can you do about any of these changes to make them less stressful than they are?

Health Assessment

Review your health. Have you had a physical examination in the last year? Frequently, emotions are related to health problems or to medications for those health problems. The development or exacerbation of health problems in yourself or those close to you can be very stressful. Many medications have a significant emotional impact, anywhere from slight agitation to hallucinations. If you are taking prescription drugs or over-the-counter drugs on a regular basis, ask your pharmacist what emotional side effects that medication may have. You may need your doctor to adjust your dosage, change the medication, or prescribe something to counterbalance the drug if it is essential for you.

Coping Strategy Analysis

Analyze your coping strategies. How do you deal with stress? Many people develop destructive coping strategies because those strategies produce some initial decrease in stress. However, they don't solve the problem but rather add to it, which is why they are viewed as destructive. Destructive coping strategies include alcohol abuse, drug abuse, smoking, infidelity, overeating, binge eating, Internet addiction, and excesses in sexual behavior and exercising. Almost anything done to an extreme can be destructive. Determining what is extreme is a value judgment, but three useful measures to determine whether it is extreme are these: Is it is harmful to your health? Does it produce shame? Does it strain relationships?

Build a Support Network

Develop a support network of people with whom you interact on a regular basis. Maintain these friendships even when you are in a romantic relationship. Camille always had several friends, but whenever she was in a romantic relationship she would abandon her friends. This left her feeling completely dependent on her romantic partner and even more alone when those relationships became troubled. When she would try to reinitiate contact with her friends, they sometimes would be reluctant to re-engage. They felt they could not count on her to not disappear again.

Increase Your Physical Activity

Make physical activity a regular part of your life. You don't have to join a gym. Just daily walks will help. Regular physical activity is one of the best things you can do for your emotional well-being.

Eat Well

Eat reasonably. Well-balanced nutrition is critical to emotional balance. Undereating and overeating disturb that balance. If anxiety is a problem for you, avoid caffeine.

Increase Your Fun

Increase your pleasurable activities. This doesn't just mean annual vacations or going to a movie once a month. This means doing something purely for pleasure that is not goal oriented for at least thirty minutes every day. Reading, watching television that you enjoy, listening to music, playing with your pets are all pleasurable activities. People who have little fun in their lives inevitably have negative emotions. Figure out how to program something pleasurable into your life as a high priority, so that you rarely skip it. At bedtime or in the morning, plan something to look forward to within the next twenty-four hours.

Sleep Regularly

Don't cheat on sleep. Most people need eight hours of sleep, some less, some more. Get what you need every night. Have a consistent routine for going to bed and getting up. Sleep deprivation makes you prone to depression and causes you to think less clearly and to overreact emotionally. Maintaining a consistent sleep schedule can have a major impact on your ability to manage your emotions.

Calm Yourself Frequently

Do a calming activity several times a day. This can be some form of meditation or it can be as simple as doing the breathing exercises described at the beginning of this chapter. Do something daily to break up the tension that builds up during the day.

Be Realistic

Set realistic expectations for yourself and others. You often are the greatest source of your own unhappiness. Are you asking too much of yourself? If you routinely exhaust yourself to meet your goals, the answer is yes. Moving your expectations down a notch can make an enormous difference emotionally and actually make you more productive because you will be less drained.

Lifestyle Analysis

Review your lifestyle. Have there been other times when you were less stressed and less emotionally reactive? If so, what was different between those times and now? Do you think that you can reduce your stress by following these suggestions, or do you need to make more dramatic changes in your lifestyle? Why do you want to maintain a lifestyle that takes the joy out of your current existence? If you truly have no choice, for example, if you are a single parent with a chronically ill child and need to work long hours to support the two of you, then be sure to follow the other suggestions here to give yourself some relief.

Listen to Your Body

Stop thinking of negative emotions and tension as symptoms. Respect them as signals from your body that you need to make some adjustments in your life. Learn to detect where physical tension resides in your body. Be aware of your breathing, so that you can tell when you are breathing more shallowly. Analyze the situation. Figure out what you are reacting to. Your emotions are your front line of communication with your body. They tell you when things are not going well. If you ignore them, you are much more likely to be contacted by your second line of bodily communication—physical discomfort or pain. Your body has a well-designed communication system. Pay attention.

Strengthen Your Emotional Competencies

You are responsible for maintaining control of your emotions and not engaging in destructive behavior to others or to yourself. You can learn all of the skills detailed in this chapter. Emotional competencies will enrich your life and the lives of those around you. A condensed version of all the procedures described in this chapter can be found in Appendix C, which you can copy and carry with you as a helpful reminder of the changes you are making.

13

Choices: Acceptance, Exits, and Forgiveness

Forgiveness frees two souls, the wronged and the wrongdoer.

You have come a long way since you began reading this book. You have learned a lot about yourself and the people who are or have been in relationships with you. Now you have some choices to make. Everyone has choices. This chapter is about your choices.

What's Enough?

You looked closely at your problematic relationships in chapter 9. You discovered how your schemas and the schemas of other people were contributing to distress in those relationships. You might have decided to change some of your schemas. But what can you do if you realize that the schemas of another person also are problematic? What if you feel that you are currently stuck in an unsatisfying relationship? What can you do about that? You have three basic options:

1. You can work on changing the relationship by making changes on your own or in conjunction with the other person.

2. You can learn to accept the relationship as it is.

3. You can end the relationship.

However, before you make any decisions you need to assess the importance this relationship has for you, the magnitude of the changes needed, and the feasibility of your different options.

When people are asked what they are unhappy about in their relationships, they often produce a litany of offenses, some of which have been occurring daily for years and other single incidents that sometimes date back decades. Often, their list of grievances drops dramatically when they are asked what are the *minimal* changes they need to be more content in the relationship. In essence, what would be enough to make them want to stay? Sometimes they want certain ongoing changes, such as less criticism or spending more time together. Others want an apology for a previous hurtful offense that was never addressed. Many want a combination of changes. If the change list shrinks, the possibility of relationship improvement usually increases, but not always, because some particular items may be very heavily weighted, for example, an act of aggression or infidelity.

People vary greatly in what they expect from their relationships and in their willingness to make changes. Your expectations and the other party's commitment to try to meet your expectations will influence your desire to continue in a relationship. However, relationship discontent is seldom a one-person affair. Most dissatisfied relationships involve two unhappy people, who each want to see changes in the other person. This dissatisfaction can result either in a mutual commitment to improve the relationship or an impasse. An impasse can result when one or both parties is unwilling or unable to make requested changes. A couple may face an impasse because the wife wants to spend their leisure time traveling and the husband does not. Whether an impasse destroys a relationship can depend on whether the parties can find compromises. In this case, the husband suggested that his wife travel with some of her single women friends, a solution that was agreeable to his wife, but such an agreement would not satisfy everyone. The viability of any compromise always depends on the people involved.

In chapter 9, you read about how Kevin experiences intense jealousy when Kimberly tells him about her flirtatious encounters. He reacts angrily and abusively. Kimberly needs Kevin to control his temper and stop his abusive language and destructive behavior. She also wants him to be less controlling and to spend more time with her. Kevin needs Kimberly to stop being flirtatious and acting cold and distant when she is unhappy with him. He wants her to let people know that she is in a committed relationship and unavailable even if she is friendly. Kevin wants her to tell him when she is unhappy with him and to try to work out compromises. He wants her to acknowledge when she hurts his feelings and to apologize when appropriate. Kimberly and Kevin agreed to try to make these changes.

Kevin and Kimberly are trying to modify their schemas and their accompanying behaviors. They each developed schema change plans and are focusing their energy on changing their own behavior, not on changing the other person's. Parts of Kevin's schema change plan are described in chapters 11 and 12. Kevin and Kimberly are not changing rapidly, but the fact that both are committed to change increases their tolerance for occasional setbacks, especially when acknowledgments and apologies accompany the setbacks. In spite of their recurrent unhappiness with each other, they both have strong positive feelings for each other and want the relationship to succeed.

This couple's example illustrates several points about how to implement successful change efforts in a relationship. Each person needs to make a commitment to the other person to work toward change. People must identify specific behaviors they need changed rather than making vague complaints. Once the parties agree on the desired changes, they need to focus on their own efforts at change, *not* on monitoring the other person. However, each needs to acknowledge the change efforts the other person is making. If it isn't noticed, the person making the change should point out examples of change. This is necessary to counteract the effects of the confirmatory bias that causes people to overlook deviations from old patterns. (If you need to refresh your memory about how confirmatory bias works, see chapter 2.)

Both people also need to realize that change, especially schema change, does not occur swiftly nor does it take place without occasional relapses. When a slip occurs, the person making the slip needs to acknowledge that, apologize for any resulting hurt or inconvenience, and make amends for whatever damage took place.

What's Enough for You?

In chapter 9 you examined your problematic relationships. Now you need to assess what changes would be necessary to move those relationships out of the problematic category. Think about the unbalanced schemas you and the other person have. What changes would be essential for both of you to move toward balanced schemas? Consider how committed you and the other person are toward improving your relationship. Review the quality of this relationship since its inception. Now, to assess your relationships, answer the following questions. Do this analysis for each relationship on separate pages of your notebook, because there are other parts to this assessment throughout the chapter that you will want to add.

1. On separate pages, write the names of those people with whom you are in painful or frustrating relationships.

2. For each person, describe how that relationship is important to you and how your life would change if the relationship ended.

3. Describe the minimal changes you would need to be satisfied with the relationship.

4. Describe what changes you think the other person wants in the relationship.

5. Write which phrase describes your attitude toward each relationship:
   - willing to make mutual changes
   - willing to make changes on my part only
   - unwilling to make changes but want other person to do so
   - do not think any changes would be enough to make this work

6. Indicate the probability the relationship will improve: high, medium, low, zero.

Acceptance

What if the other person is unwilling to compromise or make changes? Tolerance can be another road around a stalemate. Tolerance refers to accepting the difference between what you expect in a relationship and what you are getting. Even if the other person agrees to make changes, there always will be some gaps between what you want and what you get from that person. Sometimes tolerance can allow you to be content in a relationship in spite of these gaps. Your willingness to develop tolerance of the difference between what you expect and what you get depends on several aspects of the relationship: your commitment to the relationship, the quality of your relationship, what positive benefits you derive from it, your history together, your alternatives, and what costs you would experience by ending the relationship.

Developing tolerance also depends on your schemas. Those with an *Unworthy* schema may settle for very little in a relationship, because they have so few expectations. Those with an *Entitled* schema may be unwilling to suffer even minimal discrepancies from their expectations. An *Intimacy Driven* schema may decrease one's willingness to leave a relationship no matter how bad it is, whereas an *Intimacy Avoidant* schema may make leaving a relationship much easier. Sometimes an ideal role schema or ideal person schema prevents you from accepting other people as they are. You want them to match your ideal schemas and refuse to accept that no one could.

If you have been frustrated with someone for a long time for not being or doing what you want, ask yourself what makes you think he or she will change if they haven't so far. Is this something you could accept, because you have been living with it for a long time, even if you have been complaining? Apparently that person has other qualities that compensate for what you think is lacking. Or perhaps you have chosen to complain rather than leave. If so, ask yourself how complaining makes the situation any better for you. Would an alternative to complaining be worth trying?

Some degree of acceptance is essential for relationship happiness. People are not perfect and neither are their relationships. To some extent, everyone compromises with their ideals in their relationships. Acceptance acknowledges that others have a right to do things their way, which may not be your way. Acceptance recognizes the differences between you and someone else and acknowledges that person's right to not share all your preferences, interests, and values. Acceptance means viewing these differences as part of who that person is and not as something that he or she is doing to antagonize you. With acceptance you don't take differences as being personally directed at you.

People in happy relationships seldom view each other as perfect. There is a mutual recognition of their idiosyncrasies and shortcomings without a negative emotional attitude toward them. This is coupled with the awareness that the other party grants the same latitude and acceptance in return.

Remaining in a relationship out of perceived necessity but with resentment and ill will is not tolerance. Certainly people vary greatly in what is or is not acceptable to them, but some degree of acceptance is essential for any satisfying relationship. Acceptance refers to tolerating differences by accepting the other person's right to be different from you. It does not imply joyfully embracing these differences. In a marriage you might have hoped for more shared interests, greater emotional intimacy, or a more active sex life, but after years of arguing and endless tears, you have accepted that the two of you are too different to even reach a compromise that approaches your hopes. As disappointing as this loss is, if the prospect of losing the relationship is more painful, you may settle for it. If you can do that without bitterness, you have begun the process of acceptance.

Acceptance is not an instantaneous event. It's a continuing process that takes time to accomplish. The amount of time depends on the magnitude and importance of the differences between your expectations and reality. The initial process of acceptance may include a period of grieving as you face the loss of what you had hoped would be part of your relationship. When you adjust your expectations to fit the reality of the relationship as it is, your grieving is completed. Occasionally, circumstances may rekindle memories of your old expectations and associated feelings of sadness, but those experiences are fleeting. Acceptance means adjusting your expectations without feeling animosity toward the other person. Reaching this state of acceptance can take weeks, months, or years. If you are still feeling angry that the other person does not meet your expectations or longing for what you don't have, you are not there yet.

Measuring Your Acceptance

For each relationship you listed in the previous exercise, consider how you have settled. List what you have come to accept in the other person over time. Then, list what currently frustrates you but you think you could learn to accept eventually. Next, list what you think you could never come to accept. For these last items, rate the probability of the other person ever changing any of those items: high, medium, low, zero.

Since ideal person or role schemas are often obstacles to acceptance, describe any ideal person or role schemas you have that other people are not meeting. What parts are not being met? Could you try to adjust your ideal schema to be more balanced and tolerant?

Forgiveness

Sometimes a relationship impasse occurs not because of differences between you and the other person but from an act of betrayal, such as a revelation of a confidence, romantic infidelity, parental abandonment, or an act of physical violence. Acts of betrayal are difficult for people to absorb, because they usually are inconsistent with what one expects from the other person or from that particular type of relationship. Children don't expect to be abused or abandoned. Partners don't expect to be beaten. Friends don't expect friends to break promises. These acts are inconsistent with our schemas of other people or certain roles.

When an act of betrayal occurs, you have to integrate that behavior into your person schema of the individual. The more discrepant the action is from your person schema, the more difficult integration is. If you have a hyperpositive person schema of someone, an act of betrayal will appear even more discrepant. An act of betrayal may be less distressing from someone about whom you have a negative person schema, because it may seem less out of character and not be terribly inconsistent with your expectations. On the other hand, a balanced person schema might make integration of the betrayal possible, because your view of the individual already includes both strengths and weaknesses of the individual.

Other factors also influence your ability to integrate an act of betrayal into your image of a person. The extent of betrayal and the ramifications of the act are especially important. Whether the act was intentional or could have been avoided also makes a difference. How you view the person after discovering a betrayal is strongly influenced by the person's willingness to be truthful about the event, accept responsibility for his or her actions, apologize for hurting you, and make amends. The inability to integrate painful negative information about someone creates confusion and uncertainty about who this person really is. A new negative person schema is likely to emerge if integration becomes impossible.

After Shelby discovered that Dean had begun an affair with his receptionist, she was distraught (see chapter 10). However, several factors contributed to her ability to move past his betrayal and toward acceptance and forgiveness. Foremost among these was this: she had a balanced person schema of Dean. Although she loved him dearly, she also was aware of how emotionally isolated he was, how difficult it was for him to ask for help, and how hard communication was for him. She saw him as vulnerable. So, although his betrayal was clearly hurtful, she understood the circumstances contributing to it.

Furthermore, Dean did not lie about anything about his affair once Shelby confronted him, so he did not cause her sudden distrust of him to escalate. He accepted full responsibility for his actions, expressed shame and remorse, and willingly offered to go to counseling to change the factors that contributed to his betrayal. Shelby's balanced schema of Dean and his actions after the revelation allowed her to integrate his behavior into her schema system and eventually to forgive him.

Stan and Helen

For most people, forgiveness does not emerge as readily as it did for Shelby. However, if a relationship is ever to truly recover from a betrayal, forgiveness is essential. Helen's husband, Stan, had a stroke a few years ago, which left his mind somewhat diminished and his mental state confused at times. His emotions were often inconsistent with what he was saying. He continued to have mini-strokes and his alertness varied day to day. He was gradually deteriorating, but that was not the problem. The problem was worse than that. Two nights ago Stan had seemed pensive. When Helen inquired if he was alright, he said no. She asked what was wrong, and he told her. He told her he couldn't go to heaven if he didn't unburden his soul with the truth. What truth? That he had been unfaithful to her during the war when he was in Japan. He stated this with such a lack of emotion that Helen could barely comprehend his words.

He knew how upset she would be. She couldn't believe that he was telling her this. This was absolutely incongruent with who he was. He had always expressed contempt for servicemen who cheated on their wives. He had repeatedly assured Helen then and over the last five decades that he had always been faithful. When Helen pressed him for details, he gave her some, but he couldn't remember everything. He denied ever being unfaithful to her at any other time.

Helen didn't sleep at all that night. She had been pregnant with their first child when he went abroad. He had professed his undying love in daily letters while having sex with other women. She knew that infidelity was common behavior in the military. But even if every serviceman did it, it didn't matter. She wasn't married to every serviceman. She was married to Stan. Stan did it. And Stan had told her for over fifty years that he would never do it and had never done it. He disrespected men who did. Helen had always thought Stan was perfect. She had thought they had a perfect marriage. His adoration for her was so obvious that others often commented on it. Had their life been a myth? She felt ashamed and embarrassed. Unknowingly, she had participated in this deception. What else had Stan lied about? Had he not found her pretty? Was she not desirable enough for him? Had she been pregnant too many times? Had she been too exhausted by the kids too often? Had he never enjoyed their marriage the way she thought he had? Had she been too inhibited? Had all the loving things he said to her every day been a lie? Where was the line of truth? And had he always been on the wrong side of that line? Who was this man who had been so honorable, so respected, so devoted, and who had deceived her for half a century?

Stan needed to cleanse his soul. He did it by dumping his sins on her soul. Now if she did not forgive him, she would be the sinner, not he. Helen panicked. She didn't have much time to sort this out. Stan's mind was fading with each passing day. He probably would lose his mind before he lost his life. She needed to get past this. She needed to be able to forgive him while he still understood. No matter how angry she was, she didn't want Stan to die with this wall between them. She discussed the matter with her therapist, who thought that Stan's confession might not be accurate. The therapist thought there was some chance that Stan was confusing memories of what the other guys did with his own memories. Helen knew that some of the information Stan provided was inaccurate. But in her heart, she felt he was telling her the truth.

Stan's revelation challenged Helen's schemas. She had thought Stan's integrity unassailable. He was above such betrayal. Ever since they were adolescents she had never doubted his word. Her hyperpositive person schema of Stan didn't fit with this new information; neither did her hyperpositive role schema of marriage, which viewed fidelity as sacred and infidelity as unforgivable. Fidelity was revered in her family, her church, and her culture. For fifty years she had thought she was married to the perfect man and had a perfect marriage. Her relationship with Stan had always given her a strong sense of herself, which had been integral to her own *Worthy* schema. Now his view of her seemed unclear. She had never felt especially pretty but he had always made her feel beautiful. Now she wondered. Her person schema of Stan, her role schema of marriage, and her self schema of *Worthy* struggled to incorporate the meaning of Stan's infidelity.

Together Helen and her therapist explored how to make sense of this anomaly. Stan had an *Unworthy* schema that had decreased over the years, but he never got over being ashamed of his past. He had never known his father and doubted that his mother did either. As a child, he had witnessed a number of men engage in sexual encounters with his mother before he was age seven, when she was declared unfit and he was placed in an orphanage. He lived there until he graduated from high school. Although he had been an exemplary student, college was never an option, so he had enlisted in the army. He did well there and in time went through officer's training.

Helen was fourteen when she met Stan in high school. He was very shy and was never much of a talker, but she knew he liked her right away. She thought he was wonderful. He loved her family and how loving they were to each other. Stan graduated two years earlier than Helen did, but he came home on every leave to see her. They married one week after her graduation from high school. Four months later he was shipped overseas. Stan had never had a lot of confidence, but Helen had been his unwavering cheerleader for fifty years. He had a terrible fear of abandonment (*Intimacy Driven*) and needed frequent assurance that Helen loved him, which Helen knew and offered readily. Helen knew how much he needed her, but she never let him know that she knew that about him. However, his *Intimacy Driven* schema was only active with her. With everyone else his *Intimacy Avoidant* schema was dominant.

Helen thought about how vulnerable Stan had been overseas. Stan, a loner, never had a best friend in his life. He was so ashamed of his past he didn't want anyone to get to know him. His letters home described how painfully lonely he was. He missed her terribly. Her heart had ached with sadness for him when she had read his letters. She thought about how his *Unworthy, Intimacy Avoidant,* and *Restrained* schemas had always isolated him, but never more so than when he was overseas.

He had relied on her optimism and enthusiasm to pull him out of his low moods throughout his life, but overseas he had been all alone. She could see how he could have used sex to get some kind of human closeness. She knew that he must have felt ashamed and guilty of his betrayal all of his life. He had said he didn't tell her earlier because he was afraid she would leave him, and she knew that she might have done that. She knew that if she had left him it would have been the most horrifying thing that had ever happened to him. No wonder he didn't tell her.

She also thought that if she had left, she would have missed out on fifty wonderful years of love and devotion. During their marriage Stan had always been so strong and competent that Helen frequently forgot how vulnerable he was. She realized that she had been instrumental in the development of his *Worthy* and *Intimacy Comfortable* schemas that he had formed over the years, but that his unbalanced schemas had been much more powerful in his youth.

A few weeks after his confession, Stan had another stroke, making it impossible for him to talk or move. At the hospital, Helen asked him to squeeze her hand if he understood. He did. Helen told him he had been kind not to tell her fifty years ago about his infidelity. She would have been too insecure to have been able to handle it then. Now she realized that it didn't have anything to do with her. She kissed him and told him she loved him and forgave him and was grateful for every day he had loved her. He squeezed her hand back. He died a few hours later. Helen knew Stan believed her, and added, "I wasn't lying. I did forgive him . . . in my mind. I want to forgive him. I need to forgive him. And I pray that one day my heart will forgive him." And one day, several months later, it did. It still hurt when she thought about it, but she discovered that her love for her late husband was great enough to love him as he had been—even if he didn't match her perfect schema of him.

That's often the way forgiveness works. You decide that you want to forgive a transgression, but your heart and mind don't immediately fall in line. After making that decision, your hurt doesn't suddenly disappear. Nor do the memories of the betrayal. But by trying to understand the offender's perspective and weaknesses, often you are able to depersonalize the incident. You might even see that the offender had no awareness of the impact the betrayal would have on you. Witnessing the person's remorse also helps you forgive, because you can see how sad and ashamed the offender is due to how badly you have been hurt.

Sometimes you don't decide to forgive. There are no apologies offered. No explanations lessen the hurt. Nothing helps. Finally, you just set the incident aside. You have thought about it as much as you can. There are no more strands to unravel. There is no interpretation of events that will explain away the actions or soften the blow to your soul. So you set it aside. Months or years later you may discover that your heart recovered. You can think about the transgression without the nausea in your stomach or the ache in your heart. You no longer view the offender harshly. Somehow, you forgave the person the betrayal.

Sometimes you think you have finally forgiven. You have sewn up the hole in your heart and gone on. Then one day weeks, months, or years later those old feelings of anguish and despair come flooding over you. What happened? Perhaps something associated with the original betrayal triggered an old memory. Maybe a betrayal by someone else triggered emotions and memories associated with this old betrayal. Or the offender did something that reminds you of the earlier incident. Forgiving someone doesn't mean you will forget about the incident or you won't ever feel upset again, but these emotional reoccurrences become less frequent and less intense with time. As with acceptance, forgiveness is a process that can take a long, long time to complete.

Acts of Betrayal

For each of your hurtful relationships, are there any acts of betrayal that you have not been able to forgive? If so, in your notebook on separate pages, describe what they are for each relevant relationship. Then, describe why you have not been able to forgive those acts. Be sure to also describe any ideal person or role schemas you have that may be getting in the way of forgiveness. Which of your self schemas also are obstacles to forgiving?

Exits

Sometimes you can accept that others have a right to be different, but you are not willing to subject yourself to the hurt or frustration that those differences create. Ending the relationship becomes your choice. Sometimes an act of betrayal creates an impasse around which there is no detour. Ending the relationship may or may not be your choice, but the relationship ends. Whether you choose to end a relationship or the other person does, you may remain hurt and angry. However, just because a relationship has ended does not mean that you have let go of it. Letting go involves accepting that the relationship is irretrievably over and so are the dreams associated with it.

Letting go of a relationship often requires grieving. For example, a son who had been abandoned by his father as a small child entertained images of reconciliation for years, hoping his father would acknowledge what he had done to his son, regret the hurt his child had experienced, and show a desire to develop a meaningful relationship with the grown man he had become. After contacting his father and realizing that his parent had no such awareness or interest, the son finally decided to terminate further efforts toward reconciliation. Even though the contact with his father had been brief, his loss was enormous, because for years he had entertained an imaginary image that he now knew would never be realized.

Letting go is greatly impeded when an act of betrayal has been involved. In this case, the son had to deal not only with the loss of the relationship he had imagined, he also had to deal with his father's refusal to acknowledge his betrayal. Divorce often requires having to let go of a relationship after suffering betrayal. When Del discovered his wife Shirley's relationship with another church member, he was devastated (see chapter 10). When Shirley showed no remorse and moved out, Del filed for divorce. He wanted to let go of the relationship, but he was repeatedly forced to have contact with Shirley regarding their two children. Letting go is easier if you are not faced with repeated contact with the other person, but divorces often preclude that option because of children. You still need to let go, and perhaps even more so, to avoid allowing the children to become pawns in a game of vengeance.

After Del discovered his wife had been having an affair for a couple of years, Shirley moved out to pursue her other relationship. No remorse, no apologies, and no explanations were offered. Del's hyperpositive schema of Shirley made her betrayal and subsequent actions incomprehensible to him. Ultimately, he developed a negative person schema for her, and flipped back and forth between his two schemas, at times despising her and at other times longing for her return. Del ended their relationship, as Shirley had no motivation to continue the marriage.

He realized his anger toward Shirley made him vulnerable to becoming vindictive toward her, especially in regard to the kids. Del found himself thinking about her continually, her transgressions, the times she deceived him, how she used him, and how he always had been true to her. With these thoughts came anger and the desire to get even. Del is not unique. Research repeatedly has shown that ruminating about an act of betrayal is associated with an increased desire for revenge (Caprara 1986; Collins and Bell 1997; McCullough, Rachal, Sandage, et al., 1998). The suggestions in chapter 12 on how to maintain emotional control can help stop ruminations. Ruminations also can be interrupted through the process of forgiving.

Finding Forgiveness

If you are trying to recover from a betrayal in a current or previous relationship, being able to forgive can greatly enhance the quality of your life. Forgiveness is good for *you*. Psychologists have discovered that forgiveness has a powerful impact on emotional well-being. Forgiveness can reduce your depression, anxiety, and hostility and increase your self-esteem and hope (Hebl and Enright 1993; Al-Mabuk, Enright, and Cardis 1995; Enright and the Human Development Study Group 1996; Freedman and Enright 1996). Without forgiveness, the act of betrayal will continue to trap you in a victim role and produce intense emotional distress, often unpredictably and sometimes throughout your life. In the absence of forgiveness, the offender and the betrayal continue to have the power to torment you. Through the process of forgiveness, you can recapture your life, recover personal peace, and, in many instances, emerge a stronger person.

Forgiveness is essentially a two-part process. First it requires your awareness that you have been harmed emotionally, physically, or financially by someone who has betrayed your trust. There must be no efforts by you to deny the situation. Until you are able to acknowledge openly to yourself what has happened and that you have been betrayed, you cannot move forward in the process of forgiving. Without this awareness, you will remain in denial.

The second phase in the process of forgiving is that you voluntarily try to let go of your anger and your desire for revenge and replace them with understanding and compassion for the offender. Somehow you have to get in touch with the offender's basic humanity and be able to see that this is someone who also is capable of good. Needless to say, this is much easier to do with some offenders than with others.

Understanding what forgiveness is *not* is essential to understanding what forgiveness is (Enright and the Human Development Study Group 1996): It is not minimizing or discounting the act of betrayal and the subsequent harm and hurt you experienced. Forgiveness is not a denial of your right to be angry and hurt. It is not absolution of the other person's responsibility for actions taken or not taken that caused you harm. Although forgiveness involves empathy, it does not necessarily mean the restoration of positive feelings toward another person. It does mean the absence of negative, vengeful feelings. Forgiveness is not reconciliation. You can forgive someone without any obligation to reconcile with that person. Reconciliation is a separate step that you may or may not wish to pursue. Reconciliation must be based on whether you feel the other person has accepted responsibility for the betrayal, whether you can trust that individual to not betray you again, and whether *you want* to continue the relationship.

There are several factors that make forgiveness easier. A sincere apology that recognizes the harm done is especially helpful. An explanation of the sequence of events that makes the act at least comprehensible also can help. Being able to understand what the circumstances were that led to the betrayal also can expedite the process. An awareness of the other person's schemas can help you better understand how this happened. Understanding your own schemas can help you comprehend your reactions and also help you to see what may make the recovery process more or less difficult for you. Understanding what, if anything about you, made the betrayal more likely also can be useful. But even in the absence of some of these factors, forgiveness is still possible—although the journey toward it may be harder.

You are not *obligated* to forgive anyone. No one else has the right to decide whether you ought to forgive someone. Forgiving a betrayal is your choice. When someone has betrayed you, that person does not deserve your forgiveness. Your forgiveness is a gift freely given. The point here is not that you have an *obligation* to forgive anyone. The point is that forgiveness has the potential to empower you, repair your heart, and in some cases restore an important relationship.

Developing Forgiveness

The following guide was influenced by the extensive work of Dr. Robert Enright and his colleagues on forgiveness. These questions will help you work your way through the process of forgiving. As you answer the questions, remember that this procedure is a *process*, not a finite assignment. The questions are designed to help you understand more fully the betrayal you experienced and the contributing factors. You may want to skip some questions and come back to them later. Some questions will not be relevant for some relationships, so just skip those that don't apply. If you lack the information for some questions, put "don't know." Your answers can be as long or short as you want. Take your time. You can neither force nor rush forgiveness.

Before you write anything, read all the questions. You may choose to do them in a different order than presented. Use these questions however you think they will be most helpful to you. When you finish answering the questions, you may find it helpful to discuss your thoughts with someone else. You also might find reading other material on forgiveness helpful. There are numerous thoughtful books on this subject. Or you may want to set the whole incident aside for a while and let your thoughts and feelings settle.

Understanding the Impact of the Offense

Describe what the person did to betray and/or hurt you.

Describe how that act hurt and/or betrayed you.

How did you contribute to this situation in any manner, if you think you did?

Describe the impact this has had on your life. How has your life been changed?

Describe what this has cost you. What have you lost?

Describe the impact that you think this will have on you next year, and in ten, twenty, and forty years from now.

Considerations of Vengeance

How would you like to seek revenge?

How would that benefit you?

What are the risks or costs to you if you pursue revenge?

How would revenge improve the situation?

Desire for Justice

What would make you feel this situation has been handled justly?

What would need to happen for justice to be served?

What is the likelihood of that happening?

Understanding Yourself

Describe yourself before you had to deal with this situation.

Describe yourself after this situation developed.

How are you different since this situation occurred?

What has remained unchanged about you?

Are you "better" in any ways?

How has this changed your views about life, yourself, and others?

How has this changed your view of your control over your life?

Review your bonding schemas and list them here. How has this act affected any of your schemas? Also, indicate what schemas, if any, were different before this situation.

Comforting Yourself

What schemas have helped you cope with this situation?

What schemas have made coping more difficult for you?

What negative thoughts do you have about this experience on a daily basis?

How can you respond to those thoughts in a more constructive manner?

How can you contain those thoughts when they are nonproductive?

How can you comfort yourself when you are angry or sad?

How have your reactions to this event affected others?

Describe how you currently are handling this situation.

Where will your current behavior take you?

How will it affect your other relationships?

Understanding the Offender

Describe how you viewed the other person before this situation occurred.

Describe how you view the person now.

Describe what has remained unchanged about that person.

List the unbalanced schemas the other person has.

Which of these schemas contributed to this situation?

What was this person's childhood like? What were this person's parents like? What kind of problems or stress did the person have at the time of this incident? What support system did this person have? Did low self-esteem contribute to this person being vulnerable? Were there any problems at that time between the two of you?

Can you describe how the offender is/was vulnerable?

How do you think the person has felt about this incident since it took place?

What Has Not Been Lost?

Describe what drew you to that person in the beginning.

Describe how that person made you feel special and/or loved.

Describe how that person enhanced who you were in your own eyes and the eyes of others.

What was positive about your relationship in the past?

What, if anything, can continue to be positive?

What did you love or admire about this person in the past? What parts of that are still true?

What can you take from this experience and relationship that can be constructive?

Future Impact

How might this affect the rest of your life?

How do you want this to affect the rest of your life?

What can you do to increase the possibility of getting the outcome you want?

Developing Forgiveness

Have you ever loved anyone who is not perfect? How were you able to do that? What was different from this situation?

Do you have some ideal person or role schemas that make forgiveness harder? If so, how? Can you try to balance those schemas a little more?

How have you been imperfect? Selfish? Greedy? Judgmental? Unforgiving? Vindictive? Jealous? Envious? Controlling? Bossy? Do you say mean/hurtful things?

How have others forgiven your imperfections?

How have you shown compassion to others who let you down in the past?

If you think compassion is an admirable quality, what can you do to increase your ability to be compassionate?

Can you soften your position in a way that would not diminish you? How? Do you want to?

Do you want to forgive the other person? If so, are you willing to work on this?

Self-Forgiveness

Doug (see chapter 8) developed a plan to change his hyperpositive bonding schemas. As he moved from his hyperpositive schemas, his newly emerging balanced schemas made him more aware of his feelings and of his emotional impact on other people. As uncomfortable as that was at times, Doug had the courage to stick with his schema change plan, because he also was feeling the joy of emotionally connecting to other human beings who cared about him. In a letter he wrote to his children, Doug apologized for how he had not given them the care and attention they had deserved. He admitted that he had been an inadequate father by being so focused on his own needs instead of theirs. He explained that his behavior was the result of his own problems and was not because of anything they had ever done. He described how he was trying to change. His children forgave him readily, but Doug knew they had some skepticism about his sincerity.

As time passed and Doug actually did the things he said he would do, he could sense how his children were becoming more trusting of him. He could see the happiness his changes had created in them. However, the closer he grew to his children, the guiltier and more ashamed he felt about his past behavior. He experienced great regret over how much he had missed out in their lives even when they were living with him. He knew his son and daughter had forgiven him, but he felt he did not deserve their forgiveness. His problem was that he had not forgiven himself.

Forgiving yourself is no less difficult than forgiving someone else. Forgiving yourself involves acknowledging to yourself how you have harmed another, apologizing for your actions even if you know no forgiveness will be forthcoming, and trying to amend what you have damaged. Perhaps you cannot undo the hurt you have caused another. But the human heart is amazingly resilient. A heartfelt apology often can wash away the pain you inflicted and replace it with love and forgiveness.

With self-forgiveness there is another step in the process. You must acknowledge to yourself your own humanity, your own imperfect self, a self who has made choices out of selfishness or thoughtlessness. All of us are flawed. You are going to hurt and disappoint other people throughout your life. Being responsible for your actions and trying to do better is all anyone can expect of you. You should not expect more of yourself. You are not perfect. You never will be. And you aren't fooling anyone else by pretending to be. Stop trying to fool yourself.

What if you have done something that you think is simply unforgivable? Ask yourself how a lifetime of shame and self-recriminations will change the past. No matter how hard you beat your breast and tear your hair and cry, " I am guilty," you will not be able to change the past. You can try to make restitution, if not to the person harmed in the past, by other constructive actions. No matter what you have done, you cannot undo it, but you always can do better today. Withholding self-forgiveness until you have achieved some measure of penance or restitution is unfair. Isn't truly trying to be a better person worthy of forgiveness now?

Choices

Life is a series of choices intermingled unpredictably with luck, both good and bad. Some people are much less lucky than others. Having a child diagnosed with cancer or being blinded in a car accident by a drunken driver is undeniably bad luck. Nothing anyone does deserves such bad luck, but you cannot control fate. Your only freedom comes from the choices you do have, no matter how limited they are. Choices vary greatly among people. Some people have an infinite range of choices, while others may be limited to simply picking the arm in which to receive chemotherapy that day. The major purpose of this book has been to help you see that you have choices. You can choose to be present or absent in your own life and the lives of others. You can choose to face your emotions or you can hide from them for the rest of your life. You can choose to honor your relationship obligations or to dishonor them. You can choose to forgive or to remain unforgiving. You can choose to stay or leave. You can choose to change or not.

People with *Unworthy* or *Intimacy Driven* schemas tend to settle for much less than they deserve in relationships. People with *Intimacy Avoidant* or *Restrained* schemas are likely to bail out rather than struggle to work through relationship differences. Don't let your unbalanced schemas encourage you to make bad choices. Ask yourself if you had balanced schemas if you would make the same choices. Your choices do matter. They have far-reaching effects on you and the people who love you.

If you are fortunate enough to have children, there are no other choices you make that are more important than the ones you make as a parent. Certainly, some choices are easier than others. Fidelity for a millionaire sports star who has women handing him their underwear may not be as easy as for others far less vigorously pursued. Yet many wealthy athletes do remain faithful to their wives. Everyone makes choices. It doesn't matter what choices you have made in the past. You have new choices today.

Know where to invest your efforts. You cannot change someone else. You can rant and rave about other people's behavior, but you are the one who is upset—not them. You are the one who needs to change, either by changing your reactions or decreasing the amount of contact you have with people who upset you. Respect yourself. Don't make empty threats. Know what your limits are, state them, and then enforce them by taking the actions that are under your control. Be selective in whom you invest yourself. Recognize the red lights of relationship danger zones: relationships that emotionally exhaust you even if they include occasional highs; that cause your self-esteem to decrease; that make you afraid to be competent and successful; that take away your individual identity. The bulb in every red light is an unbalanced schema, whether it is your own or someone else's.

Balanced schemas are the green lights for balanced relationships. People with balanced schemas are more likely to have satisfying relationships, to feel valued, and to value others. Unbalanced schemas are a disadvantage, but they are not destiny. With time and effort, you can develop balanced schemas. Living with unbalanced schemas is like a bird trying to fly with a broken wing. You repeatedly sputter around in circles until you crash. And every time you take off, you crash again. But unlike a bird with a broken wing, you can improve your flight pattern. Life is tough enough without holding on to disadvantages that you can change. You can change your schemas. Balance them and watch how high you can soar.

Appendix A

Definitions of the Bonding Self Schemas

Worthiness Self Schemas

Unworthy: I often feel that somehow I am not as good as other people. My needs are not as important as the needs of other people. I don't deserve to be happy. The needs of other people should come before my own. I tend to feel guilty if I do nice things for myself. I also feel uncomfortable when other people do nice things for me.

Worthy: I am a worthwhile person. My needs are as important as the needs of other people, but not necessarily more so. I deserve to be as happy as everyone else. I deserve to have many of my needs met, but certainly not all of them. I can treat myself occasionally without feeling guilty. I am comfortable when other people do things for me. I like nice things, but I don't have to have the best of everything.

Entitled: I think I am as good as anyone else, if not better. I am entitled to have whatever I want. I deserve to have the best of everything. I have a right to have all my needs met. I don't think about what my needs may cost others. I am special. I think more about my own needs than how those needs may affect other people.

Intimacy Self Schemas

Intimacy Driven: I often want more closeness or greater intimacy than others give me. I seek repeated reassurance from others that I am loved. I feel lost if I am not in an intimate relationship. I have difficulty functioning if I am not involved with someone. I worry about losing people who are close to me. I worry about being abandoned. I am usually alert to any signs of rejection by others.

Intimacy Comfortable: I enjoy having close relationships, and I also enjoy my time by myself. I like emotional intimacy with certain people, but I don't like to be smothered. I am able to function fine when I am not in a close relationship even if I would prefer to be. It would be painful to lose someone close to me, but I think I could handle such an experience. I don't like rejection, but it's not the end of the world when I get it. I seldom worry about being abandoned.

Intimacy Avoidant: I prefer to keep most people at a distance. I am not comfortable being too close to other people. Relationships often seem like a burden to me. Emotional intimacy feels suffocating. Relationships aren't that important to me. I prefer not getting too attached to people.

Expressiveness Self Schemas

Unrestrained: My emotions often are overwhelming. It is difficult for me to control my emotions. People can easily tell how I am feeling. I cannot hide my emotions; they often seem out of control.

Expressive: I am comfortable expressing my feelings. I usually can control my feelings when I need to, but not always. Even if I am upset, I usually can express my thoughts calmly. I try to express my feelings constructively, so that I am not unnecessarily hurtful to others. I am not embarrassed about feeling strong emotions, but I am seldom totally unrestrained.

Restrained: I seldom show my feelings. I am uncomfortable expressing my emotions. I don't let people see how I feel. I am almost always in control of my emotions. Other people usually can't tell how I feel. I don't like other people to know when I'm feeling bad. I hate to cry in front of other people.

Interdependency Self Schemas

Dependent: I tend to be dependent. I rely on other people to help me with most things. Life is too difficult for me to handle alone. I have a hard time making decisions by myself. I frequently seek assistance from others. I do not like being completely on my own. I need other people to take care of me.

Interdependent: I can handle most things on my own, but I will ask for help if I need it. I like to make my own decisions, but am comfortable seeking advice from others.

Stubbornly Independent: I do not like to rely on anyone but myself. It is hard for me to ask for help. I don't like it when other people offer me advice or assistance. I feel irritated when someone tries to help me. I can't stand being dependent on anybody for anything. I prefer to do things on my own.

Appendix B

The Bonding Styles

The Easy Bonding Style: The Balanced Self Schemas

Worthy

I am a worthwhile person. My needs are as important as the needs of other people, but not necessarily more so. I deserve to be as happy as everyone else. I deserve to have many of my needs met, but certainly not all of them. I can treat myself occasionally without feeling guilty. I am comfortable when other people do things for me. I like nice things, but I don't have to have the best of everything.

Intimacy Comfortable

I enjoy having close relationships, and I also enjoy my time by myself. I like emotional intimacy with certain people, but I don't like to be smothered. I am able to function fine when I am not in a close relationship even if I would prefer to be. It would be painful to lose someone close to me, but I think I could handle such an experience. I don't like rejection, but it's not the end of the world when I get it. I seldom worry about being abandoned.

Expressive

I am comfortable expressing my feelings. I usually can control my feelings when I need to, but not always. Even if I am upset, I usually can express my thoughts calmly. I try to express my feelings constructively, so that I am not unnecessarily hurtful to others. I am not embarrassed about feeling strong emotions, but I am seldom totally unrestrained.

Interdependent

I can handle most things on my own, but I will ask for help if I need it. I like to make my own decisions, but am comfortable seeking advice from others.

The Anxious Bonding Style: The Negative Self Schemas

Unworthy

I often feel that somehow I am not as good as other people. My needs are not as important as the needs of other people. I don't deserve to be happy. The needs of other people should come before my own. I tend to feel guilty if I do nice things for myself. I also feel uncomfortable when other people do nice things for me.

Intimacy Driven

I often want more closeness or greater intimacy than others give me. I seek repeated reassurance from others that I am loved. I feel lost if I am not in an intimate relationship. I have difficulty functioning if I am not involved with someone. I worry about losing people who are close to me. I worry about being abandoned. I am usually alert to any signs of rejection by others.

Unrestrained

My emotions often are overwhelming. It is difficult for me to control my emotions. People can easily tell how I am feeling. I cannot hide my emotions, they often seem out of control.

Dependent

I tend to be dependent. I rely on other people to help me with most things. Life is too difficult for me to handle alone. I have a hard time making decisions by myself. I frequently seek assistance from others. I do not like being completely on my own. I need other people to take care of me.

The Distant Bonding Style: The Hyperpositive Self Schemas

Entitled

I think I am as good as anyone else, if not better. I am entitled to have whatever I want. I deserve to have the best of everything. I have a right to have all my needs met. I don't think about what my needs may cost others. I am special. I think more about my own needs than how those needs may affect other people.

Intimacy Avoidant

I prefer to keep most people at a distance. I am not comfortable being too close to other people. Relationships often seem like a burden to me. Emotional intimacy feels suffocating. Relationships aren't that important to me. I prefer not getting too attached to people.

Restrained

I seldom show my feelings. I am uncomfortable expressing my emotions. I don't let people see how I feel. I am almost always in control of my emotions. Other people usually can't tell how I feel. I don't like other people to know when I'm feeling bad. I hate to cry in front of other people.

Stubbornly Independent

I do not like to rely on anyone but myself. It is hard for me to ask for help. I don't like it when other people offer me advice or assistance. I feel irritated when someone tries to help me. I can't stand being dependent on anybody for anything. I prefer to do things on my own.

Appendix C

Managing Your Emotions

The following outline is included for quick reference at those times when you feel that you are acting or about to act in an out-of-control fashion, and you want to gain some control over your words, actions, and emotions.

Gaining Emotional Control

1. Don't react impulsively. Don't do anything until you have calmed down.
2. Calmly talk to yourself.
3. Breathe calmly, slowly inhaling and exhaling for at least five minutes.
4. Find engaging distractions. List here the activities you can use at times of emotional distress:

_____

_____

_____

Once you are calmer, analyze the problem.
1. List the facts.
2. Describe your interpretations of the facts.
3. Identify what feeling is associated with each interpretation.
4. Identify what schemas are associated with your interpretations.
5. List the evidence that supports your interpretations.
6. List the evidence that challenges your interpretations.

7. Evaluate the evidence for and against your interpretations.

8. Consider other possible interpretations of the facts. Identify at least one benign interpretation.

9. Seek clarification or additional information to assess the accuracy of your different possible interpretations. Don't blame. Don't attack. Assume innocence. Ask questions in a calm, nonaccusatory manner.

Worst-Case Preparation

1. Identify your worst-case scenario.

2. What would happen if the worst case occurred? Ask yourself how your life would change if the worst case actually took place. Identify all the possible outcomes that you fear would happen in the worst case.

3. Figure out how you could manage the worst case. Address each of the possible worst-case outcomes separately. For each possible outcome, figure out how to buffer the effects you fear. These ideas should be realistic, not Pollyanna-like suggestions.

4. Estimate how likely the worst-case scenario is.

5. Remember your resilience. Jot down a few code words here to remind you of other times when you have been resilient.

Think through any desire you may have to behave aggressively.

1. What is the goal of your aggressive behavior?

2. Do you ever get any of the responses you want when you engage in these tactics? If yes, how so? If not, what happens?

3. What could be or have been negative consequences to being aggressive?

4. How can you achieve your goals constructively?

5. Write out what you are angry about until your emotions subside.

Make a commitment not to act aggressively or abusively.

You always have a choice whether to take hurtful actions. You need to make a commitment not to do any of the following:

- Swearing, cursing, name-calling

- Being sarcastic, ridiculing others, mocking, displaying contempt

- Kicking, throwing things, breaking anything, hitting the wall, pounding the table are all included. So is speeding. If you are upset, do not drive anything with a motor. Do not engage in any physical act of aggression, whether at another living thing or an inanimate object

- Trying to get the kids to side with you
- Trying to get the kids to be nasty to their other parent
- Making your children afraid of the other parent
- Threatening other people
- Threatening to harm yourself

Stop engaging in upsetting ruminations.

Balance your negative person schemas of anyone with whom you are upset.

Remove yourself from potentially anger-inducing situations until you have learned effective self-control strategies.

After you go through the steps for gaining emotional control and you still feel angry, who can you talk to, other than the people with whom you are angry? List names and phone numbers here:

Long-Term Emotional Management

- Analyze your emotional intensity. What patterns do you see? What makes it better and worse. What stressors do you have? What can you do to buffer their impact? Answer the following questions in your notebook, and whenever you are upset, review your answers for guidance and help with the current situation.
- Review your health and medications. How do they affect your emotions?
- List constructive coping strategies you can use when you are stressed.
- List the names of people with whom you can interact on a regular basis.
- List physical activities you could make routine in your life.
- List the changes you need to make to eat a well-balanced diet.
- List the pleasurable activities that you can engage in on a daily basis.
- Select a routine sleeping schedule.
  Time to go to sleep: _____ Time to wake up: _____
- List the calming activities you can do on a daily basis.

- What unrealistic expectations do you have of yourself and others? How can you modify them?
- What changes do you need to make in your lifestyle to reduce the pressure you feel?
- List the signals your body gives you when you are stressed (headaches, upset stomach, tense neck). Pay very close attention to these signals.

References

Alberti, R., and M. Emmons. 1995. *Your Perfect Right*. 7th ed. San Luis Obispo, CA: Impact.

Al-Mabuk, R. H., R. D. Enright, and P. Cardis. 1995. A forgiveness education program with parentally love-deprived college students. *Journal of Moral Education, 24*, 427-444.

Baldwin, M. W. 1992. Relational schemas and the processing of social information. *Psychological Bulletin, 112*, 461-484.

Baldwin, M. W., and B. Fehr. 1995. On the instability of attachment style ratings. *Personal Relationships, 2*, 247-261.

Baldwin, M. W., J. P. R. Keelan, B. Fehr, V. Enns, and E. Koh-Rangarajoo. 1996. Social-cognitive conceptualization of attachment working models: Availability and accessibility effects. *Journal of Personality and Social Psychology, 71*, 94-109.

Bartholomew, K., and L. M. Horowitz. 1991. Attachment styles among young adults: A test of a four-category model. *Journal of Personality and Social Psychology, 61*, 226-244.

Bartholomew, K. 1993. From childhood to adult relationships: attachment theory and research. In S. Duck, ed. *Learning About Relationships*. 30-62. Newbury Park, CA.: Sage.

Berkman, L. F., and S. L. Syme. 1979. Social networks, host resistance, and mortality: A nine-year follow-up study of Alameda County residents. *American Journal of Epidemiology, 109*, 186-204.

Bologna, M. J., C. K. Waterman, and L. J. Dawson. 1987. *Violence in gay and lesbian relationships: Implications for practitioners and policy makers*. Paper presented at the Third National Conference of Family Violence Researchers, Durham, NH.

Caprara, G. V. 1986. Indicators of aggression: The Dissipation-Rumination Scale. *Personality and Individual Differences, 7*, 763-769.

Collins, K., and R. Bell. 1997. Personality and aggression: The Dissipation-Rumination Scale. *Personality and Individual Differences, 22*, 751-755.

Collins, N. L. 1996. Working models of attachment: Implications for explanation, emotion, and behavior. *Journal of Personality and Social Psychology, 71*, 810-832.

Colvin, C. R., and J. Block. 1994. Do positive illusions foster mental health? An examination of the Taylor and Brown formulation. *Psychological Bulletin, 116*, 3-20.

Colvin, C. R., J. Block, and D. C. Funder. 1995. Overly positive self-evaluations and personality: Negative implications for mental health. *Journal of Personality and Social Psychology, 68*, 1152-1162.

Craske, M. G. 1996. Cognitive-behavioral approaches to panic and agoraphobia. In *Advances in Cognitive-Behavioral Therapy*. K. S. Dobson and K. D. Craig, eds. 145-173. Newbury Park, CA: Sage.

Davila, J., D. Burge, and C. Hammen. 1997. Why does attachment style change? *Journal of Personality and Social Psycholgy, 73*, 826-838.

Diehl, M., A. B. Elnick, L. S. Bourbeau, and G. Labouvie-Vief. 1998. Adult attachment styles: Their relations to family context and personality. *Journal of Personality and Social Psychology, 74*, 1656-1669.

Dutton, D. G., and J. J. Browning. 1988. Power struggles and intimacy anxieties as causative factors of wife assault. In *Violence in Intimate Relationships*. I. G. Russell, ed. 163-175. Newbury Park, CA: Sage.

Dutton, D. G., K. Saunders, A. Starzomski, and K. Bartholomew. 1994. Intimacy-anger and insecure attachment as precursors of abuse in intimate relationships. *Journal of Applied Social Psychology, 24*, 1367-1386.

Elliott, C. H., and M. K. Lassen. 1998. *Why Can't I Get What I Want?* Palo Alto, CA: Davies-Black, Division of Consulting Psychologists Press.

Elliott, C. H., and M. K. Lassen. 1997. A schema polarity model for case conceptualization, intervention, and research. *Clinical Psychology: Science and Practice, 4*, 12-28.

Enright, R. D., and the Human Development Study Group. 1996. Counseling within the forgiveness triad: On forgiving, receiving forgiveness, and self-forgiveness. *Counseling and Values, 40*, 107-126.

Fiske, S. T., and S. E. Taylor. 1991. *Social Cognition*. 2nd ed. Reading, MA: Addison Wesley.

Fonagy, P., T. Leigh, M. Steele, H. Steele, R. Kennedy, G. Mattoon, M. Target, and A. Gerber. 1996. The relation of attachment status, psychiatric classification, and response to psychotherapy. *Journal of Consulting and Clinical Psychology, 64*, 22-31.

Fontana, A. F., R. D. Kerns, R. L. Rosenberg, and K. L. Colonese. 1989. Support, stress, and recovery from coronary heart disease: A longitudinal causal model. *Health Psychology, 8*, 175-193.

Frazier, P., A. L. Byer, A. R. Fischer, D. M. Wright, and K. A. DeBord. 1996. Adult attachment style and partner choice: Correlational and experimental findings. *Personal Relationships, 3,* 117-136.

Freedman, S., and R. D. Enright. 1996. Forgiveness as an intervention goal with incest survivors. *Journal of Consulting and Clinical Psychology, 64,* 983-992.

Futterman, A.D., M. E. Kemeny, D. Shapiro, W. Polonsky, and J. L. Fahey. 1992. Immunological variability associated with experimentally induced positive and negative affective states. *Psychological Medicine, 22,* 231-238.

Gottman, J. M. 1998. Psychology and the study of marital processes. *Annual Review of Psychology, 49,* 169-197.

Gross, J., and R. W. Levenson. 1997. Hiding feelings: The acute effects of inhibiting negative and positive emotions. *Journal of Abnormal Psychology, 106,* 95-103.

Hazan, C., and P. Shaver. 1987. Romantic love conceptualized as an attachment process. *Journal of Personality and Social Psychology, 52,* 511-524.

Hebl, J. H., and R. D. Enright. 1993. Forgiveness as a psychotherapeutic goal with elderly females. *Psychotherapy, 30,* 658-667.

Hendrix, H. 1988. *Getting the Love You Want: A Guide for Couples.* New York: Harper

House, J. S., C. Robbins, and H. L. Metzner. 1982. The association of social relationships and activities with mortality: Prospective evidence from the Tecumseh Community Health Study. *American Journal of Epidemiology, 116,* 123-140.

Jamner, L. D., G. E. Schwartz, and H. Leigh. 1988. The relationship between repressive and defensive coping styles and monocyte, eosinophile, and serum glucose levels: Support for the opioid peptide hypothesis of repression. *Psychosomatic Medicine, 50,* 567-575.

Keeney, B. P. 1983. *Aesthetics of Change.* New York: Guilford Press.

Kelly, G. A. 1955. *The Psychology of Personal Constructs.* Vol. I. New York: W. W. Norton.

Knapp, P. H., E. M. Levy, R. G. Giorgi, P. H. Black, B. H. Fox, and T. C. Heeren. 1992. Short-term immunological effects of induced emotion. *Psychosomatic Medicine, 54,* 133-148.

Kobak, R. R., and A. Sceery. 1988. Attachment in late adolescence: Working models, affect regulation and representations of self and others. *Child Development, 59,* 135-146.

Kulik, J. A., and H. I. M. Mahler. 1989. Social support and recovery from surgery. *Health Psychology, 8,* 221-238.

Lassen, M. K., and C. H. Elliott. 1996. The Role of Schema Polarities in Marital Discord. Presentation given at the Association for the Advancement of Behavior Therapy. New York, NY.

Levy, S. M., R. B Herberman, A. M. Maluish, B. Schlien, and M. Lippman. 1985. Prognostic risk assessment in primary breast cancer by behavioral and immunological parameters. *Health Psychology, 4,* 99-113.

Lie, G., and S. Gentlewarrior. 1991. Intimate violence in lesbian relationships: Discussion of survey findings and practice implications. *Journal of Social Service Research, 15,* 41-59.

Malik, N. M., and K. M. Lindahl. 1998. Aggression and dominance: The roles of power and culture in domestic violence. *Clinical Psychology: Science and Practice, 5,* 409-423.

McCullough, M. E., K. C. Rachal, S. J. Sandage, E. Worthington, Jr., et al. 1998. Interpersonal forgiving in close relationships: II. Theoretical elaboration and measurement. *Journal of Personality and Social Psychology, 75,* 1586-1603.

Mickelson, K. D., R. C. Kessler, and P. R. Shaver. 1997. Adult attachment in a nationally representative sample. *Journal of Personality and Social Psychology, 73,* 1092-1106.

Mikulincer, M. 1995. Attachment style and the mental representation of the self. *Journal of Personality and Social Psychology, 69,* 1203-1215.

Mikulincer, M. 1998a. Adult attachment style and affect regulation: Strategic variations in self-appraisals. *Journal of Personality and Social Psychology, 75,* 420-435.

Mikulincer, M. 1998b. Adult attachment style and individual differences in functional and dysfunctional experiences of anger. *Journal of Personality and Social Psychology, 74,* 513-524.

Petrie, K. J., R. J. Booth, and J. W. Pennebaker. 1998. The immunological effects of thought suppression. *Journal of Personality and Social Psychology, 75,* 1264-1272.

Roberts, N., and P. Noller. 1998. The associations between adult attachment and couple violence. In *Attachment Theory and Close Relationships.* J. A. Simpson and W. S. Rholes, eds. 317-350. New York: Guilford.

Schacter, D. L. 1999. The seven sins of memory. *American Psychologist, 54,* 182-203.

Shea, J. D., R. Burton, and A. Girgis. 1993. Negative affect, absorption, and immunity. *Physiological Behavior, 53,* 449-457.

Shedler, J., M. Mayman, and M. Manis. 1993. The illusion of mental health. *American Psychologist, 48,* 117-1131.

Straus, M. A., and R. J. Gelles. 1986. Societal change and change in family violence from 1975 to 1985 as revealed by two national surveys. *Journal of Marriage and the Family, 48,* 465-479.

Maureen Kirby Lassen, Ph.D., is on the graduate faculty of clinical psychology at the Fielding Institute and has had a private clinical and consulting practice in the Phoenix metropolitan area since 1978. She has been a member of the Arizona State Board of Psychologist Examiners since 1994. For over twenty years, Dr. Lassen has been training clinical psychology doctoral students in the theory and application of cognitive behavioral principles. Co-author of *Why Can't I Get What I Want?* (Davies-Black, 1998; a Behavioral Science Book Selection), Dr. Lassen has conducted workshops for professionals and lay readers on understanding the role of schemas in personal and interpersonal problems, how to deal with difficult people at home and in the workplace, assertiveness training, and relationship enhancement skills.

Some Other New Harbinger Self-Help Titles

Virtual Addiction, $12.95
After the Breakup, $13.95
Why Can't I Be the Parent I Want to Be?, $12.95
The Secret Message of Shame, $13.95
The OCD Workbook, $18.95
Tapping Your Inner Strength, $13.95
Binge No More, $14.95
When to Forgive, $12.95
Practical Dreaming, $12.95
Healthy Baby, Toxic World, $15.95
Making Hope Happen, $14.95
I'll Take Care of You, $12.95
Survivor Guilt, $14.95
Children Changed by Trauma, $13.95
Understanding Your Child's Sexual Behavior, $12.95
The Self-Esteem Companion, $10.95
The Gay and Lesbian Self-Esteem Book, $13.95
Making the Big Move, $13.95
How to Survive and Thrive in an Empty Nest, $13.95
Living Well with a Hidden Disability, $15.95
Overcoming Repetitive Motion Injuries the Rossiter Way, $15.95
What to Tell the Kids About Your Divorce, $13.95
The Divorce Book, Second Edition, $15.95
Claiming Your Creative Self: True Stories from the Everyday Lives of Women, $15.95
Six Keys to Creating the Life You Desire, $19.95
Taking Control of TMJ, $13.95
What You Need to Know About Alzheimer's, $15.95
Winning Against Relapse: A Workbook of Action Plans for Recurring Health and Emotional Problems, $14.95
Facing 30: Women Talk About Constructing a Real Life and Other Scary Rites of Passage, $12.95
The Worry Control Workbook, $15.95
Wanting What You Have: A Self-Discovery Workbook, $18.95
When Perfect Isn't Good Enough: Strategies for Coping with Perfectionism, $13.95
Earning Your Own Respect: A Handbook of Personal Responsibility, $12.95
High on Stress: A Woman's Guide to Optimizing the Stress in Her Life, $13.95
Infidelity: A Survival Guide, $13.95
Stop Walking on Eggshells, $14.95
Consumer's Guide to Psychiatric Drugs, $16.95
The Fibromyalgia Advocate: Getting the Support You Need to Cope with Fibromyalgia and Myofascial Pain, $18.95
Healing Fear: New Approaches to Overcoming Anxiety, $16.95
Working Anger: Preventing and Resolving Conflict on the Job, $12.95
Sex Smart: How Your Childhood Shaped Your Sexual Life and What to Do About It, $14.95
You Can Free Yourself From Alcohol & Drugs, $13.95
Amongst Ourselves: A Self-Help Guide to Living with Dissociative Identity Disorder, $14.95
Healthy Living with Diabetes, $13.95
Dr. Carl Robinson's Basic Baby Care, $10.95
Better Boundries: Owning and Treasuring Your Life, $13.95
Goodbye Good Girl, $12.95
Fibromyalgia & Chronic Myofascial Pain Syndrome, $19.95
The Depression Workbook: Living With Depression and Manic Depression, $17.95
Self-Esteem, Second Edition, $13.95
Angry All the Time: An Emergency Guide to Anger Control, $12.95
When Anger Hurts, $13.95
Perimenopause, $16.95
The Relaxation & Stress Reduction Workbook, Fourth Edition, $17.95
The Anxiety & Phobia Workbook, Second Edition, $18.95
I Can't Get Over It, A Handbook for Trauma Survivors, Second Edition, $16.95
Messages: The Communication Skills Workbook, Second Edition, $15.95
Thoughts & Feelings, Second Edition, $18.95
Depression: How It Happens, How It's Healed, $14.95
The Deadly Diet, Second Edition, $14.95
The Power of Two, $15.95
Living Without Depression & Manic Depression: A Workbook for Maintaining Mood Stability, $18.95
Couple Skills: Making Your Relationship Work, $14.95
Hypnosis for Change: A Manual of Proven Techniques, Third Edition, $15.95
Letting Go of Anger: The 10 Most Common Anger Styles and What to Do About Them, $12.95
Infidelity: A Survival Guide, $13.95
When Anger Hurts Your Kids, $12.95
Don't Take It Personally, $12.95
The Addiction Workbook, $17.95

Call **toll free, 1-800-748-6273,** or log on to our online bookstore at **www.newharbinger.com** to order. Have your Visa or Mastercard number ready. Or send a check for the titles you want to New Harbinger Publications, Inc., 5674 Shattuck Ave., Oakland, CA 94609. Include $3.80 for the first book and 75¢ for each additional book, to cover shipping and handling. (California residents please include appropriate sales tax.) Allow two to five weeks for delivery.

Prices subject to change without notice.